# A COMPLEX COAST

A KAYAK JOURNEY
FROM VANCOUVER ISLAND
TO ALASKA

H
HERITAGE

# A COMPLEX COAST

DAVID NORWELL

Heritage House Publishing Company Ltd.
heritagehouse.ca

*Cataloguing information available from Library and Archives Canada*

978-1-77203-449-3 (paperback)
978-1-77203-450-9 (e-book)

Edited by Marial Shea
Proofread by Renée Layberry
Cover and interior book design by Setareh Ashrafologhalai
Cover and interior photos and illustrations by David Norwell unless otherwise indicated.

The interior of this book was produced on FSC®-certified, acid-free paper, processed chlorine free, and printed with vegetable-based inks.

Heritage House gratefully acknowledges that the land on which we live and work is within the traditional territories of the Lkwungen (Esquimalt and Songhees), Malahat, Pacheedaht, Scia'new, T'Sou-ke, and W̱SÁNEĆ (Pauquachin, Tsartlip, Tsawout, Tseycum) Peoples.

We acknowledge the financial support of the Government of Canada through the Canada Book Fund (CBF) and the Canada Council for the Arts, and the Province of British Columbia through the British Columbia Arts Council and the Book Publishing Tax Credit.

27 26 25 24 23   1 2 3 4 5

Printed in China

For Esko, Chowder, Catly, Rat-face, Beauty, Flora, Kim-chow, Scorpio, Sugar, Zeek, Bell, Blueberry, Zulu, Missy, and all the other cats and dogs that make us who we are.

TRUCK DOGS IN SITKA

## DISCLAIMER

Hello and welcome to the book! Enclosed are ideas, theories, and stories from up and down the coast. Any errors or misrepresentations herein I take full responsibility for, and I ask your forgiveness, especially around Traditional Ecological Knowledge, territory names, and locations. These are tender for a settler, and I have tried to be mindful. Alas, I am small, learning, and human. I mean no harm; the goal of this book is to encourage understanding, respect, and curiosity for the Pacific Northwest.

## TERRITORY ACKNOWLEDGEMENT

This book was written on Lkwungen, Songhees, Esquimalt, and W̱SÁNEĆ traditional territory. I extend my deepest respect and gratitude to all the coastal Indigenous Peoples for your continued stewardship in the Pacific Northwest (PNW), without which this trip and story would not have been possible. Thank you.

## SUGGESTION

If you can, read this outdoors.

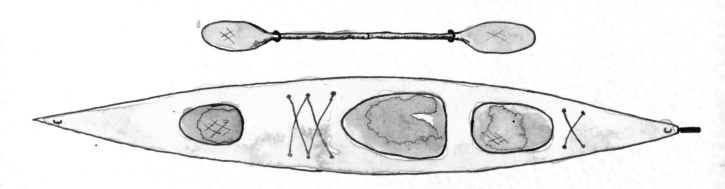

## KAYAK

Kayaks have been around for 5,000 years. The name translates to "hunter's boat." Originally built from stitched seal skin stretched over whalebone frames by the Aleuts and Inuit, for hunting seals, whales, and even caribou! These boats were an extension of the hunter—a part of them.

## SAILING

Ever since *Homo sapiens* set out on rafts to colonize the unknown, there have been sails. To harness the wind is an art, risk, and obsession.

## HATCHET

Perhaps you too were fundamentally changed after reading Gary Paulsen's *Hatchet*.

## COMPASS

Accurate navigation allows us to trade, go to war, find mates, and explore the unknown. Compasses also give us the ability to find ourselves.

## TACKLE

Humans love to seduce fish onto hooks, bludgeon them to death, roast them, and stick them in our mouths. It is a deep-rooted relationship.

## JAPANESE BUOYS

Made from recycled glass, some orbs spend ten years at sea before landfall. The hunt is on!

## CLOVE HITCH

Used for everything.

## FIRE

As fire changed our sleep pattern and fueled our cognitive revolution, humans began to tell stories.

## SALMONBERRY (*RUBUS SPECTABILIS*)

Fruits May to July and found in nitrogen-rich soil, like beside salmon streams.

BERRIES OF THE PNW: pages 32–33

## LONG-JAWED ORBWEAVER (*TETRAGNATHA*)

Long-jaws are identified by elongated bodies and stretched front legs. After birth, babies balloon and disperse on special thread.

INSECTS OF THE PNW: page 79

## RED-THROATED LOON (*GAVIA STELLATA*)

Known as the "rain goose" in the Shetland Islands, its behaviour is used by Shetlanders to predict weather. Short calls and flying inland = clear skies. Long wailing calls and flying to sea = rain.

WEATHER FORECASTING: pages 124–25

## COHO/SILVER SALMON (*ONCORHYNCHUS KISUTCH*)

Edible. Salmon are our greatest inheritance.

TROLLING: pages 154–55
FISHES OF THE PNW: pages 156–57

## ORCA (*ORCINUS ORCA*)

Cerebral cortex: 43 billion neurons. Humans have 16 billion.

MARINE MAMMALS: pages 20–21

## ORANGE PEEL NUDIBRANCH (*TOCHUINA TETRAQUETRA*)

Edible, raw or cooked.

NUDIBRANCHS OF THE PNW: pages 110–11

## DUNGENESS CRAB (*METACARCINUS MAGISTER*)

Edible. Males are attracted to pheromones in the female's urine. Upon finding a mate, the male initiates a protective "pre-mating embrace" lasting several days.

INVERTEBRATES OF THE PNW: page 82

## BULL KELP (*NEREOCYSTIS LUETKEANA*)

Edible. Bulbs and stipes pickled, blades can be dried or cooked.

TIDES: page 34
SEAWEEDS: pages 72–73

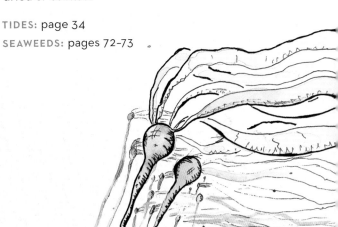

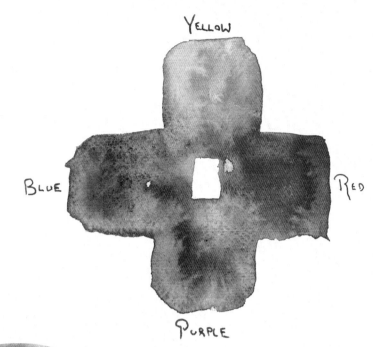

YELLOW

BLUE

RED

PURPLE

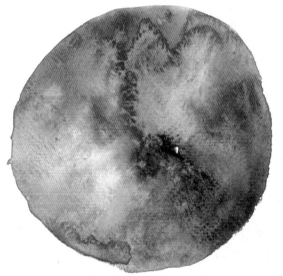

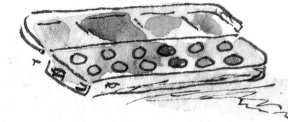

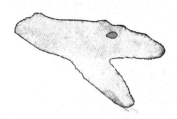

# CONTENTS

# CHART ATLAS OF THE PACIFIC NORTHWEST

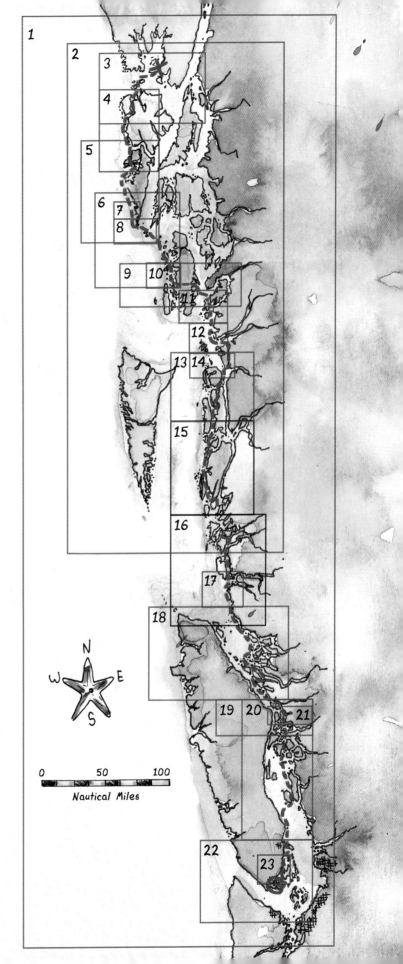

N
W    E
S

0        50       100
Nautical Miles

"The trail will only provide if you accept its offer. All of it. You must leave home. You must be broken. It will cost you your entire life as you know it. And then, and only then, can you receive. What you receive will be far greater than anything you had or anything you lost. It will change you. It might even heal you."

⌒ **BEN CRAWFORD** ⌒
*2,000 Miles Together:
The Story of the Largest Family
to Hike the Appalachian Trail*

INTRODUCTION

# LIFE IN THE BACK EDDY

# MARCH 16, 2014:

Storm clouds churning. //
Vancouver Island, BC, Canada
(Turtle Island).

Dear Journal: I'm beginning to get the feeling
this whole-big-thing is bogus. What if everything
I'm working towards is doomed to fall apart, and
everything I own really owns me? How can I trust
society if it's intoxicated by greed, delusion, and
repetition? What if there is buried treasure, but I
have to look for it... elsewhere?

Modern samsara[1]: The back eddy of pleasure and pain, gain and loss, praise and blame, success and failure, life and death.

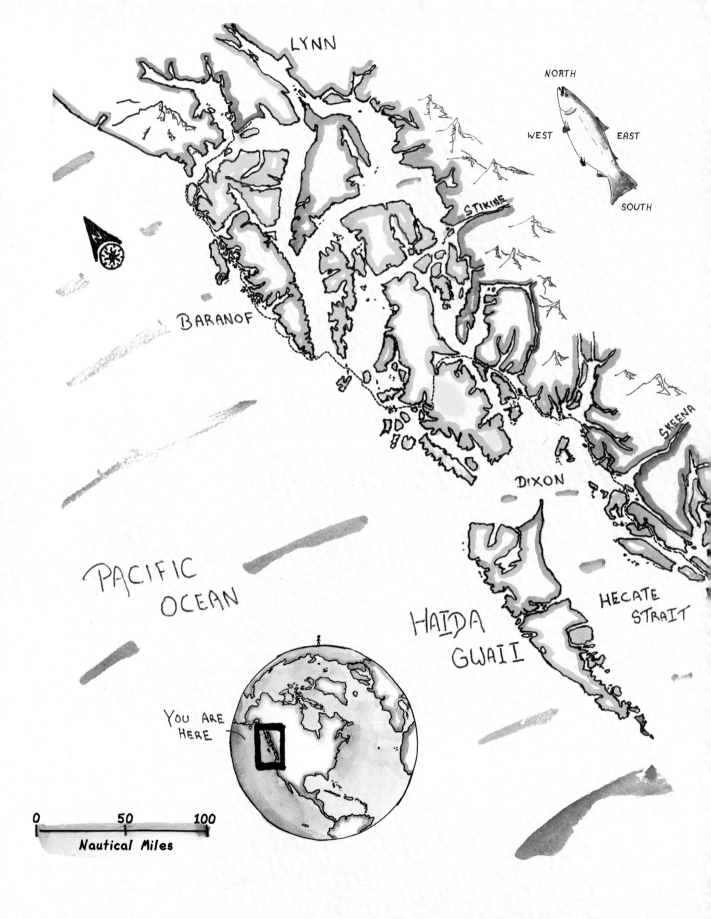

LYNN

NORTH

WEST        EAST

SOUTH

STIKINE

BARANOF

SKEENA

DIXON

PACIFIC
OCEAN

HAIDA
GWAII

HECATE
STRAIT

YOU ARE
HERE

0        50        100
Nautical Miles

# APRIL 4, 2014:

*Sun and clouds. //*
Victoria, BC, Canada (Lekwungen territory).

Waves lick cobblestones, and goosebumps migrate down my skinny, vanilla arms. To be honest, I have no idea what I'm doing. The future seems impossible: kayak to Alaska through a 1,700-kilometre (1,100-mile) maze of islands ruled by grizzlies, orcas, and wolves. *Only centimetres on the chart.* I'm nervous, but this is something I need to do.

I have questions and this journey is the only way to answer them.

Our planet is connected by trains, planes, and tech, yet many of us are lonely, stressed, and suffering. My life at university is an assembly line—wake up, poop, eat, study, fumble with relationships, protect ego, brush teeth, sleep, and repeat. *Be a good dog.* Disenchantment mounts as I struggle to find purpose.

Within solitude, I hope to find clarity.

A jigsaw of jagged mainland and thousands of islands await. The Pacific Northwest is vast, remote, under-investigated, and the last stronghold of temperate rainforest on earth. To travel here is a privilege. Indigenous Peoples have inhabited the area for over 14,000 years, and their stories are woven into the landscape. This means I'm a visitor, and my grace and attention will be required at every turn.

This journal will record inner *and* outer wilderness, and my quest to find meaning, truth, and something deeper—*something beautiful.*

Please ocean, don't eat me. I don't want to be lost at sea, leaving behind all the people I love.

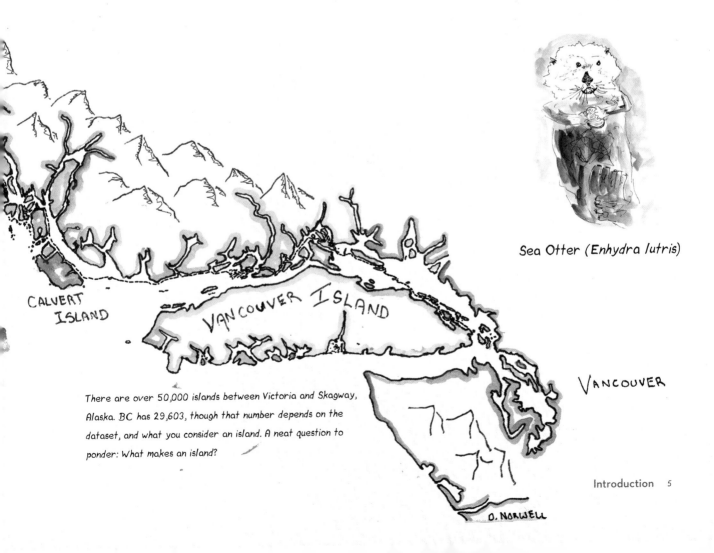

Sea Otter *(Enhydra lutris)*

CALVERT ISLAND

VANCOUVER ISLAND

VANCOUVER

There are over 50,000 islands between Victoria and Skagway, Alaska. BC has 29,603, though that number depends on the dataset, and what you consider an island. A neat question to ponder: What makes an island?

O. NORWELL

# HELLO AGAIN!

I should introduce myself. I'm David, an ordinary kid from North America. I have no superpowers, I struggle with honesty and remembering birthdays, but *I do love tide pools.* I grew up in Prince George, Kamloops, and Fort St. John, British Columbia, Canada. I collected Pokémon cards, played soccer, crashed mountain bikes, dreamed of being a wizard, and was embarrassed around, well, *everyone.* Luckily, my parents dragged my siblings—Jenny, Arron, Lexi—and me to the ocean every chance they got. We squeezed into *Vanny* and pilgrimaged to the Salish Sea. My sisters and I would dive in, daring each other farther and farther. Testing the limits of our courage *and* cold tolerance, sometimes swimming under snowflakes.

I love the ocean because it's immense *and* indifferent. We can't change it … or can we? Now living on Vancouver Island, I study geography at the University of Victoria. I skateboard to class, slackline in the quad, and spend hours in the library. My *real* education is when I slip down to the nearest bay to ponder my theories. And take an icy skinny-dip. While floating naked in the nameless-sweet-Suzan, I feel a part of the whole. It's almost spiritual. Or perhaps it's my numb nervous system shutting down.

NAME: David Thomas Norwell

BORN: August 6, 10:09 AM, 1990, Fort St. John, BC

NICKNAME FROM MOM: *Cute-Pants-Norwell.* She called me this in public all the time. *Still does.*

KAYAKING: I've paddled the Gulf Islands, and last summer I guided youth groups at Camp Thunderbird, including a nine-day journey from Nanaimo to Victoria. This required me to become

CAP

SUNNIES

WOOL/FLEECE

FLEECE

FLIP FLOPS + WOOL SOCKS

a certified Assistant Overnight Guide with the Sea Kayak Guides Alliance of BC (SKGABC). This was a week-long course that included a circumnavigation of Vargas Island outside of Tofino.

SURVIVAL: In the Yukon, I worked conducting geological surveys from remote helicopter camps. This allowed me to pay for university without going into debt (also a survival skill), and taught me many outdoor skills, including wilderness first aid and how to use a chainsaw. I learned to be comfortable alone in nature. I suck at making fires, though.

PRIVILEGE[2]: Being a white male with no disabilities and from a loving, functional family means I have opportunities others don't—like paddling to Alaska. It's a responsibility not to abuse this *cultural superpower*. Which means being a good person and pushing the paradigms of inequality. But it's tricky because I'm often ignorant of my privilege, and I'm privileged through my ignorance—*a feedback cycle*. It takes courage to be critical of a system that benefits my demographic the most. I don't have answers here, but I hope to gain perspective during the trip.

BOOKS: *The Alchemist, Lord of the Flies, 1984, Brave New World, The Stranger, Jonathan Livingston Seagull, The Fountainhead, The Dispossessed, I-ching, We, Dune, Endurance: Shackleton's Incredible Voyage, Tortilla Flat, The Art of Racing in the Rain, Moby Dick.*

ECOLOGICAL WISDOM: I'm not so good at identifying plants, animals, and fungus, but I'm learning. I've brought guidebooks for each of the three kingdoms, and I hope to improve my Latin (see the resource section at the back for guidebook tips and other endnotes).

NUMBER OF UNDERWEAR: Two.

*Opposite Clothing keeps you warm by trapping warm air beside your skin. Wet cotton ceases to insulate because the air pockets fill with water/sweat. This has given rise to the camping-expression, "cotton kills." Fleece and wool wick moisture to dry areas.*

## WHY AM I LEAVING?

Living in the city drives me totally bonkers. After three years in the urban-university-bubble, I find myself repulsed by how people treat each other *and* themselves. Constantly trying to fit in, why not stand out? I feel trapped in the carrot-race, one I never signed up for. I get nervous when I see the emotional insecurity in everyone's eyes, and the inevitable struggle we all face.

*Busy cities create busy minds.*

I'm also mad at the test-centred education system. A class filled with students could do amazing things, but my cohort is dismasted, dismantled, and discouraged to think beyond the box. "What job are you going to do after you graduate?" I came to university to change the world, but I'm having trouble changing myself.

SELF HEAL
*Prunella vulgaris*

*I was inspired to sketch by my grandfather, also named David Norwell. Before a trip to Australia, when I was eighteen, he gave me a sketch book. "Draw everything, so you learn to see the details." He also kept journals and has a mountain of watercolours. I never received formal artistic training, so please forgive any stylistic foo-pahs. I am learning.*

Charts of northern waterways and remote islands cover my bedside table and, as if an answer to my prayers, a field course—Biodiversity & Conservation of Coastal BC, taught by a certain Dr. Brian Starzomski—is starting in Bella Bella on May 7. *One month from now,* and 350 nautical miles north of Victoria. Perhaps this is the kind of classroom I'm looking for.

## SOLITUDE

As I survey society, a question barges in: *Is this it?*

Are people happy, or fooling themselves? Is there more than school, job, relationship, house, debt, kids, family, old age, illness, and death? At twenty-four years old, I've never been asked to dream beyond the conventional-life-checklist or critique the culture we hold so dear.

## WHAT ARE MY ALTERNATIVES?

This isn't the first time I've gone out alone. Wilderness is my temple *and* therapy. Western culture has wandered away from the church but failed to replace its ethical framework. Can we establish morality and a *sense-of-purpose* from science and capitalism? Do we need to? Perhaps *nature* can be our new god.

My previous expeditions into the wild have been potent. Sweet-wonders dine among mighty conifers and silent sunrises. How do we cultivate an intimate human-ecosystem relationship?

## THERE MUST BE MORE TO THIS PUZZLE.

I was eighteen on my first solo trip. For seven days I trekked through Tombstone Territorial Park in the Yukon, surviving on canned beans and peanut butter. While standing in wildflowers, surrounded by saw-toothed ridgelines, I held out my arms waiting for a revelation. *Nothing happened.* I guess it doesn't work like that. Insights do come from wild spaces, but they *can't be forced.* And sometimes the lessons seep slowly, like cold maple syrup.

I was hooked, and went out whenever I could. But nothing like this journey I'm about to take.

There is *one* other reason I'm leaving, but I haven't the courage to write about it yet. It's too embarrassing.

MT BAKER

GAZEBO AT
QUEEN ALEXANDRA BEACH

"DEPARTURE"

## PACKING LIST

There are a myriad of ways to prepare for a kayak trip. For the last week I have been scrambling in and out of dumpsters (urban-foraging), sewing rain gear with dental floss, and getting organized in a generally disorganized way. The dehydrator is filled with questionable bananas and suspicious sausages.

What you ram into the hatches is a question of comfort, capability, and resourcefulness. Some trippers insist on dry suits, toilet paper, coffee, freeze-dried meals, and camp stoves. I bought a tent off Craigslist, got a sleeping bag and fleece trousers from Value Village, borrowed a life jacket from my summer camp, and was given a fishing rod at a garage sale.

My seventeen-foot kayak, *Bell Pepper*, is a fibreglass 1991 Seaward Navigator. I wrangled it, plus a paddle and skirt, from one of my professors, Dr. Eric Higgs. To negotiate the price down to $850 from $1,150, I told him my travel intentions, baked his family banana bread, *and* said I was mostly broke—*which is true*. It was his son Logan, a fellow Camp Thunderbirder, who clinched the deal, convincing his dad I was seaworthy. *Thank you.*

Other bring-alongs[3]: Tent, tarps, VHF radio, hand pump, fibreglass repair kit, chart atlas, wool socks, dry bags, wetsuit, expired flares, and a travelling banjo crafted by my dad. Oh yes, and 15 kilograms (33 pounds) of books. Who else is going to keep me company?

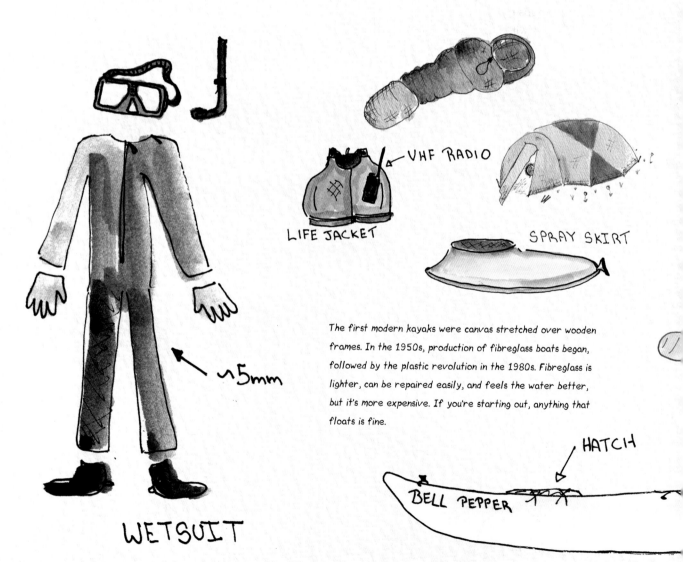

VHF RADIO

LIFE JACKET

SPRAY SKIRT

*The first modern kayaks were canvas stretched over wooden frames. In the 1950s, production of fibreglass boats began, followed by the plastic revolution in the 1980s. Fibreglass is lighter, can be repaired easily, and feels the water better, but it's more expensive. If you're starting out, anything that floats is fine.*

~5mm

WETSUIT

HATCH

BELL PEPPER

## KAYAKING 101

OK. Let's get a couple things sorted. Kayaks are not canoes. Yaks use paddles with two blades, possess a rudder or a skeg to aid in tracking (see below), and if you flip over you can roll back to the surface. The rudder in *Bell Pep* is connected to foot pedals inside the cockpit for steering. The kayak itself has one hatch in the front and one in the back that together can store 250 litres of gear and food—about a month's supplies (a trekking backpack is only 70 litres). The *skirt* goes around your torso and seals to the entrance of the cockpit. PRO TIP: *Step into* your skirt instead of pulling it on over your head, especially if you've already got your lifejacket on. *I always forget,* and end up penguining to get unstuck. The skirt keeps me from getting wet, and if I flip, I can *roll* back without flooding everything. *I hope.*

### FIRST AID KIT:

- Bandages (for knife mistakes)
- Triangle sling (I forget how to use these)
- Polysporin (for suspicious skin adventures)
- Scissors (really?)
- Tweezers (for ouchies)
- Oil of oregano (inside and outside)
- Tea tree oil (anti-viral and antifungal)
- Allergy pills (if I mysteriously start swelling)

### FISHING KIT:

- Extra fishing line (it's already tangled)
- Lures (spinners, spoons, leads. *What are these for?*)
- Extra hooks (I expect to lose my fair share)
- Leatherman (with fourteen different tools!)
- Buck knife (named Bucky)

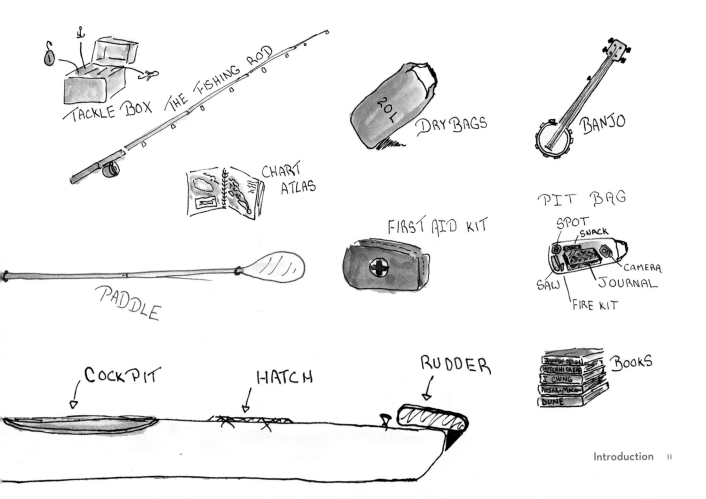

TACKLE BOX   THE FISHING ROD

CHART ATLAS

PADDLE

FIRST AID KIT

DRY BAGS   2OL

BANJO

PIT BAG
SPOT
SNACK
SAW   CAMERA
   JOURNAL
FIRE KIT

BOOKS

COCKPIT   HATCH   RUDDER

# 1

# WOLVES OF
# THE DEEP

The Southern Gulf Islands. The first day from Victoria to
Piers Island takes eight hours with a lunch stop—a speed of
2 knots (4 km/hr). This is to be my average the entire trip.
Think "snail-power."

YOU ARE
HERE

CAPE
FLATTERY

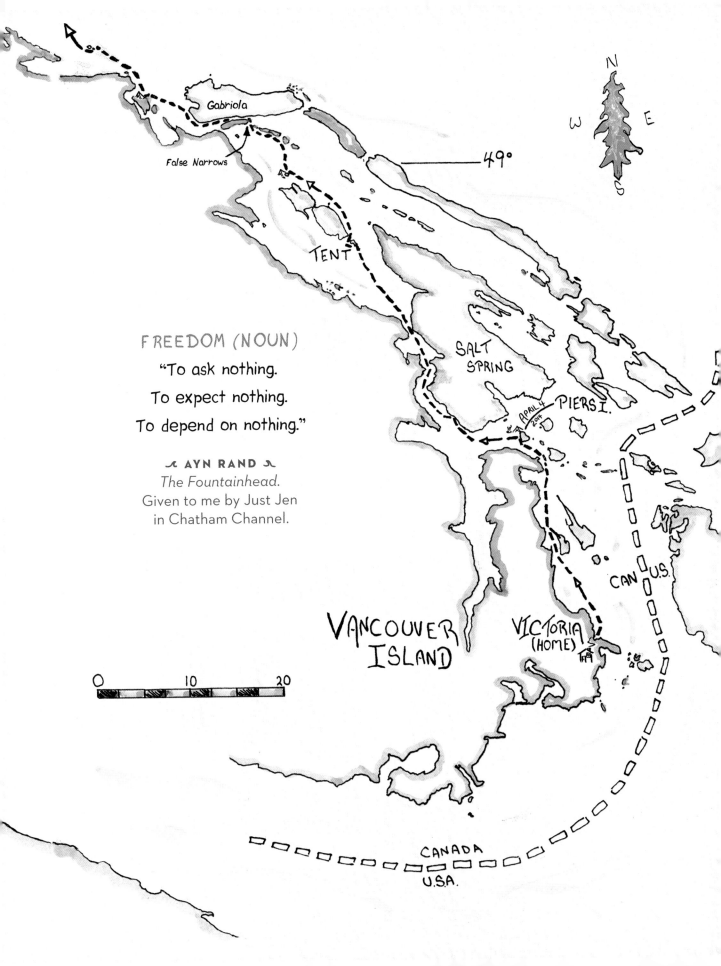

Gabriola

False Narrows

49°

N
W        E
S

TENT

SALT
SPRING

APRIL 4
2014
PIERS I.

FREEDOM (NOUN)

"To ask nothing.
To expect nothing.
To depend on nothing."

⌐ AYN RAND ⌐
*The Fountainhead.*
Given to me by Just Jen
in Chatham Channel.

VANCOUVER
ISLAND

VICTORIA
(HOME)

CAN   U.S.

0        10        20

CANADA
U.S.A.

## DAY 1, APRIL 4, 2014:

Wind SE 5–10 knots (kn). *Sunny.* // Victoria to Piers Island—WSÁNEĆ, Lekwungen, and Songhees territory— 14 nautical miles (nm).

Queen Alexandra's secret cove is ten minutes from my home in Victoria. I have *skinnied* here dozens of times. My sister Lex, the roommates, and our favourite retriever, Sugar, march down to see me off. It takes an hour to stuff everything into the hatches. I'm embarrassed at how novice and disorganized I am. My friends are not quite sure what I'm doing. "Well, I'm going… *going* to kayak to Bella Bella… *for school.*" It's a shame I have to justify my actions in the name of education. I may have no clue what I'm getting into, but I'm starting to understand what I'm leaving behind.

Hugs are passed around and I wish I was more present. As *Bell Pep* slips into the Salish Sea, my strokes are clumsy and uncoordinated. I almost flip waving goodbye. Sugar-the-dog, my skinny-dipping partner, paddles beside me until her limit is breached. *Go home fuzz-bomb, it's too far.*

Eventually I'm out of sight and my adrenaline settles. Alone—just me, my mind, and a water-body covering three-quarters of the earth. *I leave my terrestrial ties.*

### NAUTICAL MILE

Captains, coast guards, pilots, and I all use the nautical mile—a miracle in the measurement world. It's handy on the ocean because every degree of latitude is sixty nautical miles. When travelling distances affected by Earth's circular nature, this becomes the best unit of measurement.

Distance conversion:
*1 nautical mile—1.85 kilometres*
*1 nautical mile—1.15 miles*
*1 nautical mile—1 minute of latitude*
*60 nautical miles—1 degree of latitude*

### SUGAR

Sugar is an amazing dog. Once, while Sugar was swimming for a stick, a transient orca breached within metres of her. I screamed in fear, then absolute delight when I realized the whale had no dinner intentions. In Northern BC, Sugar fended off a hungry black bear while we were picking morel mushrooms. I owe her my life. POSTSCRIPT: She died in 2019 at a young age, as retrievers sometimes do.

## KAIA

Let me introduce you to Kaia. *I have a crush,* but we're in the *friend-zone*, and my feelings go undeclared.

The amoeba-shaped Piers Island (see chart on page 13) is where Kaia grew up. She was *island-schooled*—raised collectively by the salty locals and her loving parents. By 18, she was fluent in Japanese, English, karate (black-belt), and piano (eighth grade from the Royal Conservatory). She also sails, cooks, loves cats and dogs, and is good with children. AKA she is way more clever and talented than me.

Piers is my first camp spot, but Kaia is out-*in*-town, otherwise (perhaps) I would profess my emotional butterflies (but I doubt it). I leave an awkward *have-a-good-summer* note on her sailboat, *Sky* (yes, she owns a sailboat!). Then I set up camp on a nearby beach.

Last time I was here, we climbed a huge Douglas fir—her childhood tree where she would escape the adult world. Now I straddle the highest limb writing this, watching the first sunset of the trip. I won't see Kaia until September. *Eep!*

## DOUGLAS FIRS
## (*PSEUDOTSUGA MENZIESII*)

Fir bark is furrowed with deep grooves making them *+1 fire resistant*. Fir cones have mouse-like tails sticking out of the cracks. Before the logging bonanza, they grew up to 100 metres (328 feet) tall. The last mamas are ~85 metres, relegated to nature refuges. *I wish I could go back in time.*

Opposite, top **Sugar**

Above, top **Pencil sketch of Kaia, 2014.**

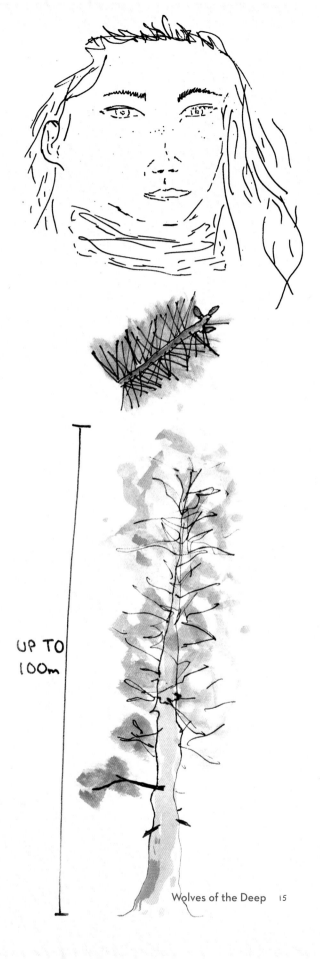

UP TO 100m

## FOOD, INGLORIOUS FOOD

As a kid, I came into the kitchen every morning to a pot of oats. This was my dad's way of saying *I love you, have a good day.* I value this now, but at the time I craved sugar-bomb-cavity-blaster cereals. Now on my own, oats are comfort food—a reminder of family. While kayaking, I plan on ~4,000 whammies (calories) a day. So oats, but also fish and intertidal treats. The catch is, I know nothing about fishing and foraging, *but* I have books that do.

Ninety percent of the food I've packed was reclaimed[1] (dumpster-dived) from grocery stores in Victoria. This saved money *and* gave me a platform to preach the pitfalls of our industrial food-rammer (which wastes ~58 percent of all edibles produced!). Another limitation: *no stove.* This means every night I must light a fire if I want hot food.

The cultural-ecological intersection of what we put in our mouths is important. This trip will explore *where* nutrition comes from, and yummy opportunities in the Pacific Northwest.

## PROVISIONS

(I sent a food restock up to Cortes Island, not included below)

- 4 kg (9 lbs) of my trail-oats master remix (look right)

- 1 kg (2.2 lbs) of chocolate (yes, it's true, and the secret to happiness)

- 4 kg (9 lbs) of dried chickpea and brown rice mix (gruffy base)

- ½ kg (1 lb) of dehydrated vegetables (it's amazing how much water veg holds)

- 1 kg (2.2 lbs) of dehydrated fruit (banana chips!)

- 2 kg (4.5 lbs) of jerky (a green grocer in Victoria throws out full roasts! Don't worry, I do a smell-check)

- 110 gummy worms (dollar-store dumpsters hold many surprises)

- 12 scuzzy hot dogs (don't ask)

- 1 kg (2.2 lbs) of peanut butter (I wish more)

- ½ kg (1 lb) of jam (raspberry, if you're curious)

- 40 granola bars (UVic dumpsters after all the kids in residence move out!)

- Vegetables (potatoes, cabbage, onions, avocados, broccoli, and bell peppers)

- Apples and oranges (I've read enough scurvy stories from colonial captains to nip this in the bud)

- Fishing rod (how does this thing work?)

I use a double ziplock system for preserves, and then the garbage-bag stuff-sack method, instead of stiff dry bags. Ramming everything into the hatches is a little-known art form, like loading trailers. Malleable items are key.

## OATS EXPLOSION

Oats with raisins, cinnamon, sugar, nuts, and love. It's not possible to convey my passion for oats in only one or two sentences. They are nature's gift to the human stomach. That is all.

## DEHYDRATED VEG BOMB

I dehydrated any vegetable I could find, even pickles. They turned out pretty weird. Anyways, it's all in this one mystery bag now. Haven't tried it yet.

## MISCELLANEOUS JERKY

There are at least four different animals in this ziplock. When you D-dive a butcher shop, sometimes you're not sure what you get. I've salted it heavy-duty to neutralize any baddies.

## THE COMMUNITY CABBAGE (*BRASSICA OLERACEA*)

Ode to the cabbage patch, teacher of shedding-layers, compactness, and strong inner fibre. Seriously, cabbage is awesome, and keeps forever (3 weeks). Just prune the outer coats when they get squiggly.

## DROP THE BEET (*BETA VULGARIS*)

Beets are cool and change the colour of your pee; the condition even has a name: beeturia. It's caused by the pigment betanin, which some humans can't digest too well, for beetter or worse.

## PEANUT BUTTER AND JAM

If there was ever a match made in heaven, a perfect couple of the condiment (spread?) world, it is these two budding philosophers. They're a seamless Venn-diagram, fulfilling the taste buds' every desire. I didn't bring bread so I'm having it on raw cabbage leaves.

## GRUFFY

Here's where it gets creative—my patented protein invention: dry garbanzo beans, lentils (orange), soybeans, brown rice, and all the spices on the rack, all in one pot. *Yet to be field tested.* Yes, I'm aware each ingredient takes different amounts of time to cook :)

## CHOCOLATE (*THEOBROMA CACAO*)

This may be the most important invention on earth. After all, chocolate sparked Homo sapiens' cognitive revolution 45,000 years ago, after which jewelry, tools, dogs, art, and music begin appearing in the archaeological record. I offer no citation.

## ONION (*ALLIUM CEPA*)

Onions are a choice while kayaking, similar to cabbage in their practicality, but so much more with a little oil on the pan. Also, if you eat them raw, the bugs stay away, so I hear.

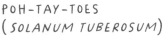

## CARROT (*DAUCUS CAROTA*)

I'm one of those people who believes in eating a variety of food colours. Cabbage—green. Beet—purple. Potato—yellow(ish?). Carrot—orange. With strategic mixing, the rest should be easy. Are there any blue vegetables?

## POH-TAY-TOES (*SOLANUM TUBEROSUM*)

"You know! Boil 'em, mash 'em, stick 'em in a stew."

**SAMWISE GAMGEE**[2]

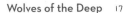

## DAY 2, APRIL 5:

Wind light with rain. //
Piers to Tent Island—Penelakut
and Quw'utsun territory—17 nm.

I wake up on Piers to an unhappy customer knocking on my tent. The public beach where I'm camped is beside private property. The lady demands to know what I'm doing here. Maybe she thought I was setting up a hippy commune.[3] I explain my trip and date of departure (today), which makes her sheepish for being standoffish.

Ownership is so strange. It creates a wall between us and the other. Aggression is justified when our things seem threatened, but curiosity, courtesy, and empathy go a long way when you meet a stranger.

Droplets shatter the fabric of the ocean and I push off. I wonder what rain looks like to a fish (Kaia came up with this question). Salt Spring Island is my next destination and I hope to get a boost through Sansum Narrows with the flooding tide. Jagged cliffs loom on either side of the channel, I'm nervous. The currents are complex and massive back eddies push the kayak against my will. My arms turn into jellyfish as I struggle to maintain control.

### Whales! ∿∿∿∿∿∿∿∿∿∿∿∿∿∿∿∿∿∿∿∿∿

PAAWWOOOOSHH! Orcas sweep from behind and I'm surrounded by a pod. Sweet Dyna! One breaches metres away, making the boat wobble. There are over twenty—they must be the resident orcas, wolves-of-the-deep. This is the marine apex predator in the Pacific Northwest and they feast exclusively on salmon. However, the transient orcas eat seals and just about everything else. Research shows they are more emotionally complex than humans and have double the neurons in their cerebral cortex. Yet some countries put them in pools to jump hoops.[4]

The ocean angels guide me through the narrows and disappear, leaving me serene and stupefied. I start crying—my body is shivering. So quickly, I've been transported to a world of whelks, whales, and whitecaps.

The light is fading as I aim for Tent Island—a reassuring name given my intentions. I'm dog-tired. Darkness falls and one of my sandals is left on the beach as I trudge my gear up. The next morning nothing remains. The tide's ability to reveal and conceal is beyond any magician.

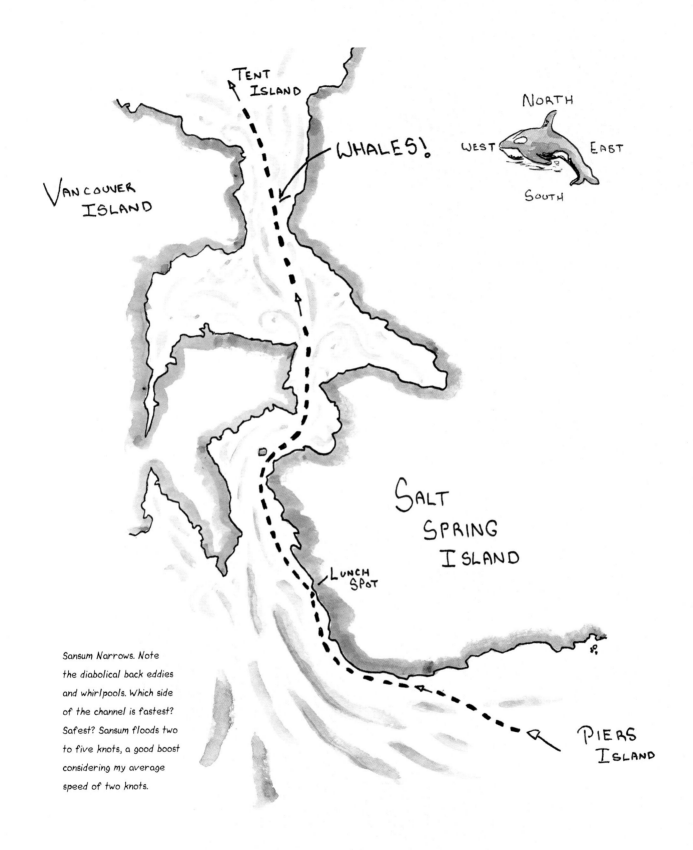

TENT
ISLAND

WHALES!

NORTH

WEST        EAST

SOUTH

VANCOUVER
ISLAND

SALT
SPRING
ISLAND

LUNCH
SPOT

Sansum Narrows. Note
the diabolical back eddies
and whirlpools. Which side
of the channel is fastest?
Safest? Sansum floods two
to five knots, a good boost
considering my average
speed of two knots.

PIERS
ISLAND

## EVOLUTIONARY CROSSROADS

Evolution gives me a major-league doozy. After millions of years crawling fin and flipper out of the ocean to establish terrestrial domination and oxygen dependency, *boop*, our mammalian cousins go back. Which took some more million years, except now, *bless their hearts*, they are hooked on $O_2$—a reminder of the world they left behind. *This is why whales and dolphins are not fish.*

What made them change their minds? *Why water?*

Gravity *is* a bit too much, and water takes a load off the body. In fact, some humans could be considered marine mammals. In Southeast Asia, the Bajau Laut people free-dive for most of their food and have specific hormonal adaptations and bigger spleens—the reserve and filter for red blood cells, handy if you're 60 metres deep and running low on oxygenated blood. If left in isolation and given a 100 million years, would the Bajau Laut become the next generation of whales?

Research by one of my professors, Dr. Chris Darimont, and his team, shows that in the Great Bear Rainforest, *island wolves are considered marine mammals*. Their diet consists of salmon brains, otter, seal, clams, and barnacles! Swimming between channels up to 13 kilometres (8 miles) wide, they are distinct from their mainland-sisters. It took these scientists over a decade to come to this conclusion, though many Indigenous Peoples had known for generations. Part of the reason they started the research was a Heiltsuk man named Chester "Lone Wolf" Starr.[5] On their first day working together, he nodded between the mainland and the islands and asked Chris, "*Which* wolves are we studying?"

And the whales? Will they evolve out of their need for air? Will we ever translate their haunting songs? What do orcas do with so much brain power?[6] *Is it possible to ride a humpback?*

If I continue bobbing for eight hours a day in the big-blue, will I become a marine mammal? Left for millennia with potential mates, what strange fate would my genes undergo?

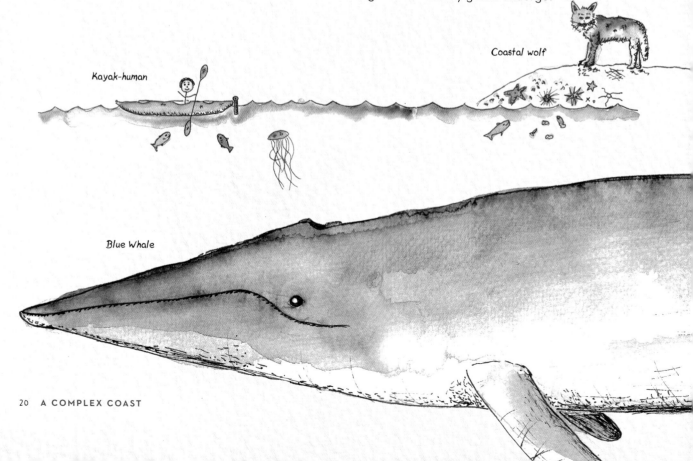

Coastal wolf

Kayak-human

Blue Whale

## BLUE WHALE (*BALAENOPTERA MUSCULUS*)

AGE: 80-90 years
WEIGHT: 150-199 tonnes (165-219 tons)
LENGTH: 30 m (100 ft)
CEREBRAL CORTEX: 15 billion neurons

## HUMPBACK WHALE[7] (*MEGAPTERA NOVAEANGLIAE*)

AGE: 80-90 years
WEIGHT: 30-40 tonnes (33-44 tons)
LENGTH: 18 m (60 ft)
CEREBRAL CORTEX: 14 billion neurons

## ORCA (*ORCINUS ORCA*)

AGE: 80-90 years
WEIGHT: 5-6 tonnes (5.5-6.6 tons)
LENGTH: 6-8 m (20-26 ft)
CEREBRAL CORTEX: 43 billion neurons

## HARBOUR PORPOISE (*PHOCOENA PHOCOENA*)

AGE: 12-20 years
WEIGHT: 50-80 kg (110-180 lbs)
LENGTH: 1-2 m (3-6 ft)
CEREBRAL CORTEX: 3 billion neurons

## PACIFIC WHITE-SIDED DOLPHIN (*LAGENORHYNCHUS OBLIQUIDENS*)

AGE: 30-40 years
WEIGHT: 100-200 kg (220-440 lbs)
LENGTH: 1.5-3 m (6-10 ft)
CEREBRAL CORTEX: 12 billion neurons

## KAYAK-HUMAN (*HOMO SAPIENS*)

AGE: 60-100 years
WEIGHT: 50-400 kg (110-880 lbs)
LENGTH: 1-2m (3-7 ft)
CEREBRAL CORTEX: 16 billion neurons

## COASTAL WOLF (*CANIS LUPUS*)

AGE: 20-30 years
WEIGHT: 30-70 kg (65-155 lbs)
LENGTH: 1-1.5 m (3-5 ft)
CEREBRAL CORTEX: 0.5 billion neurons

*Pacific white-sided dolphin*     *Harbour porpoise*

Humpback Whale

Orca

PELAGIC CORMORANT

## DAY 3, APRIL 6:
Wind light. *Sunny.* // 6.48 nm.

My *morning-brain* could talk me out of saving the world even if it only required pushing a button. I bully myself out of the sleeping bag. My wrists are sore from yesterday's race with the whales, so I *floss the tendons*, pulling the fingers up and back, then curling them down into fists, twenty times (every morning is the plan). Stretch then strengthen. Patient paddling will be the solution.

I *procrastinate*. It's late afternoon as I waddle gear to the water, four trips up and down. I leave without doing a *check-charley* and forget my sunglasses on a log.

Items lost: Sandals x 0.5, sunglasses x 1. Good start.

*Paddle, paddle, paddle.*
As stars begin their evening duty, I land on an islet the size of a tennis court. No name for it on the chart and it's ruled by gulls giving off a suspicious smell. Dry wood is easy to plunder and soon I have a rolling blaze.

Tonight's menu is *gruffy*: chickpeas, rice, lentils, soybeans, miscellaneous veg, and kelp from the tide line, cooked till mush. I eat in exhausted silence.

The ocean teems with glow-in-the-dark jellies, wiener-biters, and other mysteries-of-the-deep. To swim after sundown is my greatest fear. I resolve to overcome it. My clothing slips off in layers, and I stand naked in front of the abyss.

I repeat a mantra as the saline-universe envelopes my skin and bones: "*There is no fear when you let go of everything you know. There is no fear when you let go of everything you know. There is no fear…*"

## DAY 4, APRIL 7:
Wind SE 5 kn. *Overcast.* // Newcastle Island—Snuneymuxw territory—15 nm.

To cooperate with False Narrows, I pry open the lids before sunrise. This shallow channel floods northbound at four knots (seven kilometres/four miles per hour). Bull kelp stretches below, doing yoga in the morning rays.

On the other side, I rest on a log barge and ram down a couple peanut-butter bars. A humpback whale punctuates my thoughts, then flips its tail and bids adieu. *Alone again.*

Pelagic cormorants (*Urile pelagicus*) are underrated. They can dive 60 metres (200 feet) underwater, where they gobble rockfish, herring, and even crabs! The northwest end of Gabriola Island is some of the best nesting habitat on the coast. Out of the eroded sandstone matrix (*tafoni*), thousands of streamlined black-backs swoop. They are the fighter jet *and* submarine of the bird-world.

Newcastle Island is my destination tonight. Once I arrive, the tent click-clacks together in amber light, and I watch the Salish Sea reflect luminous ferries bound for more populated places.

STRANDED ON SANGATOR ISLAND

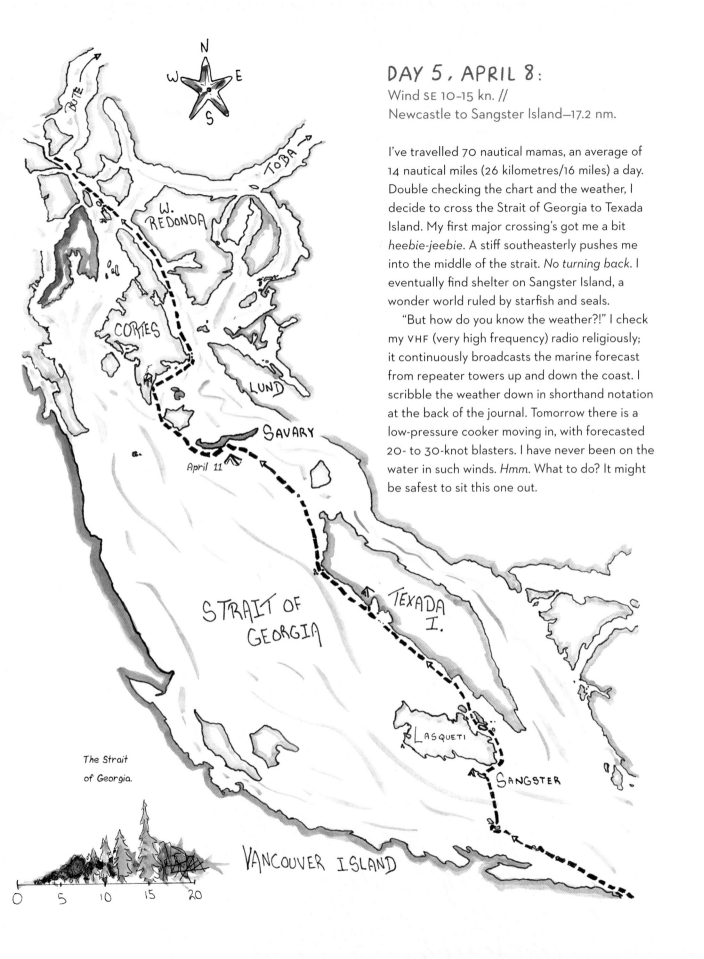

## DAY 5, APRIL 8:
Wind SE 10–15 kn. //
Newcastle to Sangster Island—17.2 nm.

I've travelled 70 nautical mamas, an average of 14 nautical miles (26 kilometres/16 miles) a day. Double checking the chart and the weather, I decide to cross the Strait of Georgia to Texada Island. My first major crossing's got me a bit *heebie-jeebie*. A stiff southeasterly pushes me into the middle of the strait. *No turning back.* I eventually find shelter on Sangster Island, a wonder world ruled by starfish and seals.

"But how do you know the weather?!" I check my VHF (very high frequency) radio religiously; it continuously broadcasts the marine forecast from repeater towers up and down the coast. I scribble the weather down in shorthand notation at the back of the journal. Tomorrow there is a low-pressure cooker moving in, with forecasted 20- to 30-knot blasters. I have never been on the water in such winds. *Hmm.* What to do? It might be safest to sit this one out.

The Strait
of Georgia.

## THE GREAT BLUE HERON (*ARDEA HERODIAS*)

**KINGDOM:** *Animalia*
**PHYLUM:** *Chordata*
**CLASS:** *Aves*
**ORDER:** *Pelecaniformes*
**FAMILY:** *Ardeidae*
**GENUS:** *Ardea*
**SPECIES:** *Herodias*

## OJISAN

Kaia's mom, Uta, calls these sea-sages *Ojisan,* which affectionately means *old man* or *uncle* in Japanese. It caught on; whenever I see one I wave happily, "Hello, Ojisan!" *They don't move.* They stay still for hours, then: Wamho! Their necks (which stretch up to three times their length) uncoil and come up with supper. They are teachers of patience, elegance, *and* agility.

Kaia's dad, Alan, met Uta while teaching in Japan, and they eventually moved to Piers. When I visit the island they welcome me warmly, despite my nervous jitters. *Thank you.* They are community builders and peace keepers on the Island and host some of the best house concerts on this coast. If you've been to one, you're lucky.

## NAVIGATION 101

Ojisans breed in colonies called heronries, and come back yearly to the same nest. Birds orient using olfactory cues, the Earth's magnetic field, the sun's position, time of sunrise and set (important for migratory birds), and maybe even the stars. Science is still far off on this.

While kayaking, there are three main navigation techniques:

1. PILOTING. Uses prominent headlands, points, coves, and beaches to match with landmarks on the chart. This method is dependent on line of sight, and can be compromised, come *Fogust* (August is *really* misty in the Pacific Northwest).

2. DEAD RECKONING. Before long (or foggy) crossings, kayakers set a *bearing* (angle) on the compass to the intended destination. To do this, check the chart's *compass rose (to calibrate for magnetic north)*. By estimating paddling speed, current direction and speed, and measuring the distance to the destination (on the chart), a kayaker *should* be able to cross anything. If there is a perpendicular current, point upwards to account for the drift. I'm pretty higgledy-piggledy (my mom's favourite word) at all this, and the thought of a blind crossing petrifies me. Perhaps I need to channel my inner Ojisan.

3. GLOBAL POSITIONING SYSTEM [GPS[8]]. I have an old Garmin handheld device that gives an accurate location of where I am, but the islands on the interface are blocky polygons with poor resolution. I couldn't figure out how to upload the proper map files. *Technology kills me.*

おじさん
~ OJISAN ~

*Herons have specialized feathers on their chest that grow continuously; they fray into a powder that is used to clean off fish slime. In breeding season, their coats turn bright blue, their irises turns red, and their yellow bills become orange. I guess people clean up and dress up for dates too.*

## CAMPSITE SHOPPING

Speaking of heronries, let me tell you about finding the perfect campsite. Each day I don't *exactly* know where I'm going. I'll have *potentials* marked on the map, but mostly I just start *shopping* around 16:00. Here's my need-want-nope checklist:

### NEEDS:

1. A suitable landing area, safe whatever the weather (this mostly means sediment beaches).

2. Fresh $H_2O$ (preferably a fast-flowing stream, then I don't have to boil it; more info on page 106).

3. A place to put the tent. This may seem like no biggie, but it's tricky to find flat real estate out here. On beaches, I level out the ground by raking the sand (I even make a pillow-bump where my head goes).

### WANTS:

1. Sunset view. This is important, and gives closure to the day. (Luckily we live on the *west* coast. No offence, Halifax, I'm sure the sunrise is dandy.)

2. Driftwood. For fire, *tarpology* (rigging up rain shelters), setting up a beach living room, and playing the-ground-is-lava.

3. A nice forest, shoreline, or tide pool. I have lots of time to chill, paint, and explore.

4. Edible goodies. Kelp, berries, and other ocean-forest munch.

### NOPES:

1. Private property. Unfortunately, there are *chowsers* on this coast who are preoccupied with guarding their temples (a note: no one owns below the high tide line). Most people are really nice and will invite me for tea. Mostly, I'd rather be alone.

2. Cliffs. I'm not a sea bird. *Yet.*

## DAY 7, APRIL 10:

Wind light. *Sunny.* //
Lasqueti Island—Tla'amin
territory—15.6 nm.

The sea has settled, the storm is over. Dismasted
kelp litters the beach.

SAVARY
ISLAND

## DAY 8, APRIL 11:

Wind SE 5-15 kn. // Savary Island—
Tla'amin territory—25 nm.

I dry out in the morning sun and stretch to the
sky; my body needs love. *Phocoena phocoena*
(Harbour porpoises) accompany me up Texada,
and soon Vivian Rock looms (see chart on page
23), infested with carnivorous sea lions, brooding.
They spot me and go *berserker.* Barking like dogs,
the harem careens into the icy water, popping
up in a rabid cluster, battling, nosing closer and
closer. I watch in disbelief as one fully ejects out
of the ocean, only to be engulfed again in the
melee. What the heavy duty… *Am I in danger?*
One thing is clear: I'm *not* camping here. With
the pressure of diminishing daylight, my only
option is a seven-mile crossing to Savary: *the
land of sand.*

*Why not?*

The clouds squeeze the last molecules from
the sun. Curious gulls circle and fly off, deciding
I'm not driftwood. The seam between ocean and
sky stitches; stars smatter the heavens.

*Uh-oh.* A southeasterly whips up and soon the
sea is a whitecap-soup. I begin surfing towards
a vague outline. I'm nervous. It's pitch black, my
headlamp is a mere freckle, and no one knows
where I am. *Onwards.*

### SPPLLAAAASHHH!

A seagull squawks and an eruption blasts beside
me. My vision calibrates—boulders! I weave
between and eventually touch sand. It's low tide
and Savary seems far off. *Distances are mutated
at night.* Gathering my gear in the dark, I plod
to the driftwood. Food + mouth. I set the tent up
backwards, take it down, *do it again.* Sleep.

Morning reflection: I've been saved by some
nameless guide. I could have nailed the reefs
last night and suffered the fate of many sailors.
*Thank you.*

### HARBOUR SEAL (*PHOCA VITULINA*)

Do you ever feel like you're being watched, only to spin round and see ripples? These munchkins follow me everywhere, *peek-a-booing* their beady, infinite eyes. I quite like their curious ways. More than anything, I'm lonely and these philosophers-of-the-deep *offer company*, however vague and mysterious.

Seals are important because they are hunters *and* hunted, mediating nutrients from kelp-dwelling fish up to the transient orcas and other apex bombers.

Off Texada, I pass a rocky islet covered in harbour seals. While switching sitting positions I jerk the kayak. *Sploosh!* My first flip of the trip. The seals plunge into the water and begin popping up everywhere. I scramble into the cockpit. *Ahhhh!* The term "wiener-biters" comes to mind, and I panic further. Eventually, I slosh in and pump out the bathtub. Jet-black domes stare back. I can almost hear them laughing.

LITTLE SEAL
Phoca vitulina

### DAY 9, APRIL 12:

Wind light. *Sun.* //
Cortes Island—We Wai Kai, Kwiakah, Homalco, and Klahoose territory—8.1 nm.

I've travelled 129 nautical miles! Pretty neat for nine days.

Cortes is isolated from mainland society by three ferries, resulting in *divergent cultural evolution*. People here have a practical and philosophical attitude, mixed with a touch of *buck-wild*. This is due to the ocean, weather, and removal from main-line civilization. Everyone wears gumboots, waves, and smiles. When in need, your neighbours help—and you do the same.

Cortes is the only place to hold an annual event called *Oyster Day* (actually "Sea Fest"). I'm staying with my friend Curtis Simpson, who grew up here. His siblings, Henri and Josie, were my roommates in Victoria, and his family has taken me in once before. Curtis invites me on the oyster rafts where he works.

The Gorge is an iconic anchorage on Cortes, scattered with oysie-planks and sketchy sailboats. Bivalve spawn hangs in increments from the rafts (see diagram opposite), which take two years to grow to commercial size. Once ready, the units are towed in on a high tide and harvested *on the low*.

We spend the morning processing littleneck clams and the afternoon harvesting oysters. Curty and I get home with a *private stash* and serious burger inspiration.

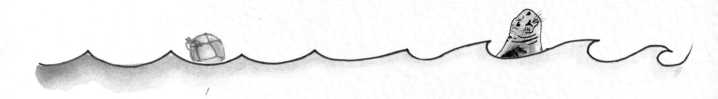

## PACIFIC OYSTER (*MAGALLANA GIGAS*)

Oysters live in one of the harshest environments on earth, the intertidal zone—waves, salt, sun, predators, and lots of competition. To prevent desiccation and survive when tides retreat, the shells squeeze shut. I learn they can survive up to three weeks without water! I also learn they change sex depending on the season, can filter five litres of water per hour, and taste different depending on habitat/water quality. Oysters are one of the biggest commercial invertebrate fisheries on earth—four billion bucks annually.

### OYSTER BURGERS

5–7 bivalves (from ocean)
2 eggs (from chickens)
creative spice mix (cayenne, salt, pepper)
½ cup cornmeal (breading mix)
½ cup flour
milk
bunning digs: tomatoes, cheese, lettuce, pickles, love (go full-wild)

1. Shuck[9] using necessary means—insert knife in the *soft spot* at back, and twist.

2. Soak oysters in milk for 15 minutes (I dunno why).

3. Dunk oysters in eggs and spices (like French toast).

4. Bread 'em with flour, spices, and cornmeal (coat 'em up).

5. Sizzle-fry with oil.

6. Bun-time: toppings and condiments (remember: full-wild).

7. Nourish (eat slow, and say thanks to the ocean).

8. Repeat Tuesday, Thursday, and Saturday (as bivalve population permits).

9. Enjoy the zinc, calcium, magnesium, protein, selenium, vitamin A, and B12 (lots of B12).

10. Careful of red tide.[10]

PACIFIC OYSTER
*Crassostrea gigas*

*Above* Oysies produce 50 to 200 million eggs during spawning. Once fertilized, the larva finds a rock and begins excreting "cement" from its "foot," then it shells its gonads and other squishy parts, meaning it takes calcium and salt from the ocean and mixes it with proteins from the oyster.

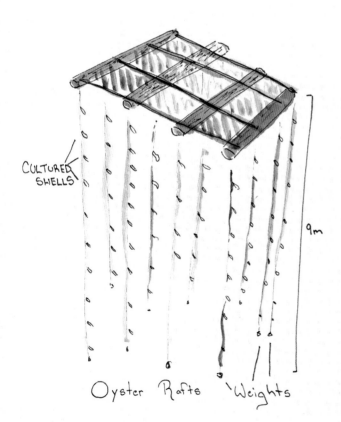

CULTURED SHELLS

9m

Oyster Rafts   'Weights'

# 2
# CAPE
# CAUTION

"The sea is emotion incarnate. It loves, hates, and weeps. It defies all attempts to capture it with words and rejects all shackles. No matter what you say about it, there is always that which you can't."

～ **CHRISTOPHER PAOLINI** ～
*Eragon*

QUEEN CHARLOTTE
STRAIT

NORTH

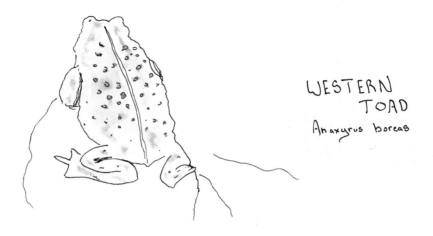

WESTERN
TOAD
*Anaxyrus boreas*

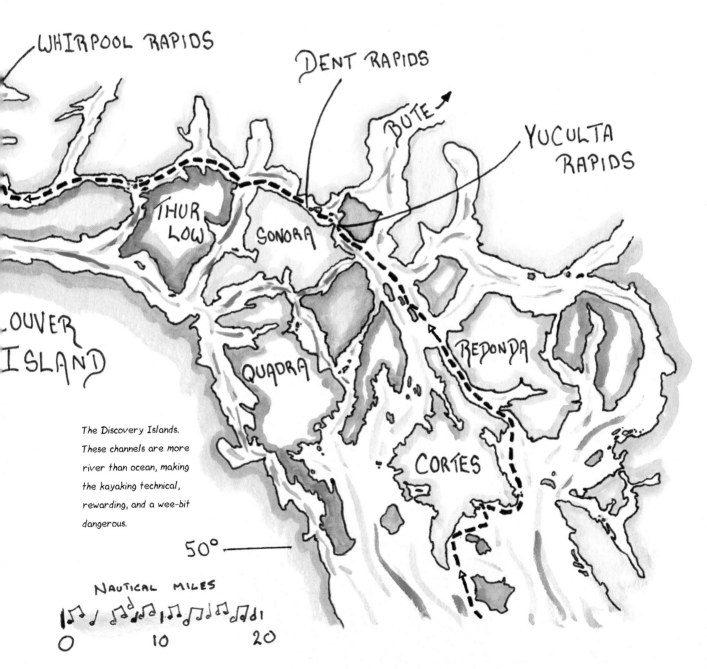

WHIRPOOL RAPIDS

DENT RAPIDS

BUTE →

YUCULTA
RAPIDS

THUR
LOW

SONORA

VAN COUVER
ISLAND

QUADRA

REDONDA

CORTES

The Discovery Islands.
These channels are more
river than ocean, making
the kayaking technical,
rewarding, and a wee-bit
dangerous.

50° ——————

NAUTICAL MILES

0          10          20

# BERRIES OF THE PACIFIC NORTHWEST

## SALMONBERRIES (*RUBUS SPECTABILIS*)

Salmonberries give a vitamin boost (C, A, B6), and are *generally lovable*. Identified by their pink flowers and jagged, arrow-shaped leaves, they begin in May and don't stop until July, making them the *earliest* fruit on the coast. As nitrogen-loving plants, they are abundant near salmon-bearing streams and midden sites (shell deposits from Indigenous habitation). The one downside *(and upside)* to these mouth-wompers is their *mushyness*—they must be processed or eaten quickly.

I found salmonberries all the way to Alaska.

## THIMBLEBERRIES (*RUBUS PARVIFLORUS*)

Thimbles require nimble fingers, otherwise the orbs are happily smooshed. Without boiling down, I add sugar for preservation and sweetness, and squish them inside ziplock, turning them into jam for later. Good patches appear in disturbed areas like recent fire sites and clear-cuts.

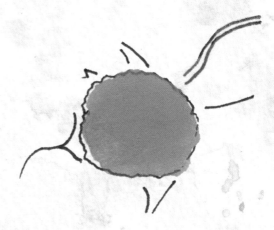

## SALAL (*GAULTHERIA SHALLON*)

Salal is a crafty lover and the classic understorey in the PNW. It reigns dominant and almost impenetrable in young forests. The berries are the latest-bloomers, good into November, depending on latitude. Young salal leaves are a hunger suppressant, useful on long hikes (or for whining kids). The leaves can be brewed into a tea with anti-inflammatory properties that treat bladder infections and menstrual cramps.

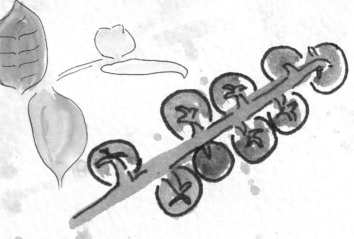

## RED HUCKLEBERRIES (*VACCINIUM PARVIFOLIUM*)

On Hurricane Island, I explored an Indigenous midden site, ripe with secrets. Ancient house beams lay coated in moss, and Sitka spruce giants blotted the sun. Red huckleberries braided the entire understorey, reaching well above my head, dripping with wonder-balls—a huckleberry orchard! I boiled them into syrup for a pleasant oat-experience.

R-huckles are firm and keep well. Tasty stuffed in fish.

## TARP PICKING[1]

This is the best way to mega-pick. Set up a tarp at the base of a loaded bush, and comb through the branches. This technique works best with red huckles. Once the berries cascade onto the tarp, funnel them into a container.

# DAY 12, APRIL 15:

*Winds light. //*
Cortes to Rendezvous Island—15.2 nm.

Orcas are breaching in the bay—the most pleasant alarm clock in the universe? Cortes has given me a taste of humanity *and* oven-cooked meals; I even had a soak in the hot tub! I'm refuelled and back in business. The whales stream north, motivating me to finish my oats and get on with it. The currents are favourable, so I fall asleep, *slumped in the cockpit,* letting the ebb take me north. I now live a life ruled by the moon.

At the Rendezvous Islands, I reconnect with my whale buds, who now pursue a lone sea lion. The transient killers swerve and sweep the shallows. The sea lion conducts a fantastic leap during the chase, and eventually the orcas give up.

Plunging into the ocean for a snorkel, I'm amazed by the diversity. Urchins, cukes, and tubeworm-thingies mingle and jingle. Lingcod and kelp greenlings eye my bare feet. I sleep without the tent at first, but the mosquitoes are too much.

## TIDES

"Just how do tides work?" I ask this almost *philosophically.* Tides on the coast of BC can be greater than ten metres, some of the biggest in the world (#1 is the Bay of Fundy, at fifteen metres). The PNW has a *mixed* tide cycle, which means *two highs and two lows* each day. These are a function of the Earth's position and distance from the sun *and* moon (see diagram).

Basically, the moon and sun are in a tug-o-war gravity-battle with the Earth, and the oceans are caught in between, unable to decide.

## TIDES LEVEL TWO

"Why are tides greater on the full and new moon? And what does that mean for intimate relationships?" The moon takes twenty-eight days to orbit the Earth, and *lines up* with the sun twice each cycle. When the lunar and solar tides coincide, it *magnifies* the tug, making the oceans rise higher, thus that much closer to touching the moon. Neap tides are when sun and moon cancel each other out; spring tides are when highs and lows are maxed.

Not sure about the intimate relationships. I'm just a beginner.

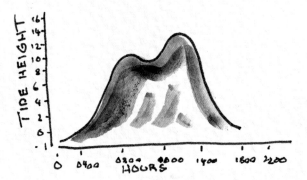

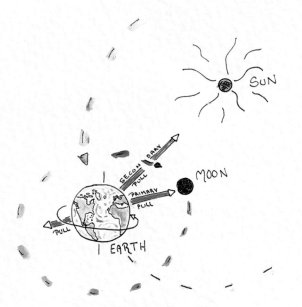

*Above Gravity rules our lives—and the oceans.*

*Opposite Sunset snorkle with friends. Can you find them all? Red urchin, eel grass, lion's mane jelly, copper rockfish, lingcod, sea cuke, bull kelp, and a cormorant diving for herring. *Kaia painted the cormorant.*

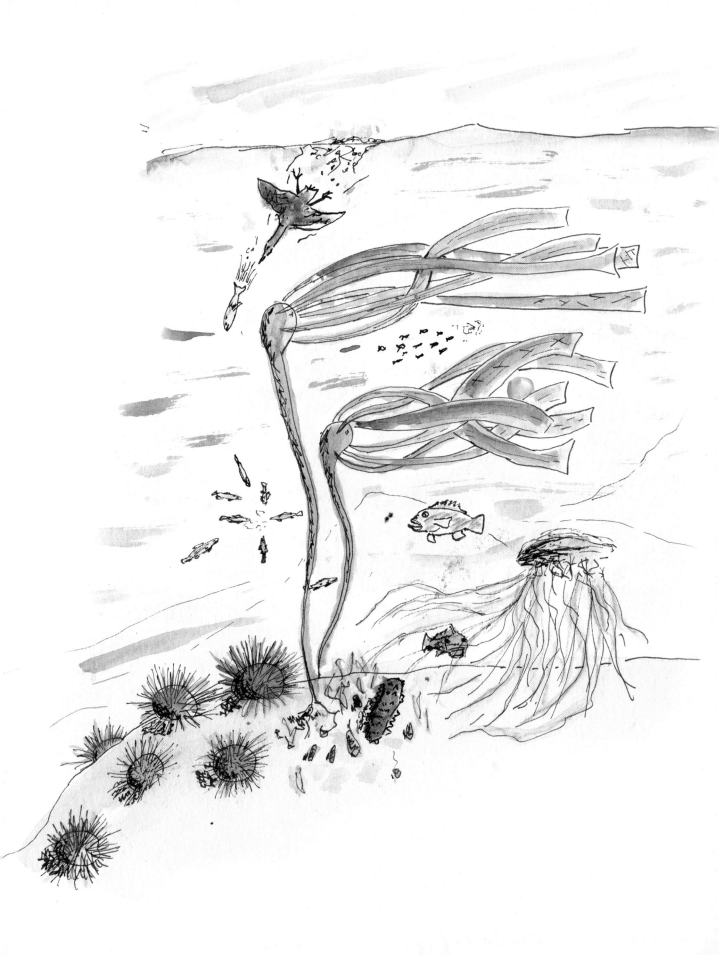

# DAY 13, APRIL 16:

Winds light to SE 5. //
Rendezvous to Dent Rapids—
Kwiakah territory—10.8 nm.

Two eagles drift on a log, ferocious ridgelines slice clouds in two, and my mind struggles to hold onto anything definite.

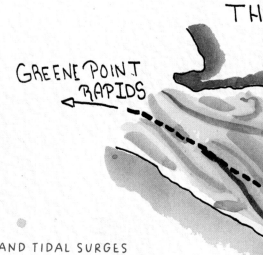

GREENE POINT RAPIDS

TH

OK, next lesson. Tidal currents here are full-bonkers and unlike anywhere on the planet, giving the Pacific Northwest its character *and* biological diversity. The fastest tidal surge in the world is Nakwakto Rapids, peaking at 17 knots (31 km/h)! This is in Gwa'sala and 'Nakwaxda'xw territory, which covers the north end of Vancouver Island and the adjacent mainland. Yuculta, Dent, and Arran Rapids are up on the list too (see opposite).

I use the back eddies to glide up *the inside* of Stuart Island. Wherever you have currents, you have back eddies (parallel opposite flows). This is helpful for kayakers, who can sneak up channels. Eventually the water ebbs, and I careen through Yuculta towards Dent. *Yippee!* It's a dangerous rollercoaster, but I've done a bit of white-water, which comes in handy. I pull off into a little parking spot before the next gnarly section. Dent needs slack tide, to be on the safe side. I watch from shore as a one-metre waterfall forms!

## CURRENTS[2] AND TIDAL SURGES

Narrow bottlenecks sink countless vessels each year—from kayaks to ferries. It's all about equilibrium with these puppies. Visualize a thirty-metre-wide river that encounters a five-metre constriction, then *opens again* to thirty metres. The water builds up in height, speed, and pressure as it cooks through, then a complex-chaos of relief after the narrows, creating whirlpools, back eddies, turbulence, and other mysteries-of-physics. Then imagine the flow switching direction and doing it again—four times a day (every six hours). The final kicker: it's not a *river*, it's the amoral, indifferent, Mighty Pacific.

Sound scary? It is, but fascinatingly fun. I have been moving with favourable currents, paddling north for six hours then taking a siesta. An intimate relationship with the moon is developing—my midnight lover. When I lack strength, it pulls me on.

PIDS

N

DAY 13 CAMP

TURNBACK PT

ARRAN RAPIDS
• FLOOD: 14kn
• EBB: 10kn

BIG BAY

DENT

DENT RAPIDS
• FLOOD: 11kn
• EBB: 8kn

STUART ISLAND

YUCULTA RAPIDS
• FLOOD: 10kn
• EBB: 8kn

SONORA ISLAND

Stuart Island is one of the only islands with its own airport and golf course. It's home to exclusive fishing lodges and rich bigwigs. The reason the fishing is so good? The currents.

# On Solitude

## ON SOLITUDE

*What's the longest you have been alone? Only talking to trees? Crying without a second shoulder, and searching for secrets in the moon-lit pines?*

With only islands, weather, and the duties of survival, I cannot escape my mind—ruthlessly boring, repetitive, lustful, and delusional. Is everyone this unstable!? Repeating stories of the past and fantasies of the future, it's insatiable. The insanity-potential I possess is daunting. *However*, my inner-wilderness *is* settling (a little).

*The true needs of an individual become apparent when the wants of society are removed.* This seems holy. Our culture has a fear of solitude. We grow up with expectations, care, and inspiration of others. Evolutionarily, this is why we prospered—*we worked together.* But our monkey cousins also went solo from time to time, to find food and territory. And perhaps, *something more?* Perhaps that's why we are no longer monkeys.

Friends and strangers bring out the beautiful parts in me, but also prevent me from being authentic. At university, I was following cultural orders—afraid to show vulnerability, femininity, and my ignorance.

Many Indigenous traditions have rites-of-passage where individuals set out in nature to find their true self and commune with the *creator.* These experiences instil maturity, survival skills, and a profound sense of purpose. In ancient India (and today also), spiritual seekers set out on pilgrimages thousands of kilometres long—*with bare feet.* Neighbouring nations would let holy-searchers pass through unharmed. *It was beyond politics*—a universal mission.

We Western settlers give our kids cell phones at twelve, new cars at sixteen, and alcohol at nineteen. Then we send them to university to amass debt, career-fever, and messy-sexual-encounters. Are these freedoms or vices? Where's the context, vision, and quest?

Out here, I am finding *something*, although it's hard to translate. Often, my mind is too loud to truly soak in my surroundings. But there are times when everything goes quiet—*a glitch in the matrix.* I'm not religious, but if there is a god, it lies buried here: between lonely timbers and lipstick lichen (*Cladonia macilenta*). *I'll keep looking.*

Solitude cultivates authenticity. Upon returning home, I hope this new light shines and awakens the same light glowing deeply in everyone.

## DAY 19, APRIL 22:

*Sun and clouds. //*
Chatham Channel—21.6 nm.

Johnstone Strait held stiff northwesterlies that had me rigged up on Poyntz Island, journaling and waiting for calm waters. Today, I squeak through and turn into the protected Chatham Channel. Supposedly, there is a post office here. I spot a dock and the familiar Canada Post sign. *Civilization!* Hmmmm, a weird place to send mail from.

### "JUST JEN"

Jen declares proudly and somewhat philosophically that she has no last name. "It's. Just. Jen." Over the decades, husbands have come and gone, leaving her last name too mixed up to note. She lives alone with her dog, Bruce, etched into the side of Chatham Channel. This is one of the most remote post offices in Canada and sends out mail every Wednesday *via seaplane*. It is visited more by bears than people. There used to be a village on nearby Minstrel Island, but it's deserted now. A couple prawners stay with her during the season, but that's about it.

Wild grey hair lifts and tangles on her wool sweater, reminding me of *Usnea australis* (old man's beard, a lichen, which is a symbiotic relationship between fungus and algae). She is weathered, kind, and thoughtful. I find out she has been running the post office for the last ten years *by herself*. At first, she knew little of the coast, and recalls frozen pipe fiascos, pesky

JUST JEN IN CHATHAM CHANNEL

black bears looting the garden, and her dogs kidnapped by cougars. Bruce seems to know what he's doing.

I show her my journal and she gets excited, striding across the room to get her art-gear. "You need to learn about shading." Paint is how she passes time on rainy days. Which is most of the winter.

After writing letters to loved ones, I'm embarrassed to admit I have no money to buy stamps. She smiles, gives a wink, and takes the envelopes. To spend time with another human after weeks alone does wonders for the soul. I leave smiling and full of energy.

*Shading mountains with Jen.*

## ON GOD

Imagine a school where ethics, philosophy, and religion are at the *centre*. Rabbis, monks, priests, philosophers, imams, physicists, logicians, and evolutionary biologists all plead their perspective, prophetic tales, and everything else one needs to make an informed decision. Then kids can carve their own way. Ultimately, the aim would be to create tolerance around worldviews and a diversity of belief-systems in our homogenous society. *We need new angles.*

This would have been better than my colonial-social-studies class.

I don't know if God exists, or if the great philosophers were right. To be honest, that's why I'm here: *to do research.* I'm on a modern pilgrimage. Just as Jesus stumbled into the desert, and Kierkegaard marched through Copenhagen's crooked streets. Just as Buddha renounced the palace, and Mohammed—peace be upon him—began to fast. I paddle my little boat into open water to ponder reality.

I think wilderness builds character. It's a chance to find what is good, true, and holy. Many summer-longers on the PCT, Appalachian, and El Camino Santiago are doing the same—looking for truth. Our western world is devoid of formal coming-of-age ceremonies, so we have made our own. What about you?

My family was open-minded. We had Bibles, Buddhas, and biology texts all lined up together.

This helped, and if you're a parent reading this: make sure to be open about religion and philosophy. Don't shovel your dogma. Let kids explore.

Yes, religion seems corrupted by power, and most philosophy is contextual. But what we believe in matters; it transforms everything we know and love. Even if we opt out of faith and philosophy, it's worth understanding where we came from.

We all have a belief-system, even if it's scientific-capitalistic-materialism. And science is not solid! Remember when the earth was flat and there were no tectonic plates? Remember when a particle couldn't simultaneously be in two places at once? Can science also be dogmatic and considered a religion? One good thing about science is that it has mechanisms to challenge and evaluate its findings, something most religions lack.

There's a lot we don't know; it's humbling. Take human consciousness. New studies show our physical and mental systems work like algorithms, and researchers admit they don't really know how or why. There are parts of cognitive research, quantum physics, and evolutionary biology that are beyond us—so far out of reach, the math stops making sense, and so do the scientists[3].

My current belief: *question everything,* in a good way.

## WESTERN RED CEDAR
## (*THUJA PLICATA*)

When I was small, Dad used to split cedar into pieces so I could carve swords. It's the smell and sound I remember. *Crack!* A perfect material. Out here, I use it for tarp-supports, mindless whittling, and making fires. When everything is wet, cedar splits to reveal a dry interior, because of superpower-chemicals making it resistant to rot, moisture, and fungus.

Indigenous Peoples use it for paddles, long-houses, clothing, *canoes,* and fish nets braided from bark strands. This is amazing, one tree for everything: a real-life giving tree.

## DENDROCHRONOLOGY
## (DENDRO = TREE / CHRONO = TIME)

*Sweet tree-time.* Each ring represents one year of growth. The dark section represents fall and winter, when trees toughen up for the cold. The lighter part shows the summer growth-spurt. *How old is this puppy?*

In dendro, we can learn more than birthdays, like the dates of drought years, wildfires, and landslides, and how climate is changing. It's an objective history book. Cedars can live 1,500 solar-mamas. *That's a lot of stories.*

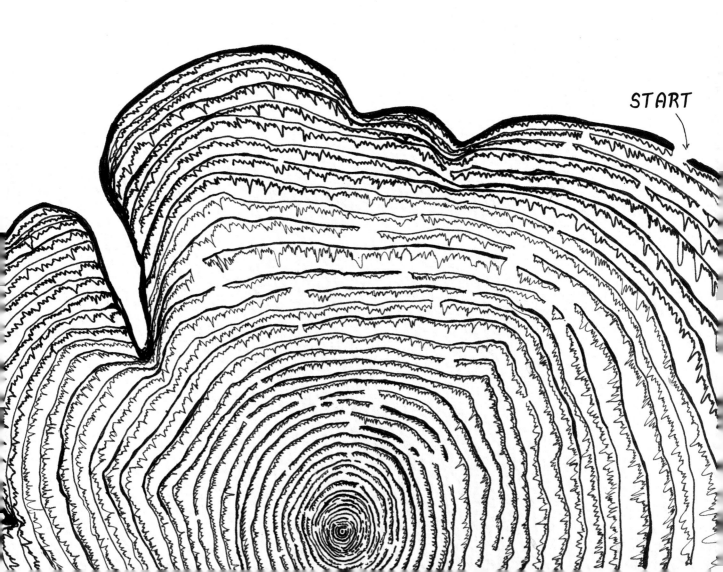

START

# DAY 21, APRIL 24:

*Rain.* // Minstrel Island,
Tlowitsis territory, 18.9 nm.

If all societies collapse, what will happen to us?

Minstrel is a stark reminder of impermanence; this place used to be a metropolis. During the logging boom, thousands of workers lived and restocked here. In awe, I pick berries and dumpster dive from the wreckage: one full jar of PB, spices, cornmeal, rudder cables, and a wool sock. *How old is this stuff?* Vines and creepers crawl into broken windows; support beams rust and decompose. Rodents, bears, and bugs recolonize their home.

How will Vancouver and Seattle look 100 years after humans?

What made Minstrel unsustainable? Is there some structural fault in how *Homo sapiens* relate to nature and its "resources"? Capitalism leads to innovation, but does it create lasting, respectful relationships with the places we depend on? The inherent value of these ecosystems seems lost in the economic confluence of greed, property, profit, and competition.

Leaving the forest to its slow-motion reclamation, I head out on a flat-water-mirror reflecting fir boughs and clouds. *Lagenorhynchus obliquidens* (Pacific white-sided dolphins) tease my bow and play with the sea-sky interface. Rain sputters. I arrive at Compton Island, wet, tired, hungry, and with a brutal case of kayak-legs (a bit like after riding a horse). I eat yesterday's gruffy and pass out half inside the sleeping bag.

BARNACLE BOTTLES

As civilizations expand and complexify, they fall ill from the inside. Scientists call this process diminishing return. A hypothesis by the anthropologist Joseph Tainter[4] in 1988 states: As population increases, control structures decrease. Societies use religion, capitalism, materialism, fascism, or any other "ism" to maintain control, but ultimately, they implode after a certain threshold. So human communities don't collapse because of drought, famine, war, or disease; those are symptoms of an unstable population no longer able to adapt. What happens if the society is global?

## DAY 24, APRIL 27:
Winds light. *Sunny.* // Broughton archipelago—Kwakwaka'wakw territory—13.5 nm.

No-chart day. Navigating usually requires referencing the chart atlas in a ziplock on the deck. I meander through the Broughtons using the sun as a compass. It's a maze, but eventually I'm staring out at the mighty Pacific. *No protection remains.*

## DAY 26, APRIL 29:
Wind NW 15–25 kn. // Browning Islands—Gwa'Sala-'Nakwaxda'xw territory—9.72 nm.

Ten hours to make ten nautical miles. *I'm exhausted.* My daily schedule is unpredictable, trying, and adaptive—a mix of gut feelings, alarm-clock discipline, and coincidence.

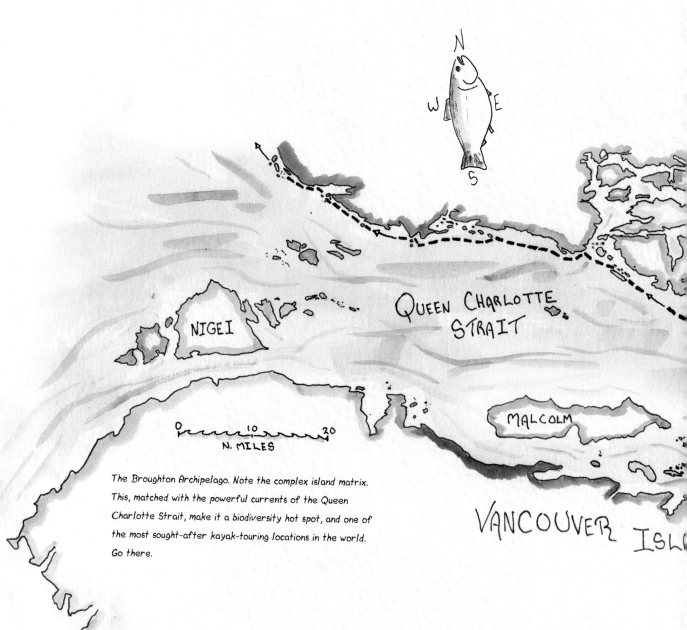

NIGEI

QUEEN CHARLOTTE STRAIT

MALCOLM

VANCOUVER ISL

0 · · · · · 10 · · · · · 20
N. MILES

The Broughton Archipelago. Note the complex island matrix. This, matched with the powerful currents of the Queen Charlotte Strait, make it a biodiversity hot spot, and one of the most sought-after kayak-touring locations in the world. Go there.

# DAY 27, APRIL 30:

Wind NW 20–30 kn. // Arm Island—21 nm.

04:00. My mind struggles out of dream-world, my hands wrestle the sleeping-bag into the stuff-sack, and my willpower decompartmentalizes the tent and lugs *everything* down. This muddy bay is 500 kilometres (306 miles) from home. I feel strange and disembodied. My brain is quiet, saving energy for necessity.

No sunrise, only a grey dimmer-switch. I move quickly, knowing the morning calm won't last. The VHF forecast is bleak—*high opposing winds.*

I'm past Vancouver Island and there is no turning back. Exposure is my only companion.

08:00. The swell is three to five metres and whitecaps are everywhere.

A lone man from a fish farm rushes out in his dingy. "You all by yourself out here!?" His words are scattered by wind and spray. Convincing him "I'm OK!" and reluctantly turning down coffee at the fish farm, I push on.

09:30. Conditions are deadly. I seek shoreline, and curl up in a cave for six hours, moaning quietly. *I don't know why,* but I've been making lots of weird noises lately. My inner-animal is breaching through. The sun traverses the sky without me.

15:00. I awake, disoriented and alone. Tomorrow, I paddle around Cape Caution, pushing the boundaries of my boundaries. *I hope I don't die.*

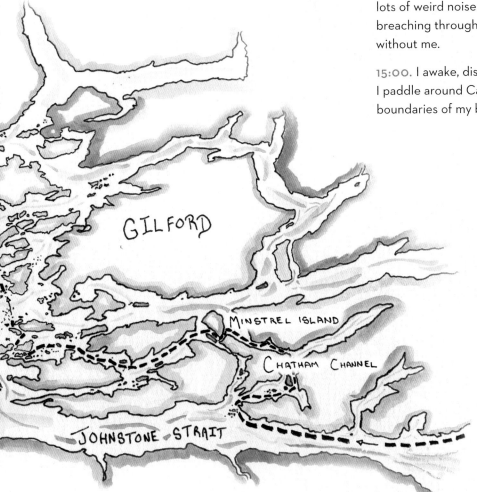

GILFORD

MINSTREL ISLAND

CHATHAM CHANNEL

JOHNSTONE STRAIT

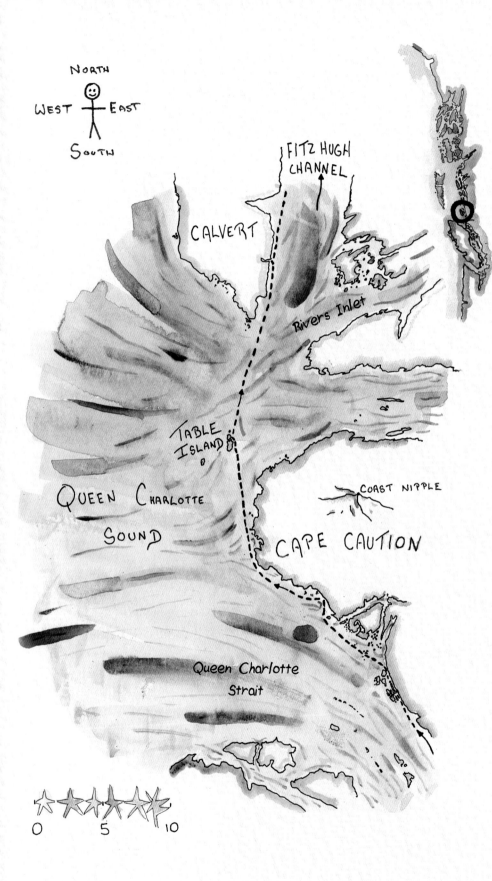

NORTH
WEST — EAST
SOUTH

CALVERT

FITZ HUGH CHANNEL

Rivers Inlet

TABLE ISLAND

QUEEN CHARLOTTE SOUND

COAST NIPPLE

CAPE CAUTION

Queen Charlotte Strait

0          5          10

## TABLE ISLAND POEM

These logs are
battered and
infested with sand.
They test my balance,
and offer me a
seat to think
Eternal meditators.
From standing to fallen
from seed to sea
from salt to sand.
One day
we too
will wash up
on the beach
of oblivion.

Cape Caution. Visualize the
currents on an incoming and
outgoing tide. How do you
plan your kayak traverse?
What's your route if a gale
comes in from the Pacific,
or stiff north westerlies?
An extra note: the island
west of Table is called Egg
Island, and has a lighthouse,
and a lighthouse keeper.
Imagine living there.

# DAY 29, MAY 1:

Winds NW 5–10 kn. *Overcast.* //
Table Island—20.2 nm.

Cape-C is a volatile headland openly defying the Pacific and, perhaps, *even god.* Currents from the Rivers Inlet and Queen Charlotte Strait often rebel and wrestle with westerly swell and gale-force winds. Conditions can change without warning. The biggest challenge: *exposure.* There is no shelter here, no safe haven, no retreat.

In 1793, ol' George Van nearly lost the HMS *Discovery* close by, inspiring the name *Cape Caution.*

*But don't worry.* All treachery has seeds of purity. I have been watching the weather and studying the charts like a bible. I plan to use the currents *to my advantage.* I just hope the wind doesn't kick up.

04:00. I weave through explosive reefs and let the tide push me north. After a morning of *paddle-paddle-paddle,* I coordinate with the crashing waves of Burnett Bay. Trundling up to driftwood, I shovel food into the furnace. The sand is littered with wolf tracks; I follow them and shiver warmth back into my soul.

Neptune's kingdom looks manageable, so I push off and smash through the surf. Then, *the infamous cape.*

Threading the Cape Caut needle takes five uneventful, arduous hours. Table Island, an enclave covered with 45-degree rock and timber, is my salvation. I try to land on the first decent rock ledge, and *Bell* flips in a sudden swell as I'm getting out. Gear dumps out of the cockpit and I scramble to recover everything. *This island is untameable,* where do I camp? Around the next headland, I yelp in delight—the perfect sandy beach. *Yippee!* Refuge comes in unlikely spaces, at unlikely times, and often when we need it most.

I pry *Mytilus californianus* (California mussels) off the rocks, and after fire-roasting the blue-shell-mamas a thick sleep overcomes me. Two hours later, I urgently need to *poop, vomit, and pee at the same time. I do*—right beside my tent. *Eeeeewwww!* The mussels are exacting revenge—*or I'm allergic.* I pass the night in delirium, but with the morning sun comes gastrointestinal salvation.

CAPE CAUTION

THE MIGHTY PACIFIC

* I later try other shellfish in small doses and have similar symptoms. A definite shellfish allergy. Oysters are OK.

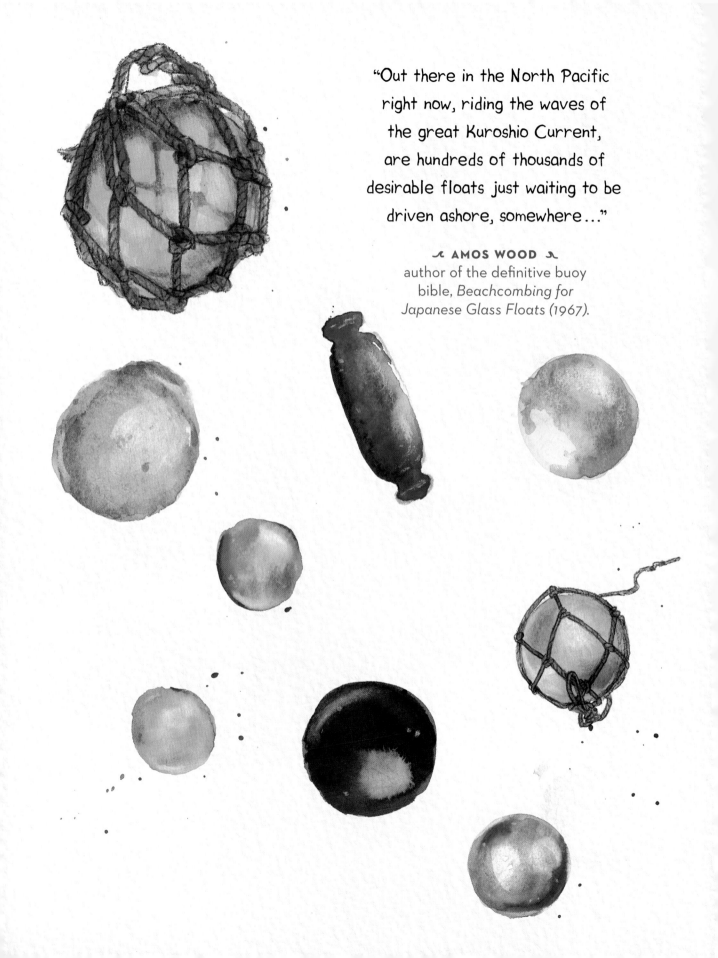

"Out there in the North Pacific right now, riding the waves of the great Kuroshio Current, are hundreds of thousands of desirable floats just waiting to be driven ashore, somewhere…"

꜀ **AMOS WOOD** ꜁
author of the definitive buoy bible, *Beachcombing for Japanese Glass Floats (1967).*

These paintings were created by Adrienne Rempel, an amazingly skilled artist from Vancouver, BC. She is an honoured member of the Norwell family and has deep relationships with all my siblings. If I painted these, they would have looked drowsy and less jaw-dropping. Thank you, Adrienne! Each one is a universe to ponder.

## JAPANESE BUOYS

These fishing floats were blown from melted-down recycled glass into rough spheres. Ranging from blues and greens to pink and yellow, the orbs have a charm, elegance, and mystery that has seduced me into obsession. Perhaps it's because they are fragile and have traveled so far. Many have been at sea for ten years, *waiting*. They are "Easter eggs" tucked among the drift-wood and seaweed. Always out of reach, just under the next log. Today I screamed in delight only to find a half-buried lightbulb, which, interestingly, was also from Japan.

There is treasure everywhere. Inside. Outside. It's just a matter of seeing things in the right light.

Speaking of a hunt, there are fifty-six orbs hidden in the pages of this book: Good luck with the hunt; "gotta catch 'em all."

## GEORGIA KLAP

*Zooooooommmm!* Another *Rufous* scares the *jeebies* out of me. To impress potential soulmates, hummingbirds plummet at breakneck, pulling out at the last second (the "J" dive)—sometimes within centimetres of my cranium. They are attracted to cliffs and the edges of forests, making the coast prime for witnessing their flirtatious dance moves.

Hummingbirds remind me of my friend Georgia, who died in a house fire a year before the trip.

There was this Valentine's Day-themed party. Candles decorated the window shelves and were scattered throughout the house. Sometime during the night, a couch caught fire and was put out, but embers lingered. After everyone left, Georgia and her flatmates went to bed. The hundred-year-old Johnson Street house went up in a flash. At 4 AM the police and firefighters could not enter the building because of the extreme heat. The blaze caused a nearby van to catch fire. Neighbours and onlookers screamed from the street, *There are people inside.* Nothing could be done to save Georgia's life. Also in the house were Emily Morin, 20, and Mark Mitchell, 26. Young souls budding with passion, love, and change-making.

Georgia was the same age as me at the time (22) and capable of anything. The hummingbird was a symbol of her presence throughout the gatherings to celebrate her life. Hummingbirds will always be a sign of hope and creativity to me.

I dedicate this trip to her, and everyone else taken from our hands without warning.

Georgia lives on in the gardens, trees, and bees of Southern Vancouver Island.

Can anyone escape death's wandering ways?

## FIRE

Every night, I haul *Bell Breezy* above the tide line, set up the tent, and light a fire. *It's ritual.* Each

RUFOUS
HUMMING BIRD
Selasphorus rufus

MATING SEASON

THE 'J' DIVE

*Above* The rufous hummingbird (Selasphorus rufus) makes one of the farthest migrations of any bird on earth in relation to body length, flying 784,500 body lengths (6,200 km / 3,900 miles) from Alaska to Mexico.

beach has different fuel stocks and requires a scavenger hunt. I lean towards the *teepee* setup with my kindling, but also use the *log-cabin* technique. The key is putting down flat pieces of wood as a foundation for the fire to burn onto, and to keep it off the damp sand. These base pieces combust into coals that hold steady heat to warm the pot.

PRO TIP: On cold nights I pull a sizable hot rock from the embers, wrap it in a scarf, and take it into the sleeping bag. Sometimes I take two, one by my feet and one beside my core. Often they are still warm in the morning. Be careful: once I melted my sleeping bag.

TINDER: Cedar shavings, dried old man's beard, dry spruce needles.

**KINDLING:** Split cedar, dead spruce branches (break from bottom of live tree), dead salal stems.

**WOOD:** Cedar driftwood and whatever else looks dry. One time, I accidentally threw in a piece of treated timber (an old telephone pole). The fumes made me gag, and I had to put out the fire and start again.

### GRUFFY RECIPE

Perhaps you have been wondering about my magical *gruffy*. It's more an attitude than a recipe, but I'll try my best:

1. Collect salt water from the ocean, and combine with fresh water. I use a fifty-fifty mix for all cooking.

1. Add whatever veg, beans, lentils, and grains you have (use some discretion, but not much).

2. Search the tide line for relatively fresh or dried-out kelp (as long as there's no fly's buzzing, it should be good). Add it to the pot.

3. Find a pinch of old man's beard (a lichen, remember). Add that too (for vitamin C).

4. Heat over the fire and cook to a pleasant *inconsistency*. It could take hours, depending on if you soaked the beans or not. I always forget, and my cooking routine goes long into the evening. I don't mind sitting around the fire; what else am I going to do?

5. Find a nice spoon-shell or carve a spork out of driftwood.

6. Enjoy with mouth, eat with gratitude, and imagine serving the dish in a restaurant, and whatever you would call it on the menu, if *gruffy* doesn't seem marketable.

7. Make enough for tomorrow's lunch.

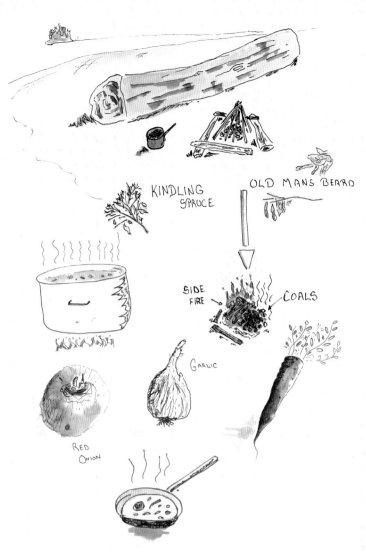

Garlic, onions, carrots, and potatoes last longer than I thought in the hatches (three weeks if kept dry). The dehydrated veg and jerky help immensely.

### THE NEXT BITE

Eating alone is wonderful, and I've observed an interesting habit. Rather than savouring each mouthful, it seems I'm consuming the *expectation of the next bite*. Immediately after beginning to chew one food-nugget, I'm preparing the next. My mind is constantly one foot/fork in the future. Why can't I be in the present? *Hmm...*

# DAY 32, MAY 4:

Day off. Winds NW 5–10 kn. //
The Trap—Heiltsuk territory.

EAGLE TALON

Total distance from Victoria: 347 nm.

I'm on the home stretch, only 21 kilometres
(13 miles) to Bella Bella. It's been a month, but
the days have melted into dotted ink lines, camp-
fires, and clamshells. My clothes are filled with
sand and salt. My hands and feet are carved by
cuts and bruises. But I'm healing wounds deeper
than those on the surface. *I feel right and holy
and beautiful.*

It's back to school and society. Back to expectations and accountability. *Back to people.* Part
of me wants to stay.

## WHAT HAVE I LEARNED SO FAR?

- *Each moment is unique*—a gift to be honoured
  and enjoyed. Food is sacred. Anything is
  possible.

- *To be disciplined takes discipline* and perhaps
  a watch. The ego is nothing more than one's
  attachment to an idea.

- *Accept and transcend.*

- *Take responsibility for your situation,* and be
  patient. The world is working in your favour.
  But it takes a while for the lessons to emerge.

- *Smile when things go sideways.* Life points
  out when you're too invested in the future.
  Roll with the waves.

- *Do one thing at a time,* or else you burn
  the lentils.

- *Take care of the body. Calm the mind.*

- *Fall asleep in weird places,* preferably close
  to water.

THE M
PAC

*Getting to Bella Bella.
This is beautiful paddling.
If I was brave, I would
have gone on the outside
of Hunter. Which way would
you have gone?*

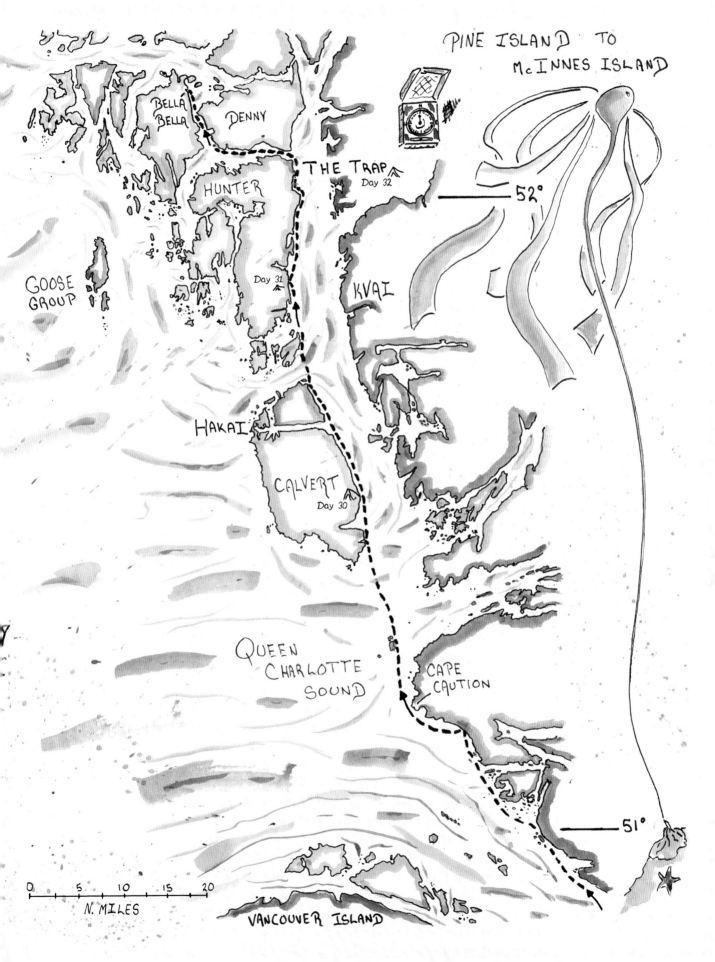

# DAY 33, MAY 5:

Winds NW 5. // Bella Bella—13.5 nm.

"*Bell Pepper,* meet Bella Bella!" I've been rehearsing this line for a while.

The last four days were a trial. I'm tired but eager to reintegrate with humanity. Coming around the last headland, Bella-B slides into view. Colourful houses blend with the shoreline—seamlessly. Young boys pitch themselves off the dock, making their mark on the ocean's infinitude. A lone man casts lines from the breakwater, fishing for springs and silvers. This is the home of the *Heiltsuk First Nation.*

An *Antigone canadensis* (sandhill crane) greets me at the beach. I step onto hot sand and take a moment: *I made it.* I didn't capsize or get eaten by wiener-biters. I didn't get lost or lose my mind. I made it! Savouring my existence, my story, my pride… *and* anxiety? Yes, I'm nervous. I have been through this *whole-big-thing.* Now *what?*

I walk through town in a daze, as brown bodies frolic in a field. A woman smiles from her doorway. A neighbourhood dog nuzzles into my crotch, wiggling his tail, *hello.* My senses are overwhelmed, but I'm elated to be back in the warm belly of humanity. I smile openly.

The Heiltsuk are strong, compassionate, and practical. Folks here still travel in traditional canoes and know the hardship of open boats in open water, so they appreciate my labours to get here and they make me feel welcome. In two weeks, Bella Bella is hosting Tribal Canoe Journeys, where communities up and down the coast will paddle here to meet, commune, and potlatch.

The field course I signed up for *starts tomorrow!* The class will fly or take the water taxi from Port Hardy, taking a day to travel what took me a month. How do I translate my experience? *Do I have to? Should I show them my journal?*

Classmates arrive and hugs are abundant. *I'm so happy to see them all.* They are a little silent around me, or perhaps I am silent myself. Finally, my friend Matt leans over: *Dude, what happened out there?*

Once everyone arrives we are formally welcomed to the territory at the Heiltsuk Integrated Resource Management Department (HIRMD). They convey responsibility and stewardship: "This ecosystem is not *wild* but *shared.*" The take-home message: *Be gentle and listen to the landscape. Try to think outside the worldview that encases you.* Our group heads to the docks, and classmates help me load *Bell* onto the shuttle boat bound for the Hakai Beach Institute on Calvert Island. This is where our studies will take place.

A new chapter begins.

I think it's hard for settlers like myself to understand the relationship between people and place. All over the Central Coast are archeological sites ranging from 6,000 to 14,000 years old—a lot of generations. My family is three generations in Canada, and we've moved five times. What does it mean to have 14,000-year-old roots in one ecosystem? What knowledge is required to sustain a society like this? How come the Heiltsuk and other Indigenous communities didn't collapse like the community on Minstrel Island and past civilizations all around the world?

BELLA

SAND HILL CRANE
Antigone canadensis

## 3 MONTHS LATER, AUGUST 2014:

Hakai, Calvert Island—Heiltsuk territory.

Summer has slipped through my fingers! It feels like I got to Calvert yesterday. The Hakai Beach Institute is a research station where scientists try to quantify and understand the coastline's complexity. Our course was amazing. Matt Morrison (my best friend), Andrew Sheriff (an awesome human who's great with stats), and I researched the impacts of river otters (*Lutra canadensis*) on the surrounding ecosystem. Our motion-detection cameras caught the mustelids "partying" and excavating burrows in the middle of the night. The class loved it, and our instructor Brian Starzomki was impressed. He inspired all of us to learn about species for the pure joy of having a relationship with them. *This is how education should be.*

After the field school, I thought to paddle north to Haida Gwaii and Alaska, but the idea felt lonely and dangerous. I'll save it for another summer. Instead, I hatched a plan to continue working on Calvert. I followed old career advice from my mom: *Just be keen.*

I asked the scientists if they needed help with their fieldwork, and found Maartje, a Dutch hydrologist, sampling streams for organic matter. She offered to have me as an assistant for the rest of the summer. *Yippee!* Another researcher, Julia Fisher, a master's student in Brian's lab, asked if I would join her team for a two-week kayak research trip to study ecology at archeological midden sites. I couldn't believe it—*perfect.*

The months blur into seashells, raging streams, and nipple-twisting skinny-dips. On time off, I paddled to Koeye River, where the Heiltsuk have a cultural camp for kids. I helped my other best friend, Audrey Lane, with her duties in the garden, and banged boards with the carpenters to craft new cabins.

Now the leaves are changing. I load *Bell* on the top of the shuttle boat heading south. Back to Victoria and another year of studies. Also, *Kaia*. We've exchanged emails and *I think she likes me*. I'm curious, scared, and confused. The butterflies in my heart migrate often.

My journey took me halfway up the coast; I must return to finish the job, and paddle to Alaska.

I will write soon, *I promise!*

## +1 EASTER EGG!

*Oh ya!* Audrey and I found a Japanese fishing buoy! On a long weekend, we took the ferry to Haida Gwaii to rock the Edge of the World Music Festival and visit my sister Alexis and friend Amanda Cook. Only there was no scheduled ferry back to the Central Coast, so we hitch-hiked on a sailboat (thank you, Ben and Debby McLeod from Orcas Island!). We were three days late for work, but along the way, we spotted the orb floating beside Promise Island (Hartley Bay area). Gazing into its eroded surface, you can see across the Pacific into the eyes of a Japanese fisherwoman.

BS

MK

MM

JF

## 4 MONTHS LATER, DECEMBER 2014:

Victoria, BC—Lekwungen territory.

It's been four months since Calvert, and I must tell my tale. Kaia and I have begun to see *each other! Yipee!* We climb buildings to escape the horizontal campus, and even camped overnight up top.

Her 25-foot C&C sailboat, *Sky*, is our home, and I'm learning to sail! We are anchored in Cadboro Bay (a five-minute bicycle from UVic), and hoist the sails on mornings with favourable wind. This is a cheap (free to anchor) and awesome way to live. If you're starting studies in a coastal community, consider it.

Oh ya, I graduated! To be honest, it doesn't seem important. A piece of paper, another day, another box on the adult-life-list. I consider my privilege: Am I spoiled, lucky, karma-blessed? Or just white, able-bodied, and male?

## 5 MONTHS LATER, MAY 2015:

Spring again. // Calvert Island, again.

*We did it!* Kaia and I sailed sweet blue *Sky* to Calvert, and only used the engine once (when we almost crashed into Mitlenatch Island during a midnight moon sail). It's wonderful to share the coast. Kaia is attending a wildlife monitoring field school with Dr. Chris Darimont, and I'm working with a team led by Erin Rechsteiner investigating sea otter populations and their foraging behaviour. Another magical summer awaits!

*Sky under sail.*

## 1 MONTH LATER, JUNE 2015:

Koeye River.

*"Dear Grampa, you inspired me to write. I'm grateful you taught me the value of reflection and honesty. When pondering my relationship with you, I smile. You were passionate and acted with conviction. You always had time to laugh and share a moment, as well as cookies. Thank you for being you, and letting everyone share your spirit."*

My grampa died. I can't get back to the funeral in time. I send the above note to be read at the service. What to do? *What to do!?* I need space. The last months have been intense. This relationship happened *fast*. I've had no time to reflect. Kaia has a year of school left, and I'm graduated; we are in different chapters. I need time alone. We can still write letters and be friends, right? Hmmm. I love her, but I also love my freedom and the opportunities it offers. Am I making a huge mistake?

We separate and both fail to communicate our feelings. It's almost easier not to talk about my leaving, but more tricky and tender in the end. Kaia remains on the coast and ends up sailing home single-handed.[4] Well not totally alone: she adopted a kitten—Numa.

*Little sad dudes, and a crab-baby riding a water jelly. On our trip north, Kaia and I would dip buckets off the side of Sky to collect jellyfish samples.*

## 7 MONTHS LATER, JANUARY 2016:

Whitecourt, Alberta—Treaty 8 territory.

The logging industry and government are at war with the mountain pine beetle (*Dendroctonus ponderosae*). I spend daylight hours felling and burning "green attack" (recently infested trees). It doesn't make sense—we can't play god in these ecosystems. It's cold, I'm lonely, and my coworkers are out-of-work oil-riggers (no offense, just different world views). My body *and* heart ache.

Kaia is in Japan. We have been writing letters, and the A-symmetry in my heart creates no end of tears. I don't know what to do, but I *need* to see her again. Why does it hurt? What evolutionary purpose does the broken heart serve? How does one navigate the tide pool of love, youth, and regret?

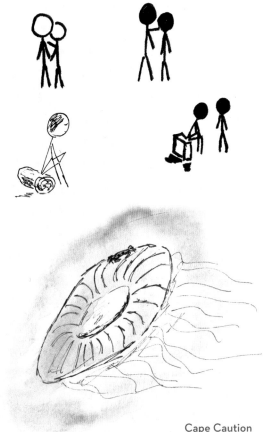

JOURNAL ONE:
VICTORIA → BELLA BELLA

FALL IN LOVE ( KAIA

SPRING 2014          SUMMER 2014          FALL 2014

## RELATIONSHIP TIMELINE: SCIENCE⁶ VS LOVE

### THE CRUSH PHASE

During this phase there is a *decrease* of activity in the prefrontal cortex, the analytical mind that creates negative assessments of others. It's a *judgment-override process* to push us towards connection without thinking about consequences. It also reduces inhibitions. Think: just-do-it. Just go say *hi*. Just write her a poem. Just get her attention, by *any means necessary*. How many times have you clumsily approached a potential mate with a question you already knew the answer to?

### THE FALLING PHASE

This phase is dominated by testosterone and estrogen, *the sex-drive hormones*, pushing us to reproduce. There are three other friends in this phase:

**ADRENALINE:** *The stress-response hormone.* Makes the heart beat faster, resulting in more energy and focused attention on our potential mate. It can also heighten nervousness—the butterflies.

**DOPAMINE:** *The happiness (reward) hormone.* To initiate motivation, attraction, and desire. If dopamine levels are extremely high, people may feel an addiction to their lover. In some relationships, the level of dopamine is the same as using cocaine.

**SEROTONIN:** *The regulator hormone.* For balancing mood, appetite, sleep, and sexual desire. In the beginning of relationships serotonin is erratic, creating out-of-whack sleep schedules and lack of appetite.

### THE ATTACHMENT PHASE

After the initial love-storm, oxytocin and vasopressin begin to predominate.

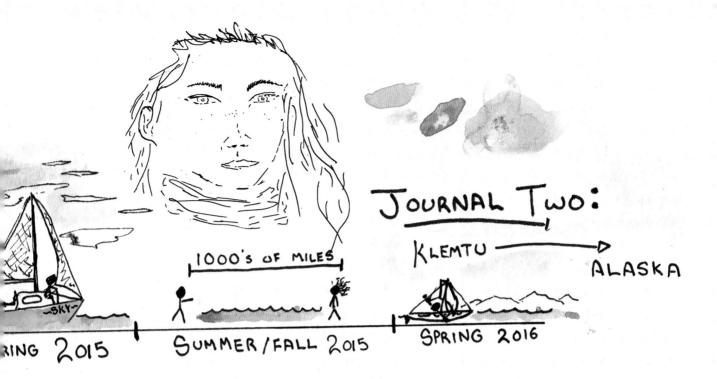

JOURNAL TWO:

KLEMTU ⟶ ALASKA

1000's OF MILES

-SKY-

RING 2015    SUMMER/FALL 2015    SPRING 2016

OXYTOCIN: *The cuddle hormone.* This makes us feel safe and creates trust between partners, to promote monogamy and commitment. *And cuddling.*

VASOPRESSIN: *The attachment hormone.* Released during physical touch, it creates emotional bonding and the desire to protect one another. Also present with family, especially mothers and children.

### THE BREAKUP-THEN-MISS-YOU-COMPLETE-DISASTER PHASE

*I'm a mess.* My heart is in knots, and it feels like I've been hit by a bus. But I've done this to myself. What do I do?! Is there no book on how to navigate relationships smoothly? Why is there no Relationships 101 at university?

When couples separate, they go through withdrawal from all the hormones we mentioned. The higher the high, the truer the love, the more painful the fall.

ADRENALINE: Before it created focus on our loved one, now it makes us bonkers. In excess, along with cortisol, it can make the heart swell, leading to the medically real broken heart syndrome.

CORTISOL: *The fight-or-flight hormone.* At erratic levels it causes inflammation, sore muscles, chronic stress, acne, and hair loss.

So why do we have these biologically unpleasant responses to breaking up? To make us get back together? To be more cautious with our heart in the future? Or is it just the price we pay?

*Wait, so are we all hormone-robots searching to reproduce? Or is there something more than body sensations, neural fireworks, and raging hormones? I don't mean to science-bomb love; perhaps this is one piece in a larger picture.* *(For another perspective, see page 114.)*

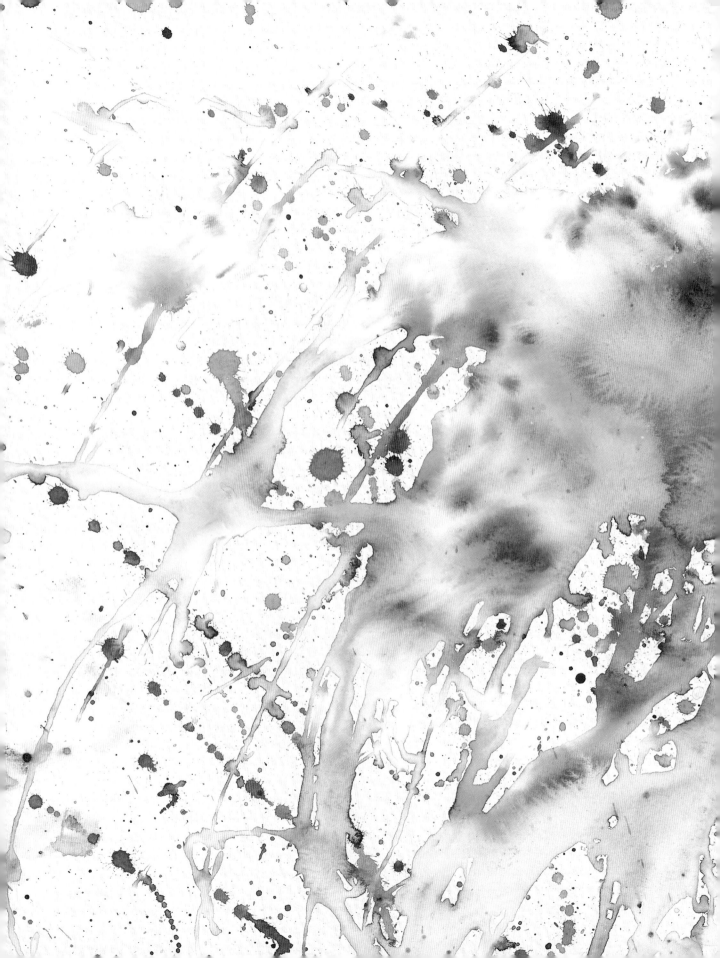

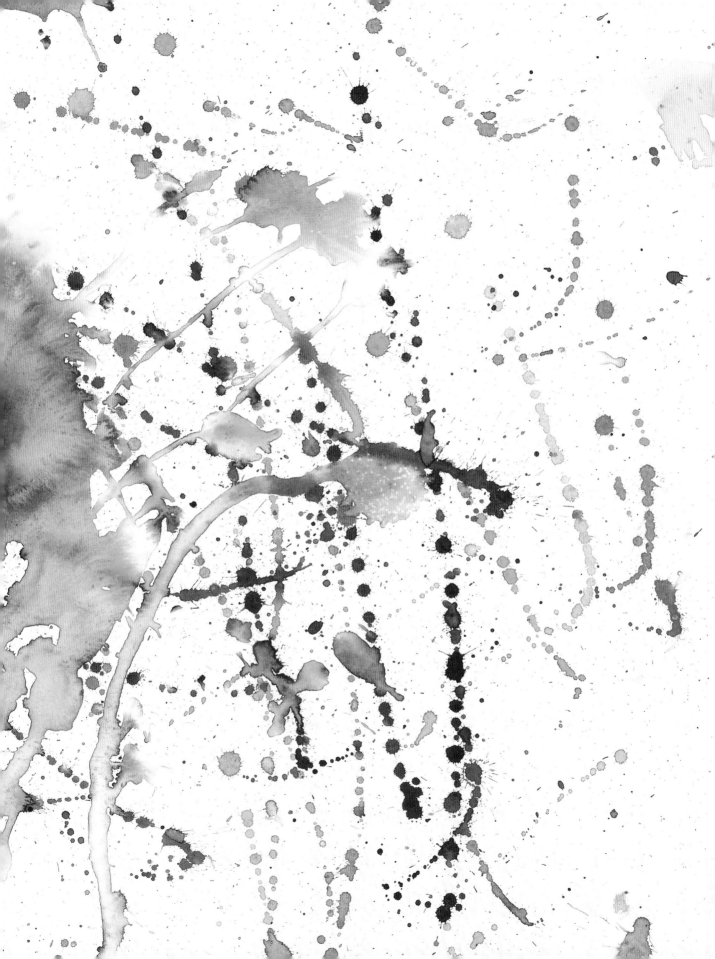

# 3

# LET GO OF EVERYTHING

"If you stick around, people
will just start feeding you."

↲ **LAWRENCE** ↲
a Klemtu local, telling me of the
generous hospitality his
ocean people humbly possess.

(Kitasoo/Xai'xais territory)

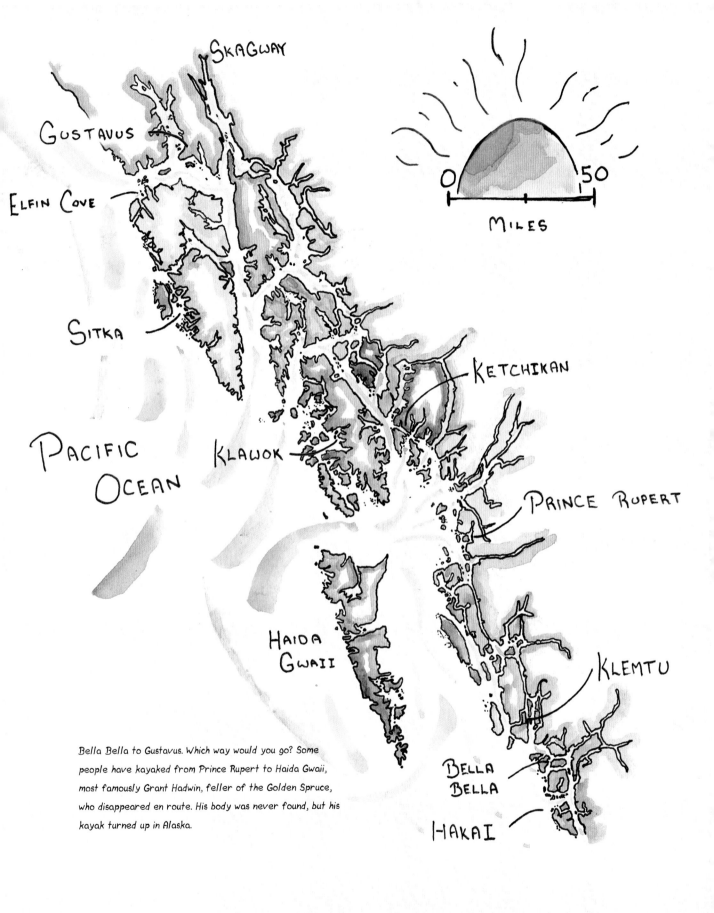

SKAGWAY

GUSTAVUS

ELFIN COVE

SITKA

PACIFIC
OCEAN

KLAWOK

KETCHIKAN

PRINCE RUPERT

HAIDA
GWAII

KLEMTU

BELLA
BELLA

HAKAI

0 — 50
MILES

*Bella Bella to Gustavus. Which way would you go? Some*
*people have kayaked from Prince Rupert to Haida Gwaii,*
*most famously Grant Hadwin, feller of the Golden Spruce,*
*who disappeared en route. His body was never found, but his*
*kayak turned up in Alaska.*

# FITZ HUGH CHANNEL:

Two years since my first trip. // Plan: Klemtu to Skagway, Alaska. // Distance: 600 nm.

The ferry from Port Hardy streams north—a city-of-lights plowing through the darkness. *Bell* hides below on the car deck, ready to swim again through the complex coast. It's been two years since my first journey. In that time, I've learned that my heart and mind often don't cooperate. Kaia was in Japan for the last year, and I don't know where we're at. I want to talk with her about *everything*, but haven't the courage or certainty. Do I want to be alone or together? I'm hoping this trip will create clarity. We saw each other for a moment before my departure and I promised to write and to consider coming home at the end of this ocean-madness.

This leg will pick up where I left off, and stitch together north-coast BC with southeast Alaska. My destination is Skagway, 600 nautical mamas from Klemtu, the next village north of Bella Bella. My goal for this journal is to delve deeper into the biology of the Pacific Northwest, and record my mind as I dive into isolation.

I'm still looking for answers. Let's see what the cedars can teach me this time.

## KNOTS OF THE PACIFIC NORTHWEST

The week-long kayak course I did had a whole section on tarpology—how to set up tents and other jury-rigs to keep the rain off. Sailing on *Sky*, Kaia and I needed to be fluent with ropes; our lives depended on them. Knot-tying is a good skill to know, and it's an art. There are thousands of knots, but the ones we learned are enough for just about every use.

Practice until you can do them blindfolded, in the pouring rain, clinging halfway up a tree.

### BOWLINE

- The "king of knots."
- Used to make a secure loop.
- For sheet lines to sails.
- Also hammocks.
- Releasable.

### FISHIN' "CLINCH" KNOT

- Used for catching chowies.
- This figure shows the "7 up" technique.

### TRUCKER'S HITCH

- Used for tightening down loads from a hard point.
- Yes, truckers actually used this before the invention of ratchet straps.

### ROLLING HITCH

- I now use this knot instead of the trucker's. Same purpose, but is easily adjustable.
- Used for all tarp tech.

### SHEET BEND

- To mend and extend.
- I use the "rabbit through the hole" method.

### FIGURE OF EIGHT

- Used to securely make a loop or attach two ropes.
- The "climber's angel."

### CLOVE HITCH

- Used for *everything*, including securing boats to docks.
- So amazing it's hard to believe it exists at all.

*For the dedicated knot-smith please track down a copy of The Ashley Book of Knots—the bible of knotdom. With over 7,000 illustrations, it is Mr. Ashley's life's work, and a treat for the eyes, even if you're not curious about knots.*

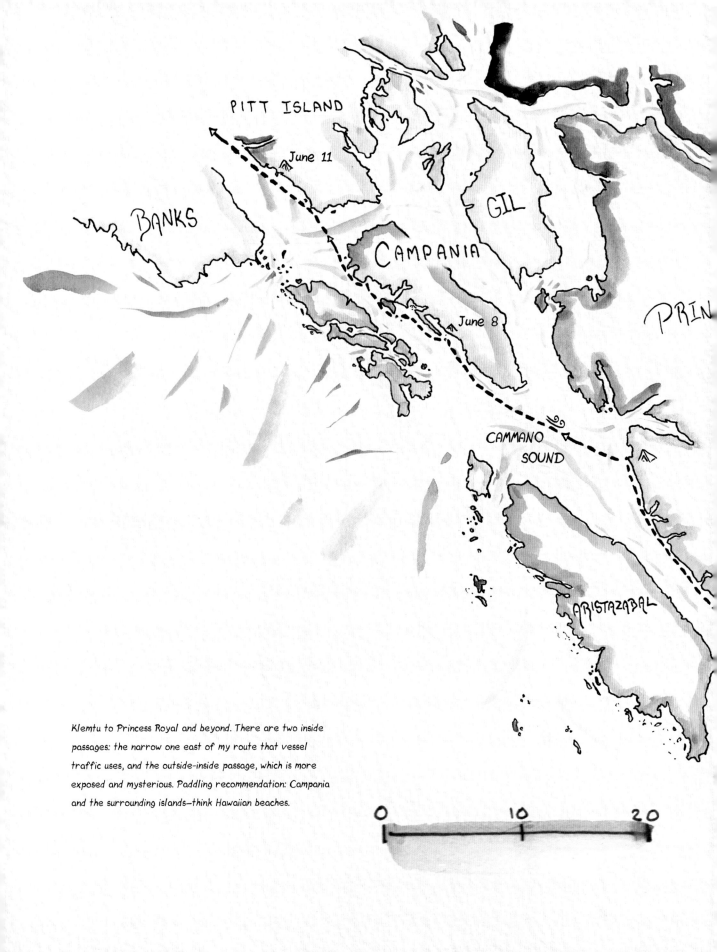

PITT ISLAND

June 11

BANKS

GIL

CAMPANIA

PRIN

June 8

CAMMANO
SOUND

ARISTAZABAL

Klemtu to Princess Royal and beyond. There are two inside
passages: the narrow one east of my route that vessel
traffic uses, and the outside-inside passage, which is more
exposed and mysterious. Paddling recommendation: Campania
and the surrounding islands—think Hawaiian beaches.

0          10          20

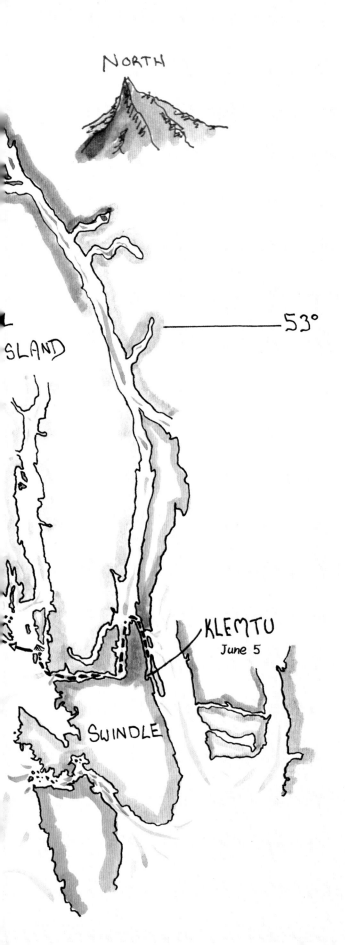

NORTH

53°

SLAND

SWINDLE

KLEMTU
June 5

## DAY 1, JUNE 5, 2016:

Wind light to S 10. *Sunny.* // Klemtu to Princess Royal Island—17 nm.

*People are watching.* I grab a quiet hand to carry *Pep* off the ferry. Klemtu greets the weekly connection eagerly—provisions are Tetrised into salt-weathered vans and rusty trucks. I add myself to the chain. And soon, I'm alone at the terminal with a stray dog, *BP*, and my mission.

Klemtu is a fishing village, home to the *Kitasoo First Nation*. The town is sleepy at 8 AM. I hold a couple conversations and gather it is challenging to live and love in an isolated island town. However, a rich sense of community is borne out of this challenge, and many urbanites would benefit from adopting similar principles of mutual aid.

Lawrence sits alone watching *Gavia stellata* (red-throated loons) dive for fish. He is 86 and used to cast gill nets in front of town, where birds resurface with tasty morsels. He nods at my journal and tells me he never learned to read or write because he was always out with his family catching and smoking fish. He gets up early to study the birds, weather, and ocean—*a different kind of literacy*. As I bid him farewell, he tells me he will see me again. I hope so.

Slipping *Bell* into the water, I close my eyes and say a prayer to the ocean-gods. *Please don't eat me.* Keep me safe. I mean no harm. *I seek guidance.*

## DAY 2, JUNE 6:

Wind light. // Princess Royal Island—21 nm.

*My muscles ache.* I thought my body could pick up where I left off. Thick fog saturates the morning and sticks to my skin. There is no sun, no sky, no sense of self. *Nothing to anchor reality.* I navigate by compass. The acoustic landscape is void, but then: *PPOOOSSSSHHH!* Two humpbacks are gasping within metres of me, but visibility is too low to locate them. I love whales. *Whales and tide pools.* Did you know humpback songs can last hours and are heard 10,000 kilometres (6,200 miles) away? *Bonkers.*

The haze lifts, exposing the stunted trees and wave-shattered shores of Aristazabal Island. The winters here are ruled by gales. It takes a lot of energy to bend a tree sideways.

I arrive at a cozy tombolo—an island connected to land by a sediment bridge. My evening puzzle is to figure out where the high tide line is. I'm not sure in the end, and I make up my tent on a sandy pad among the boulders.

My mental alarm clock goes off at two in the morning, an hour before high tide. I need to make sure the ocean is not going to flood me. Scuffling out of the zippers, I find a sky freckled with a million stars, and rising water that will engulf my spot within the hour. Madly, I drag the tent and its contents into the forest. Wide-awake, I find no need for sleep. I prop up on a log and contemplate the cosmos while the beach is enveloped by my salty lover.

*Tides are teachers.*

Sea lettuce (*Ulva lactuca*) brought up by the high tide glistens in the morning sun. A tasty vitamin-C-filled treat, sea lettuce can be dehydrated to last for months. I take a full day off to dry the lettuce on hot rocks. The work results in a ziplock filled with crunchy goodness (vitamins A, C, B1, magnesium, and antioxidants).

## MEDITATION

I survived a 10-day silent Vipassana retreat this spring, and I hope the daily meditation practice helps my mental stability. But my brain is often co-opted by monkeys.

I aim to sit for *an hour*, observing body and breath. Mostly it's an all-out-war, my mind coming up with any excuse to bail: "You're tired, your legs are numb, this is stupid, DO ANYTHING BUT THIS!" Why is it so hard to observe the breath?

There is *something* deep here. It's one thing to go off in the woods, but if you have no method to maintain stability, your mind could be absorbed by the wild. *You could go crazy.*

ANAPANASATI: Concentrate on the small area below the nostrils. Create continuous *friction* between your awareness and the breath. Like a guard defending a citadel, you must thoroughly examine every breath that enters and leaves. Keep going until your mind becomes single-pointed. Investigation questions: "Is the in-breath or the out-breath warmer? Which nostril is air moving through? At what point during the breath do thoughts tend to arise?" This might seem boring, but I'm intrigued. And a little intimidated by "my" lack of control. Where *do* thoughts come from?

VIPASSANA: Scan the body from head to toe. Remain equanimous to all sensations. Try to observe their impermanence. Just look at the characteristics—hot, cold, stinging, tingling, aching, etc. Have no judgment. Don't identify with sensations. Keep going until everything dissolves!?[1]

METTA: "I seek forgiveness from anyone I have hurt … I forgive anyone who has hurt me … May I be happy, peaceful, and free. May all beings be happy, peaceful, and free." Really *feel* it and imagine sending the feelings out.

~20cm

HOLD FAST

*Above* Spring is the best time for collecting seaweed. Large storms and upwellings in the winter stir up nutrients, and the April sun allows for photosynthesis.

*Below* This 10-day course profoundly changed me. There are two Vipassana centres in BC and hundreds around the world. Courses are by donation, and run by volunteers. If you are curious, try it.

NOSE

INHALE

EXHALE

### BULL KELP (*NEREOCYSTIS LUETKEANA*)

The hollow stipe of Nereocystis can be made into a didgeridoo, which aids me in my habit of making weird noises.

1. Find a recently washed-up specimen and cut one to two metres (three to six feet) in length.

2. Purse your lips and blow like a fish from the corner of your mouth.

While kayaking, I cut them from underwater forests and have floating ocean sessions.

Yes, edible. Eat all parts. Except the hold-fast, I think.

### GIANT KELP (*MACROCYSTIS PYRIFERA*)

Giant kelp is the marine-macroscopic-algae-boss of the Pacific Northwest. It grows up to 35 centimetres a day in spring and reaches a max of 50 metres. Remember, old-growth Dougies are 85 metres. Giant kelp is the fastest-growing organism on earth.

Can be dried and crushed to powder and added to everything (think kelp smoothie). Also, try using the blades for lasagna kelp-noodles!

Famous for inside-out sushi, which is herring roe on kelp. If you've tried this delicacy, you are lucky.

### BLACK GOLD (*NORI*) (*PYROPIA ABBOTTIAE*)

A pillar food for coastal Indigenous Peoples, harvested in May. When I paddled into Bella Bella, the roofs were covered in sun-drying Pyropia.

A vitamin-booster for all dishes—fish, rice, spaghetti, etc. Sometimes fried into "seaweed chips."

- Protein (50 percent of its dried weight)
- Vitamin A (one sheet = 3 eggs!)
- High in vitamin C
- High calorie count

### ROCKWEED / BLADDERWRACK (*FUCUS DISTICHUS*)

A tough intertidal dominator, rockweed has its own camel-back for long hours in the sun. It also survives freezing temperatures, allowing a range from Cali to the Arctic.

And of course, it's edible!

- High in sugars.
- Contains mannitol, which reduces the rise in blood sug.
- Choicey for fermenting due to sugar content (think seaweed-kimchi!)

### TURKISH TOWEL (*CHONDRACANTHUS EXASPERATUS*)

People don't eat this, but you could (no seaweed will kill you, though some are acidic). As the name suggests, this one has a different super-power: it's a scrubby! Yes, seaweeds do that.

I struggle to stay scientific here. It has spiny papillae… scrubbers.

T-towel has an ingenious marketing strategy, coming in pink, red, yellow, and green. OK, I'll stop.

### BEACH WRACK (*GARDENOUS DELIGHTOUS*)

The best way to learn seaweeds is by taking long walks on the beach. And if you have a garden, you can bring it home for compost or mulch.

- For mulching, pile 4–6 inches (it shrinks).
- Reapply as needed.
- If you can, rinse first with fresh water.

Black gold
(*Pyropia sp.*)

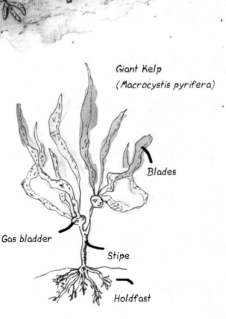

Giant Kelp
(*Macrocystis pyrifera*)

Blades

Gas bladder

Stipe

Holdfast

A big thank you to Sara Wickham, who patiently kelp-guided me. For her master's thesis she went to 100 remote islands on the central coast to sample beach wrack and its effects on terrestrial ecosystems. Basically, she did her master's on beachcombing, and her team found three Japanese orbs in the process!

# DAY 4, JUNE 8:

Winds N 15 veering to S 10–20. *Overcast to sun.* // Campania / Lax Ka'gaas Island— Gitga'at and Gitxaala territory—17 nm.

Out of challenge emerges creativity.

It takes all of me to lug *Bell* and my belongings down the boulder beach at 3 AM. No stars or moon penetrate overcast skies; I use my headlamp. An early start is required to catch the north flooding currents. Cammano Sound is a nine-mile crossing known for its confusing currents and exposure to Hecate Strait.

After two hours, a *headwind* kicks up. *Uh-oh, spaghettio!* The breeze is consistent and takes enormous fortitude to battle.

Swollen tendons rub raw, my scapula aches. *The pain escalates.* The wind is pushing me backwards and every stroke is agony. *I don't want to make it worse,* but it's ten kilometres (six miles) to shore! I panic. What if the weather turns evil? What if I'm swept out to sea! I have to do *something.* Immobilized and scared, I float alone—a dot to be erased. I stretch my shoulder and change stroke techniques. *Nothing.* For an hour I sit scared and alone, drifting slowly into Hecate Strait.

The wind veers then begins to push from behind. *A miracle!* If only I could sail.

A six-foot tarp is under my bum as a cushion. Sliding it out, I rig up a Jimmy—see diagram). It scoops the wind like a rocket—six knots! The wind picks up and soon I'm surfing three foot whities. *Holy macaroni and chhheeeesse!* This is the fastest, *ever.* I'm not wearing a skirt due to the setup and get a couple soakers. The headlamp in my pocket gargles kaput.

Rounding the cape of Campania Island, I beach the boat on glorious white sand. It's 10 AM and I've gone 32 kilometres (20 miles)! I send out my SPOT OK-message and pass out for a five-hour recovery.

Massaging my shoulder and exploring the pain, I find the area inflamed. *My body is so squishy!* I'll have to be careful for the rest of the trip and warm up before 3 AM departures. Sailing might be my saving grace.

RIGHT
BY
LEFT

PADDLE MAST

LINES FROM
ALL CORNERS OF TARP

*Opposite Jimmy-rig sailing and wrinkly hands. My hands take the greatest toll while kayaking—constantly wet, baking in the sun, and rubbing on the paddle. Many kayakers wear gloves to shield themselves from the elements. I prefer to feel it, but I pay the price.*

## SPOT

So I have this new gizmo, a one-way satellite check-in device. It sends a message saying "I-am-OK," along with my location, to 10 preset emails: my family and Kaia. If things go totally-trouble, I can send an SOS to the coast guard. This, plus my VHF and six-year-expired flares, are my lifeline. Is it enough?

## HOW TO SAIL A KAYAK

Harnessing the wind is one of our oldest obsessions. The exact origins are unknown, but it makes sense that as soon as there were rafts, there were also sails. Before leaving, I researched how to sail a kayak, but found no practical solutions.[2] A week before leaving, I met an old-timer who knew the coast well. He drew diagrams in my journal, creating a sail out of cedar driftwood, beach rope, and a tarp. The A-frame comes up and down on pulleys and can be operated from the cockpit.

It works *too* well, and an hour into sailing I'm judo-kicked by a gust. The mast is blasted into the water and my kayak flips. The sail sinks slowly and I submerge. I try to flip upright, but the rigging is engulfed. I pull the skirt and let the ocean into the cockpit.

Luckily, I'm close to shore and it's not totally bonkers. Sorting the rigging, I re-enter, pump out, and paddle to shore like a wet cat.

Gear is scattered over the rocks, drying in the sun  a yard sale for birds and bears. Both hatches breached, soaking my lentils. I recuperate, dry out, and sail another six kilometres (four miles) before pulling in for the day. The bay is covered in *Salicornia* (sea asparagus), which is perfect with the gruffy.

PUMP

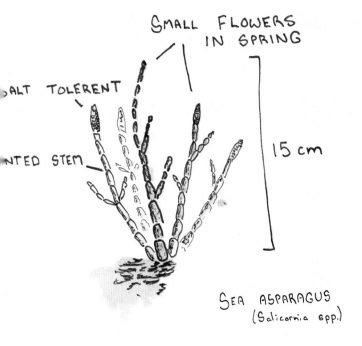

SMALL FLOWERS
IN SPRING

ALT TOLERENT

NTED STEM

15 cm

SEA ASPARAGUS
(Salicornia spp.)

## SEA ASPARAGUS
### (*SALICORNIA PACIFICA*)

Sea asparagus is an intertidal plant commonly pickled or eaten in salads. It is a halophytic (salt-tolerant) succulent flowering plant. In French-Canada it has the name "tétines de souris," which roughly translates to "mouse titties." In restaurants you might see it as "sea beans."

## GOING TO THE WASHROOM

You might be wondering about the best way to do business while roaming the coast. I mostly use the water-bottle method: pee in bottle, pour out, rinse, repeat. The *side-blaster* is efficient *and* playful, but can be dangerous if the ocean doesn't cooperate. This technique is as it sounds. I peed my pants once while guiding for Camp Thunderbird. I had been holding my pee for hours and when our group got startled by an oncoming sailboat, *I let go*. When we got to shore, I quickly jumped in for a swim.

Going *number two* is technical and should be avoided, unless you like it. Undress, jump in, aqua-poo, re-enter. You can imagine the difficulties arising (literally). There is one other way, called the *partner-poop*. This requires a friend to stabilize your boat while you yoga-bum over the side.

On shore, I *do-do* beside tide pools, then rinse with salt water (which frees me from toilet paper). High tide flushes everything to the fishes. It's nice to know I'm giving back to the ecosystem.

SAILING SET-UP
2.0

# DAY 6, JUNE 10:

Winds W 10-20. // Campania Island—5 nm.

*I flip again.* The winds are westerly so I try a beam-reach (where the wind hits perpendicular to the boat), but a sudden swell-gust combo flattens me. The wind shifted from light to 15 knots in 30 minutes; I didn't reef in time. It's worse than ever. Having eight-foot pieces of cedar and a six-foot tarp tied to your paddle while underwater is *a bit* tricky. From now on, I will carry the buck knife (Bucky) on my life jacket to cut the mess.

Currently, the chart atlas is in pieces and each page dries individually over the fire. Waterproofing the hatches will be necessary if I keep flipping.

# DAY 7, JUNE 11:

Wind S 5-10 to W 5-15 to S 20-30. // Campania to Pitt Island—18 nm.

I need to figure out how to sail this boat. Around noon, I push onto the water after waterproofing the hatch covers with additional tarping, and creating dagger boards for sailing stability. Today, I'm wearing the wetsuit, *just in case.* Winds are ideal and the new tech is dandy. *Yahhhoooo! Sailing is liberation.* Three-quarters of the way, I list to port and my paddle catches an edge. It pulls the sail down hard. *Noooooooooooo!* At least I'm wearing my wetsuit. *Cut ties.* Bail out. Paddle to shore. Determined to keep going *and, perhaps,* determined to defy the ocean itself, I re-tie and sail on.

The breeze veers south and sailing prevails. Contouring Pitt Island, I begin to make love with the wind. At the end of the day, I'm exhausted, wet, cold, and awestruck—the forces at work are raw and real. They possess me; *I submit.*

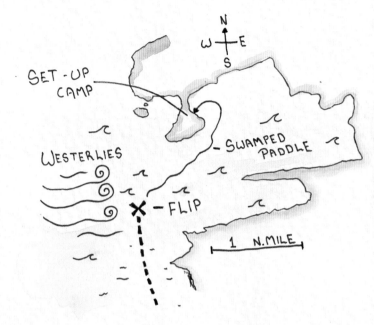

*Above* Wet-exiting a kayak is traumatic. Inside the cockpit is a false sense of security in an ocean of risks.

*Below* It's a flippy setup, best suited for down-wind blasting. To reef (reduce sail area), I roll the tarp around the gaff rig, and lower the main halyard. To be honest, I don't think I would recommend this rig, unless you are quite adventurous, mechanical, and have previous sailing experience. Or go for it :) The good thing is, it can be adapted, and many sail configurations are possible.

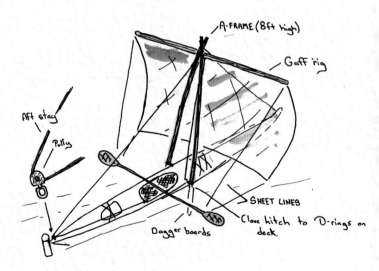

# INSECTS OF THE PACIFIC NORTHWEST

My tent is a great habitat for "insecting" (like birding, but bugs). Many six- to-eight-leggers get stuck inside and set up their *own* camp on my roof. The study of insects is really called entomology (entomon = insect/logia = study), and can teach us deep lessons.

## BEES (*ANTHOPHILA SP.*)

Most Hymenoptera species (sawflies, wasps, ants, and bees) live in extraordinary social complexity, and don't kill, steal, or lie to each other. There are over 500 bee species in the Pacific Northwest. They communicate with body language. You may know how some bees notify others of food locations through dance moves. Smell is the other biggie when you're dealing with flowers all day. Pheromones act like social media, a way for bees to send messages; for example, one bee will communicate "there is danger" and other bees will emit the same pheromone (think "liking") to ampli-fly the message. The queen uses scents to execute larger commands over the community and her eggs.

## BLACK FLIES (*SIMULIIDAE SP.*)

There are over 100 species of black flies in the PNW. Yes, they bite, and inject an anticoagulant so you keep bleeding; if you have an allergic reaction it's usually to this protein. Sometimes they carry diseases (mostly tropic species), and some bites can get infected. Yes, they make an irritating noise (worse than people complaining about them? I'm not sure) and get stuck in the eyes, ears, nose, mouth, and notebook. Yes, they have a purpose: they nourish bats, birds, fish, and other bugs; transmit diseases, keeping populations in check; and pollinate. Research on their anticoagulant proteins helps heart attack patients.

## MOSQUITOES (*CULICIDAE SP.*)

Also, why can't something exist for its own sake? Does it need a list of ecosystem contributions to gain our respect and be spared insecticides? Maybe. Mosquitoes live for five to six months and have a similar resume as black flies, but affect human lives even more. They are the deadliest animal (to humans), being the vector for malaria, dengue, zika, yellow fever, and other big-hitters (about 750,000 deaths per year). This culls our weak and keeps us in touch with death, no?

Mosquitoes can detect your $CO_2$ seventy-five feet away. So remember, eating garlic works to repel them, thanks to the allyl methyl sulfide that masks their sense of smell. Also, scientists study the proboscis of mosquitoes to better design hypodermic needles.

## LONG-JAWED ORB WEAVER (*TETRAGNATHIDAE SP.*)

This is my favorite spider family, mainly because they are easy to ID. They have elongated bodies and their front legs span out. They also love water and can usually be found at docks and marinas.

OK, a word about arachnids. They almost always have eight legs (insects have six). They have two main body parts (not three, like insects) but don't always have eight eyes. They also don't have antennae or wings.

The coolest thing about spiderlings is how they disperse after birth. To avoid crowding and being eaten by their mom, they release silk thread and wait for favorable winds. They can travel hundreds of kilometres and have been found five kilometres (three miles) above earth riding atmospheric currents. This is why they are usually the first species to colonize newly formed volcanic islands in the middle of the Pacific.

## CONTRAST

It seems *everything* has an opposite, especially emotions. Sometimes I'm happy, but oh, how fast things go: up, down, up down, *sideways*. Happy, sad. Desire, disgust. Pride, shame. Maybe *this* is evolution. Every time I push from one extreme to another, I expand my threshold for discomfort and gain perspective about the nature of reality: *this too shall pass.*

So it's *good* when things go "bad."

The ability to experience contrast is what makes us human. If a person is continuously happy, is it happiness, or delusion? Emotions are relative and have value in contrast to their polar-sisters. It's the *transition* from edge to edge that creates depth, character, wisdom, and capacity.

I need struggle *and* love.

What happens if we *seek* contrast? By putting ourselves in precarious situations, will we grow? Does new life linger in dark spaces?

The thing is, change is awkward and emotional.

Stability in routine, housing, finances, and relationships are seductive because they give a sense of control, comfort, and pleasure. Everyone struggles, but *the degree* is created by privilege and circumstance. If I embrace discomfort and renounce the holy cappuccino, will I find contentment? *Empathy?* Love for all beings? It can't hurt. Or can it?

A clever intervention deliberately removes ease, denies habits, and demands presence of mind. It requires *letting go*—relinquishing attachment of self, possessions, and others. Salvation from the mundane is not offered by the holiday, weekend-party-binge, or visit to church, but by *interruption of the routine.* Interventions are all around us, and work in both directions. The habits we adopt matter and create lifestyles that feed back into society. Interventions can be voluntary or imposed. Imposed ones happen every day—we miss the bus, the power goes out, a loved one dies, we get sick. To be conscious of how we respond is key. Do we laugh or cry, smile or frown? By putting ourselves in voluntary discomfort, we practice a balanced reaction.

What do *you* think? Do we *need* discomfort to grow? I've made my choice. I'm out here to poke holes in myself, and see what remains.

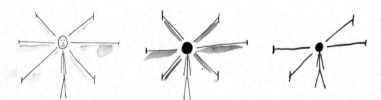

*Opposite  Pitt Island is the only island in BC known to host a resident population of moose. Perhaps they too are a coastal subspecies with saline adaptations? The island is also home to the elusive Spirit Bear,[3] a white-furred black bear subspecies called a Kermode bear (Ursus americanus kermodei). Only around one hundred exist.*

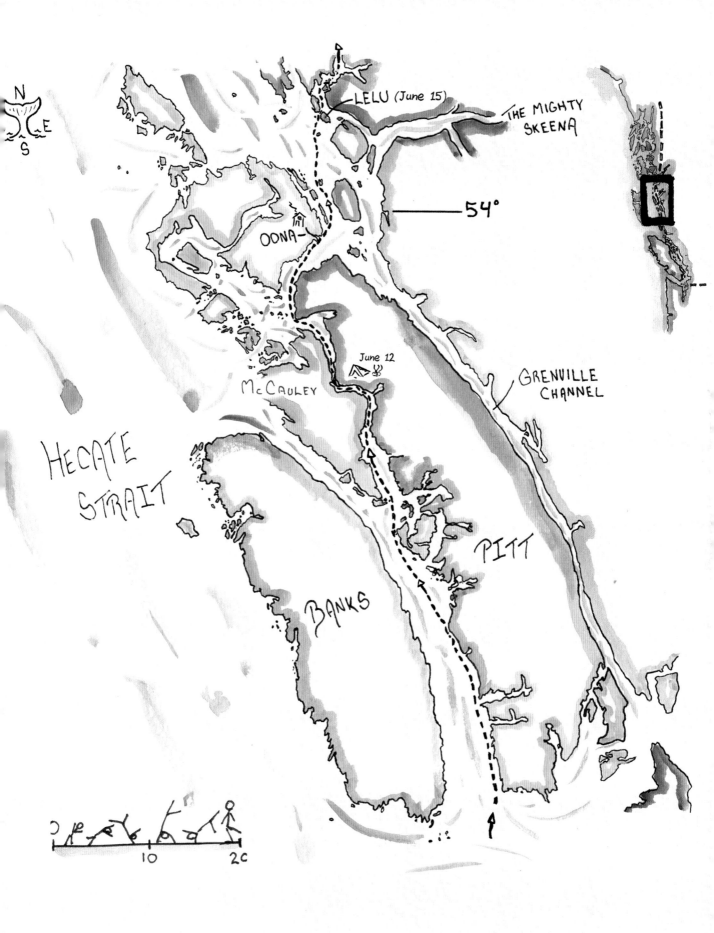

N E S

LELU (June 15)

THE MIGHTY
SKEENA

54°

OONA

June 12

McCAULEY

GRENVILLE
CHANNEL

HECATE
STRAIT

PITT

BANKS

10    2C

# INVERTEBRATES OF THE PACIFIC NORTHWEST

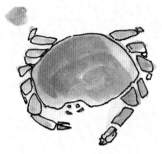

## BUTTER CLAM
*Saxidamus gigantea*

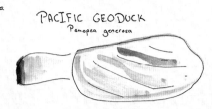

## PACIFIC GEODUCK
*Panopea generosa*

## MOLLUSKS

It turns out I'm allergic to butter clams and geoducks, but I like the *idea* of them. Watching clams squirt in a muddy bay is fascinating, and geoducks are the best protein invention on this coast.

## CRABS

Crabitat is synonymous with eelgrass beds and soft sediment. Dungys and red rocks are the biggest, and sought after commercially. Kelp crabs are tasty too, and can be caught from the kayak, paddling over kelp forests. In Thailand, people even eat shore crabs!

To process: Cut in half with a hatchet—right in the middle of the "lighthouse" shape on the belly (which ensures it's a male). Then clean and boil the two halves. Some people eat the guts too—why not?

- You can make pull-traps with cordage and a basket structure. Just bait with fish heads and pull up after 15 minutes.

- The honest way is to dive with a mask. Swim out and comb the eelgrass. When you find a sizable target, dive down and grab it. Neoprene gloves help; pincers can draw blood and don't let go in crisis. You can use this to your advantage and dive with a stick.

## SEA CUCUMBERS

Sea cucumbers are messy, squishy, and, except in their phallic shape, *nothing* like cucumbers. Firstly, they escape out their anus when handled. Second, they are red and filled with goo. I have only tried them once, and the lateral muscles lining the inside wall were not worth the oh-my-glob factor.

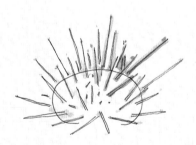

## RED URCHINS

Diving for urchins is a great pastime. A stick helps pry them off rocks. The best advice I got about what part to eat: "*You'll know when you see it.*" However, *I didn't know*, and ate just about everything *except* the orange gonads, then threw up. Use a clam shell to scrape the *orange goodness.*

There are four species of urchins (red, purple, green, white), and there are only three creatures effective at killing these spiky hand-grenades: starfish, humans, and sea otters. So when we killed the otters in the 1700s, the urchin pop went bazooka, destroying much of the PNW kelp forests. (For more information on kelp-urchin-otter politics, see pages 128–29.)

## TIDE-POOL SOUP

My friend Fin Bones makes a nice tide-pool soup. I've never tried it, but I'm 50 percent sure it would be edible. The directions are as the name suggests. Fin recommends:

- Limpets (delicious, but be quick with the knife, they're wary)

- Kelp (don't forget your greens! See page 72)

- Purple shore crabs (mmm... crunchy)

- Isopods (enjoy the legs)

- Sculpins (they're quick, use your monkey brain)

- Mussels (the most edible of the bunch)

- Gooseneck barnacles (juicy! Use a knife for these fellas.)

- Fin says, "Now chop onions and root-veg, if you got 'em. Spice with pepper, chilies, oil, and salt water. Cook 'till nothing crawls out. Twist a lime and begin. Crunch, munch, and don't forget to chew. Eat slow. Say your prayers for the little ones."

*Fin is one my best friends. This recipe and sketch are taken from his journal on a solo kayak trip to the Brooks Peninsula. He paddled with his surfboard for a couple weeks to catch the most remote waves on Vancouver Island. He now lives on Haida Gwaii. In 2021, while rappelling from a 120-foot Sitka spruce he fell and broke his spine. Engulfed by searing pain and numb legs, Fin was flown to Vancouver, operated on, and given back to his parents. Although told he may never recover feeling in his right leg, one year later he is surfing again.*

# DAY 8, JUNE 12:

Wind S 25–35. *Heavy rain.* // McCauley Island—Tsimshian/Gitxaala territory—27 nm.

The tent is thrashing. 05:00 and no hint of morning, the sky a mess of charcoal, the ocean writhing. If I could go with the flow, I could travel major miles.

Let's give it a shot.

A storm jib is stowed and ready, but my paddles are catching enough wind. *Everything is heading north today. It's not a day to flip.* The swell boosts my progress with intense moments of acceleration. Surfing is tricky—when a wave catches you, it can push your stern sideways. Shoulder-checking, and timing my strokes with the rollers, I spot a set of biggies. I surf the first two, but the last one manhandles me, and *Bell* catches the edge. I flip—*upside down.* And the howling is muted.

For a moment, total silence.

Immense clarity lies underwater. Ever since I was a kid, it was the one place I felt at ease. Like being in a big cathedral or an old-growth forest. *No outside thoughts allowed.* Opening my eyes, the blurry surface seems impossible to reach. Survival is my only focus. Back to basics: *I need air.* To right myself I must leverage *Bell* and my body using a paddle-pull and hip-flick. Arranging the blade, I pull down hard. My torso twists. *Gaasssp!*

The rocky shores are a mile away, and there is no one but me. It's 06:00. If I hadn't rolled successfully I would have faced extinction. To re-enter a kayak in this mess would be a life-and-death situation. *Chowser. (*This is the closest I came to dying on the trip. It rewired me deep-down.)*

In the lee of a small island, the shore is too jagged to land so I tie up to a patch of bull kelp. My body slumps over. *Awkward kayak sleep.*

A drop of rain on my nose. *Onwards.*

It's cats and dogs as I finally find a suitable camping spot at 18:00. Everything is soaked except the essentials (but even those are moist). I find little rest, comfort, or solace. My mind toils and my body is crawling. My toes itch, the wool scratches. I'm damp everywhere, and desperately lonely. My only *way out* is thinking of Kaia and home—imagining I'm *anywhere but here.* My experience is a bad dream. But for a weird moment there is peace. *I cannot run from this, I must accept.*

Perhaps there are two kinds of happiness: that which comes from possessing what we desire—food, family, fame, fortune, sex, and stuff; and happiness that comes from having nothing—the willful acceptance of what we lack.

# DAY 9. JUNE 13:

Wind L to NW 10-20. *Heavy rain.* //
Pitt Island—3 nm.

Hemlocks and Sitka spruce offer protection to a point, but after full-saturation, nothing escapes the deluge. All morning I huddle out the weather; I cannot risk getting my last clothing wet. Finally the sun emerges from its sabbatical and I dry what I can, including the lentils, which I spread on a tarp. I leave late and paddle a measly five kilometres (three miles) into the wind. *There is no point.*

My numb fingers fumble with the wet wood. After an hour, I walk away swearing. As if to mock me, the smouldering logs come to life on their own. Once I finish setting up the tent, I see it is beside a mound of bear scat.

I feel like an animal—acting, reacting, smelling, swearing, sweating, sleeping. Old instincts are rising to the surface.

Giant Pacific Octopus

(*Enteroctopus dofleini*)

## AN ODE TO BOOKS

Books are reliable. They give without expecting anything. I traverse cultures, landscapes, and philosophy without leaving the tent. I can live many lives. Books are the best parts of people, and never change their opinion. To read is to be with someone, without fear of judgment.

I deep-down believe a good book can change the world.

My 20-litre book bag has been worth hauling up and down the beaches. Every night, I crank on the headlamp and read till my lids turn to cannonballs. This is also when I write, paint, and plan. I scour the charts until tomorrow's possibilities are memorized. I consider retreat routes, water points, fishing potential, and camping options. It's fun, and it keeps me busy. Without my book-friends I would be lonely.

The book that changed my world was *Dinotopia*, by James Gurney. It deeply affected me as an artist, a storyteller, and a human. If you like the format of this book, I learned it from *Dinotopia*. Read it as soon as possible. It's not a children's book, although kids like it. I think we need more illustrated books. Thanks to printing conventions and cost, we are stuck with text-based snore-machines, where the only picture is on the cover. We are visual learners—let's create an illustration-revolution.

## OONA RIVER

Bob pulls up to the dock in a sketchy Chevy. I'm eating leftover porridge with a cedar stick. *"Welcome to Oona River"*—an old fish an' timber stronghold on Porcher Island. More boats waste away on the beach than are tied to the dock. A couple souls survive here throughout the year. I help Bob unload fuel drums and take him up on coffee at Jan's (which is a daily ritual). Jan is another ambassador of Porcher and has run the salmon enhancement program for twenty years. After java and biscuits, I head to the hatchery and meet the summer students Jan hopes will take over her role. She's getting old and no longer has the energy to take care of all the eggs, alevins, fry, parr, and smolt.

Salmon are the key to life on this coast. The aluminum tanks in the hatchery are filled with coho fry building up strength before their four-year migration to sea and back. Most juveniles in the wild die within weeks; hatcheries increase the chances of survival. After a tour of the tanks, the summer students—Jas, Vera, and Jaimie—invite me for a waterfall hike. The stream running by the hatchery is rich with cedars and Sitka spruce.

After two hours navigating a non-existent trail along prime spawning banks, thunder emerges. Moss-coated cliffs surround us and water cascades into a freezing pool. Grinning at the torrent, Jaimie points out, "This is as far as the salmon get."

## WATER DEFENDERS

It's been pouring for the last five hours and my feet are freezing (flip-flops don't offer much insulation). In the time it took us to walk upstream, the water rose six inches. Back at the hatchery, they invite my sorry soul to stay the night—"You can't camp in this." We spread out charts of the area and chat about Lelu Island—next to Prince Rupert—where *water defenders* are standing up against a proposed Liquefied Natural Gas (LNG) project. Lelu is in the mouth of the Skeena River, which holds the second-largest sockeye run in Canada. I plan to visit the camp and learn what it takes to challenge the status quo.

CLOVE HITCH

Oona River Wreck

23645

I adore decomposing human construction, especially boats. I
like imagining all the voyages, storms, and love stories this
boat weathered before rotting back to which it came.

"If you are unwilling to defend your right to your own lives, then you are merely mice trying to argue with owls. You think their ways are wrong. They think you are dinner."

꒜ **TERRY GOODKIND** ꒜
*Naked Empire*

## MONEY, MONEY, MONEY

Capitalism is the powerhouse-train on which we ride. But do we trust the vessel? Can we count on the rails? And where exactly are we going? I'm honestly not sure. My first job was delivering newspapers at five in the morning. I made eighty bucks a month, and after two years I saved fifteen hundred dollars, enough to buy a full-suspension Specialized Big-Hit (a mountain bike, in case you're wondering).

Work equals money. Money equals power and possessions. I was 12 years old, it stuck with me. I kept getting jobs. At 18, I started summer shifts in the Yukon, for a mineral exploration company, GroundTruth. We were looking for gold and the end vision was stock market success and an open-pit mine. I loved the job because we got to explore remote ecosystems in the untamed north—the same wilderness I aimed to exploit. The paradox was not lost on me.

But it wasn't black and white. There were jobs, governments, debt, speculation, caribou, Indigenous Peoples, forests, fish, archeology, and rivers at stake. *It was messy.* People wanted to do the right thing, but money is powerful. I learned a lot about resource management and living in tents. After four summers, I left. If I wanted to go out in nature, I could do it without the moral quandary.

Up and down the coast, projects export oil and gas, harvest timber, hunt bears (banned in 2018 for BC, but Alaska is still open), hunt wolves, and amass fish—often surpassing regeneration rates. Supply and demand is problematic when we don't account for the ecosystems (or ozone) we degrade. It has this special term.

### ENVIRONMENTAL EXTERNALITIES (NOUN):

1. The extra consequences of industrial activity that affects an ecosystem without being reflected in market prices. For example, a logging company might harvest timber, and replant the forest (usually with a monoculture of profitable softwood), but what about the loss of animal habitat, biodiversity, and carbon sequestration? Who pays for that? And if the trees were old growth, can we put a value on the ecosystem services they provided?

On Lelu, the Malaysian oil and gas company, Petronas, has proposed an LNG compression plant and export facility. It will be the terminal of a pipeline from northeast BC's shale gas fields. These non-conventional gas reserves can only be extracted through hydraulic fracturing (fracking): injecting high-pressure liquids into bore holes.

Lelu is under the traditional and current title of the Lax Kw'alaams First Nation, who oppose the project. The island is occupied by a resistance camp initiated by members of the Nation, preventing survey teams from conducting their work.

The Skeena River supports the food security of three Indigenous communities and over seventeen communities. Sockeye are the lifeblood of people, bears, whales, and everything else. Can we put a dollar value on that?

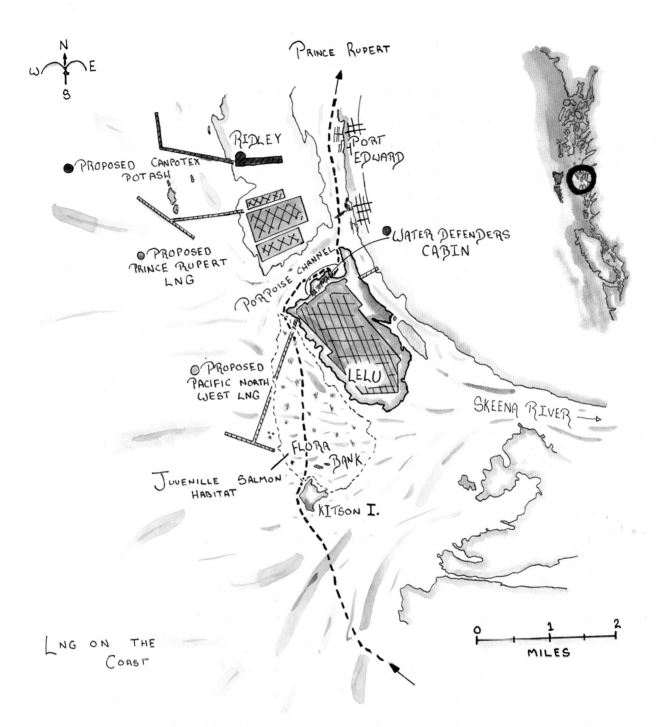

The estuary of the Skeena is an anomaly. The underwater bank, made of glacial till left from the last ice age, has been held in homeostasis by the outgoing current of the Skeena and the complex flows from Hecate Strait. Coated with eelgrass, Flora Bank, which is connected to Lelu, is prime juvenile habitat. Sockeye smolt depend on Flora for protection, food, and habitat while becoming accustomed to the salt water (requiring a neat process called osmoregulation,[4] which takes weeks). The compression plant will dredge and destroy this unique ecosystem.

With vested interests on both sides, there is bound to be a battle.

# DAY 11, JUNE 15:

Wind S 20. *Stormy.* //
Oona river to Lelu Island—29 nm.

A fury of eagles dive-bomb beside me. A teepee and cabin merge into view, and I'm greeted by a Gitxsan woman who smiles, but in a serious manner. The free and prior informed consent protocol requires me to float in my kayak, waiting, until I have answered five questions before being invited onto the territory. These questions are:

1. Who are you and where are you from?

2. Why are you here?

3. How is your presence going to benefit the Gitwilgyoots people (translating to "people of the place of kelp")?

4. Do you or have you worked for the oil and gas industry or the government?

5. How long do you intend to stay?

I tell the truth and join for a meal. We spend the night swapping stories, ideas, and philosophy. Everyone has different reasons for standing up against the capitalistic-juggernaut.

Christy, the camp leader for the week, is of the Gitxsan First Nation (their territory is 150 kilometres / 93 miles upstream). Although the LNG facility is not on her territory, the river is. She tells me the Skeena connects her people to the salmon, which is what allows the Gitxsan to survive and flourish.

## FACES OF LELU

A Cree couple from Saskatchewan are there with their two teenage girls who had never seen the ocean. Tired of oil companies taking advantage of their land and resources back on the prairies, the family is meeting other land defenders in BC to share strategies.

Neeka has raven-black hair and eyes like river stones. She is up from Cali learning about decolonization and how to take a stand for the

environment. My heart leaps the way hearts do—my spontaneous love going undeclared. I feel guilty after, thinking of Kaia. There are so many beautiful souls; I want to meet them all!

I was worried I wouldn't have anything to contribute to the camp, but after telling my tale, I'm told my experience is *just* what's at stake. This journey has value, and being able to share it can be transformative for folks who could never visit. This sits with me heavy-duty. *Hmmm.* Maybe this is why I write.

## HOW TO HEAL

My toes are mangled sausages. Red blisters have popped into infected sores, oozing pus. Repeated exposure to near-freezing water has damaged the blood vessels. I later learn the medical term: *perniosis.*

I don't take care of myself too well. I've broken eight bones, mostly doing stupid things—snowboarding, mountain-biking, skateboarding. It's not the activities that are unintelligent, *but me.* Trying to impress. Trying to be heroic. *Trying* to be reckless. In some monkey-way these injuries created status and stories. They made me feel *seen and special* in a culture devoid of significance. One thing I'm learning: It doesn't matter what other people think.

My body is this tender, squishy, sensitive thing. When I'm *in it* for the wrong reasons, it tells me. If you got a bad feeling about something: say *no.*

My pain reaches a climax between Oona and Lelu. I have my worst flip yet—I won't go into the embarrassing details. After trying to re-enter four times in sloppy swell, I finally succeed, and spend the next hours shivering in my tent, reclaiming heat.

Back on the water, my feet go absolute-bonkers, as though fire-ants are laying eggs under my skin. *Imagine the most itchy you've ever been, and multiply it by a gazillion.*

*I'm trapped in this boat, in this body, in this ocean.* A wave of claustrophobia assaults me. I scream, at everything. I would rather cut off my legs than endure. Whipping off the skirt, I dunk both feet in the salty water—temporary relief. And after, it's worse.

There are no hospitals here. *I have to take care of myself.*

Pain is a signal to prevent overuse and injury. It shows my bad habits. Mostly I ignore pain, and pop P-killers. Rarely do I sit and have tea with it. Medicine reduces symptoms but prevents examination of the roots. Injuries can be mentors or monsters; it's a bit scary how thin the line is.

I hope this doesn't get worse.

At 12, I broke my leg riding down metal stairs on a bicycle. At 16, I snapped my arm snowboarding; the bone healed funny and is still sideways. Ages 17 to 26, I broke both wrists, an elbow, my arm (again), and collar bone—almost one fracture a year. My identity relied on being risky and able-bodied, but each injury forced me to look in the mirror and ask: Who am I really? When I can't rock climb, snowboard, and skateboard, what will I do? And are those activities creating lasting happiness? Or just tools to ego boost? What about sea kayaking?

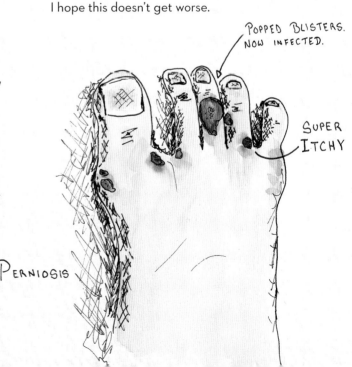

POPPED BLISTERS. NOW INFECTED.

SUPER ITCHY

PERNIOSIS

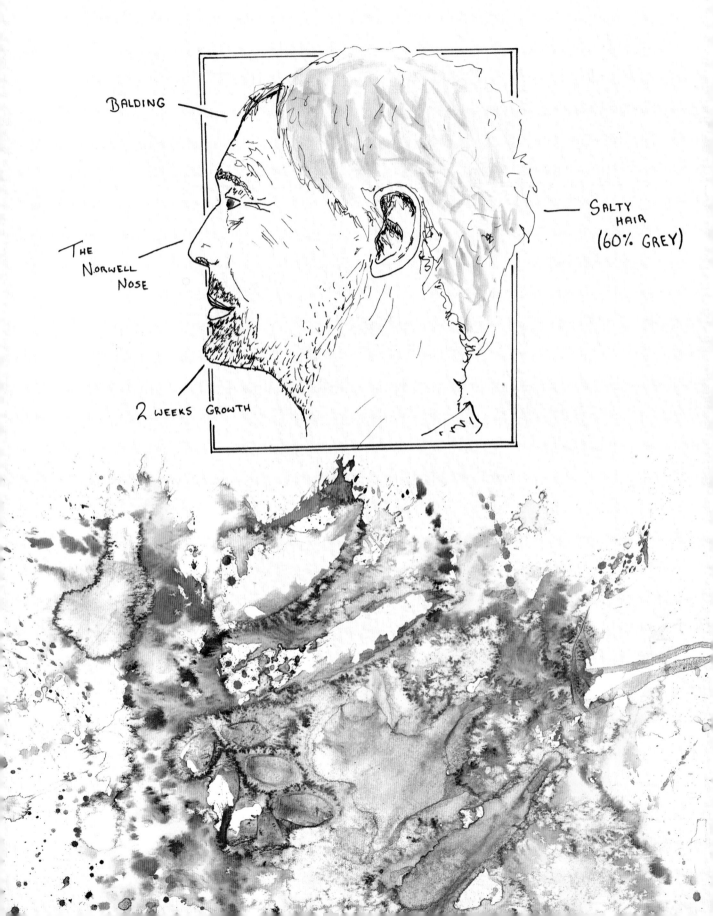

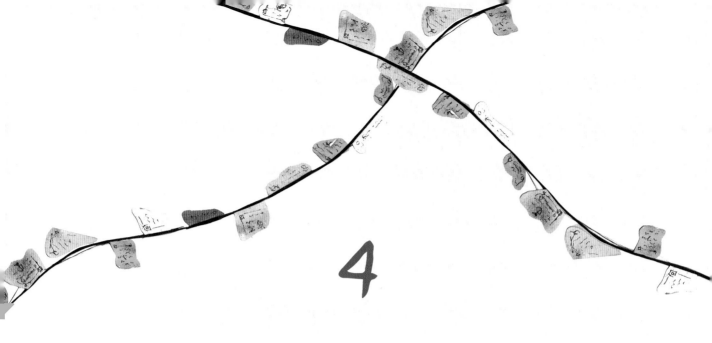

# 4

# MY DAD

"Whether one is rich or poor, educated or
illiterate, religious or non-believing, man or woman,
black, white, or brown, we are all the same. Physically,
emotionally, and mentally, we are all equal. We all
share basic needs for food, shelter, safety, and love.
We all aspire to happiness and we all shun suffering.
Each of us has hopes, worries, fears, and dreams. Each
of us wants the best for our family and loved
ones. We all experience pain when we suffer loss
and joy when we achieve what we seek."

ঽ **GYALWA RINPOCHE, HHDL** ঽ
*Toward a True Kinship of Faiths: How
the World's Religions Can Come Together*
Dad and I are both really into HHDL.

## PRINCE RUPERT WITH DAD

I need medicine—my feet are strange and emitting fluids. I ride the currents from Lelu and pull into Prince Rupert. A port town weathered by a century of shipping, fishing, and logging, it is home to all the associated characters.

A lady at the visitor centre points at my banana-slug toes. *"Oh my god. Do you need help?!"* At the grocery store, I purchase tea tree oil and Polysporin, and apply both liberally. I look up the condition online: "To heal, keep your feet dry and warm." Could be difficult.

My dad is a strange cookie. He enjoys knitting,[1] making soap, and other niche handicrafts. It's cool. He taught me to be creative, crafty, and not care what other people think. As a kid, I was embarrassed by him. I regret that now.

I invited Pops to join for a leg of the journey. We will traverse the Alaskan border to Ketchikan—160 kilometres (100 miles)—then he will take the ferry home.

To share time will be a special treat, but I'm nervous. I always feel like a little boy when I'm with him. Old roles lie deep and dormant, despite the growth I've been through. I hope we can build a new friendship and understanding. We meet at a bed and breakfast and grab a beer from a back-door brewery. He is nervous too. At 62 years old, he's never kayaked on the ocean before.

I stop at a mailbox and send a letter to Kaia. I miss her, and love her, and tell her so (in a vague and philosophical way). She's the only one back home who understands this coast like I do.

We sort our gear on a sunny dock safeguarding fish boats from the storms of Dixon Entrance. Dad has packed a wealth of tasty munch, and I have already made a dent in the gorp (trail mix). Loading kayaks takes more time than you think, but eventually our gear is stowed and we push off, launching into a new father-son relationship.

## AN OMINOUS BEGINNING

The first challenge is the narrows by Metlakatla, where the currents are, of course, against us. The sun collapses and we look for a place to camp. The islets in front of Metlakatla are sacred burial grounds to Indigenous Peoples. We want to give respectful distance, but we mix up the chart, and by the time Dad uncovers gravestones, it's dark.

Indigenous Peoples have operated in the Pacific Northwest from time immemorial; the best we can do is paddle gracefully and mindfully through the landscape—even when we accidentally sleep in the wrong place. We light a fire and apologize to the nameless presence we both feel. *Sorry.*

*Opposite* *Dad made this banjo from a birch he milled in the yard! He's like that, always building. His job-job is a forester for the BC government. He mediates talks with Indigenous communities. My mom and dad had their own forestry consulting company before getting government jobs. They wanted to change the clear-cut mentality. Now they try to influence the system from inside but seem to be getting disenchanted. I still don't know, is it better to change something from the inside or the outside? Or just let it be?*

## DAY 13, JUNE 17:
Wind L to NW 10-15. // Metlakatla—4 nm.

**05:00.** The routine is new to Dad. We are hoping to get a boost with the flood and avoid the afternoon wind. The tides around Prince Rupert are up to seven metres vertical, which means a hundred-metre horizontal slog down the beach. *What a workout!* We paddle for three hours until an opposing wind kicks up, forcing us to pull off. Dad needs a cup of tea and I need a nap. A slow start to our first full day. Dad drops his phone in the water, it gargles and dies. No need for gizmos anyway.

## DAY 14, JUNE 18:
Wind W 15 to L. // Some Random Bay—6 nm.

Westerlies whip unconditionally over wicked seas while a grizzly wanders the low tide, digging up clams. A patient gull waits for leftovers.

GRIZZLY BEAR
*Ursus arctos*

*Opposite* Dixon Entrance. Lax Kw'alaams translates to *"place of the wild roses." It is an ancient camping spot of the Gispaxlo'ots People.*

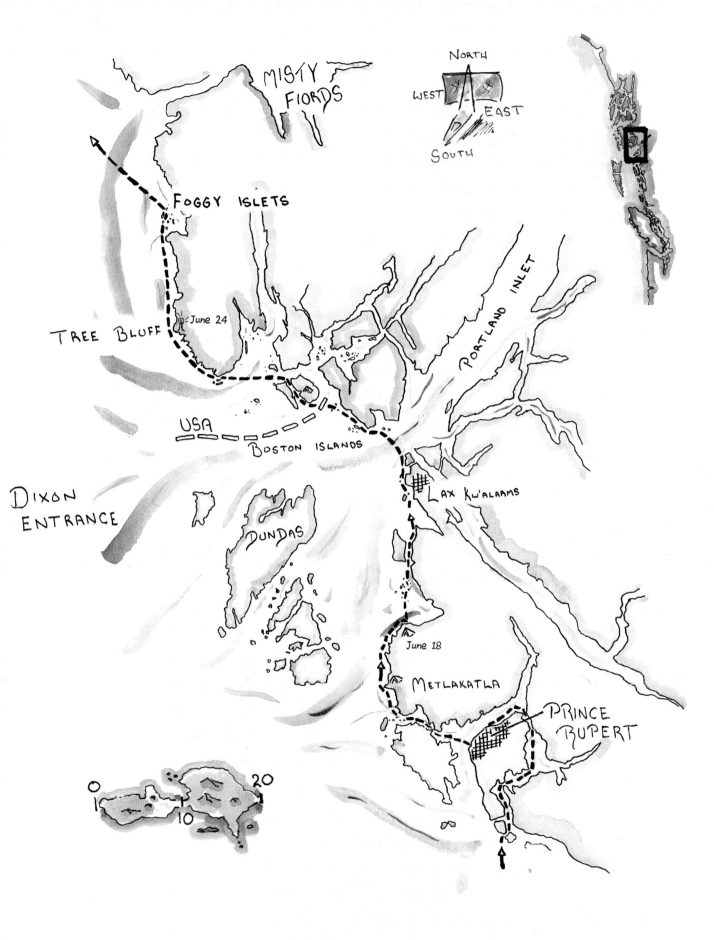

## DAY 15, JUNE 19:
Wind W 5 to L. //
Lax Kw'alaams—10 nm.


My feet are healing.

## DAY 17, JUNE 21:
Wind NW 10. *Summer solstice.* //
Boston Islands—9 nm.


A *Sebastes caurinus* (copper rockfish) jumps on
the line and begins to struggle. The vibrations
make it to my hands—I feel its desperation. Dad
paddles over and supports my boat while I reel in

Copper rockfish
(Sebastes caurinus)

the umbilical cord. Rockfish are spiky specimens that secrete poison from their needle-sharp fins. I manhandle the squirmer onto the deck, and for a moment I catch its mad, darting eyes—a fish out of water. Then I smash its skull until the spasms become faint and hollow.

Dad and I stare in silence. Blood drips down and is diluted by the salty water from which it came. Killing things is profound and spiritual. We paddle to shore, light a fire, and watch the scales crackle. A deep, evolutionary process has taken over. We say a prayer and devour our prize. I feel sad, raw, and exhilarated. The hunter is victorious, and the lover weeps.

## DAY 18, JUNE 22:
Wind Light to NW 10–15. //
Boston Island to Nameless Bay—5 nm.

Water. Yes, *water*. It's hard to believe it exists at
all. I float on it, it rains on me, I drink it, and pee
it out. It's everywhere—*except for this islet we've
camped on.* Dad marches into the forest to fill
up from a gnarly swamp, and introduces a cool
treatment solution. Water in a clear bottle left in
UVs (sunshine) kills all biotic material in six hours—
solar disinfection. Note: this technique does not
treat toxins.

It's a valid question: Where *do* you get water?
And did you ever drink your own pee? Until now
I haven't treated water once; I collect from quick-
moving streams, which are abundant on this
coastline. No pee, *not yet.*

Dad sets up an A-frame for sailing. I go swimming and scrub myself to get rid of a dubious smell.

We leave for Alaska in the late afternoon,
hoping to get a boost from the flooding tide.
*Borders are irrelevant here.* No hint of political or
cultural change. I think you are supposed to call
ahead to customs before crossing, but it seems
like no one could possibly notice or care.

We are welcomed most ceremoniously by a
humpback's tail.

*Welcome to Alaska.*

## DAY 20, JUNE 24:
Wind SW 20 to Light. // Tree point—8 nm.

Cape Fox sounds like a terrific place to picnic. *It's
not.* Nudging into Dixon Entrance, the cape gets
smashed by aggressive weather combos and
strange currents. Dad and I maroon ourselves
and wait for the winds.

The sea settles and we make it to the abandoned lighthouse[2] on Tree Bluff, which was built
in 1903 (engraved on a moss-covered stone). We
tiptoe through the wreckage; the structures are
rotten and the forest is Jurassic. A precarious
railway snakes through the trees linking the boat-
house to the lighthouse. Nature is taking these
artifacts back into its womb. My imagination
stretches back in time—this would have been a
treacherous *and* beautiful place to call home.

I climb up and peer over the edge of
the world.

## TLINGIT TERRITORY

Southeast Alaska is home to the Tlingit First Nations, a conglomeration of around twenty tribes. The territory connects to the interior via the Alsek, Tatshenshini, Chilkat, Taku, and Stikine watersheds. These river highways allowed trading with Athabascan and interior Indigenous Peoples, creating the framework for complex political systems, mind-bending artistic endeavours, linguistic diversity, and philosophical evolution.

From what I understand, Tlingit people are split into two moieties (clans): Raven and Eagle. This is further divided into house groups (lineages) with their own animal symbols. Indigenous Peoples...hmmm, this isn't my story.

My story is rooted in colonization—the systematic (and ongoing) assimilation of Indigenous Peoples. I have mixed feelings. My ancestors immigrated to Vancouver under false pretexts; they were told the land was wild and undomesticated—a narrative sold by governments looking to undermine the rich culture of Indigenous Peoples. In my travels, I have witnessed ancient fish traps and active clam gardens. I met folks who know the traditional names and medicinal uses for the plants in the forest. This coast wasn't *and* isn't wild; it's shared, cultivated, and respected.

Ignorance is no justification. Reconciliation is tricky and takes time. And trust. For me, this means being a better listener, better human, and trying to engage where appropriate. Canada and America's history of societally sanctioned genocide is horrific. We settlers must make the effort to learn and witness our shared history. Radical empathy requires being uncomfortable (sometimes deeply). The *Kuper Island* podcast on CBC helped my process and sobered my privileged smile. This is not ancient history. Penelakut's residential school (south of Nanaimo, formerly Kuper Island) closed in 1975, others in Alaska and BC as recently as the 1990s. Children were raped by priests and nuns. In these schools, there are records and stories from Elders that a quarter of the children died. Imagine if this happened at a public school today?

More than anything, settlers must engage in reconciliation *on Indigenous Peoples' terms*. The Heiltsuk Nation have created their own framework and process for reconciliation. It's called: Haíɫcístut. Look it up.[3]

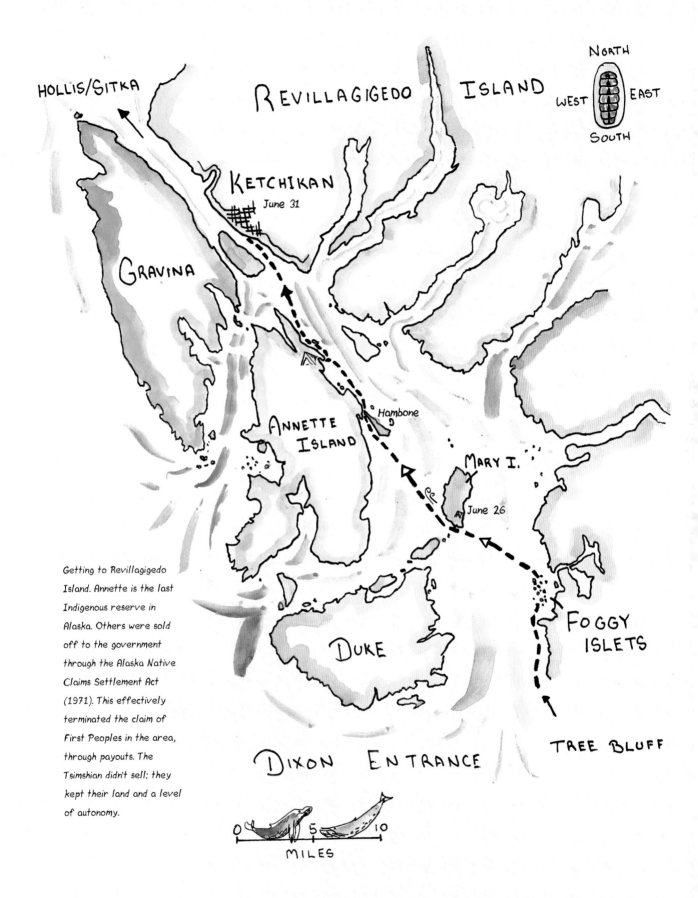

HOLLIS/SITKA

REVILLAGIGEDO ISLAND

NORTH
WEST EAST
SOUTH

KETCHIKAN
June 31

GRAVINA

ANNETTE ISLAND

Hambone

MARY I.
June 26

DUKE

FOGGY ISLETS

TREE BLUFF

DIXON ENTRANCE

Getting to Revillagigedo Island. Annette is the last Indigenous reserve in Alaska. Others were sold off to the government through the Alaska Native Claims Settlement Act (1971). This effectively terminated the claim of First Peoples in the area, through payouts. The Tsimshian didn't sell: they kept their land and a level of autonomy.

0          5          10
MILES

## NUDIBRANCHS OF THE PACIFIC NORTHWEST

Dad and I have been *tide-pooling* into the invertebrate universe. Nudis are gastropods. Basically, sea snails who threw away their shells in favour of rainbow displays and slug culture. They are my favourite inverts, oozing around, using their superpowers. Yes, *superpowers. Aeolida papillosa* (shag-rug nudi) eats toxic stinging anemones, *steals their stingers*, and attaches them to their own back for defence. *What the mega-murphy?!* How do you figure that life-hack out?

Nude-bombs are mind-bendingly slow, so they need to be ready to mate when the chance arises. It helps to have *both* private parts. As hermaphrodites, they slug-love without worrying about the gender of the one other nudist in the pool.

It gets weirder. Some NBs eat coral rich in algae and absorb the chloroplast, which *continues to photosynthesize.*[4] Then they run on solar power. *Are you kidding me!?*

Lastly, nudibranchs are carnivores—fish eggs, barnacles, other nudis, sea pens, sponges, and similar gooey-wooeys. They take on the colour of what they eat, like the green-algal-mama discussed above. That's why they are beyond imagination in appearance; it tells predators, "Hey, I'm toxic. *Back off.* Get your own slug-sandwich."

Nudi = *naked*. Branch = *gills*.

### HOODED NUDIBRANCH (*MELIBE LEONINE*)
SUPERPOWER: Uses hood to capture prey like a Venus fly trap. It swims jellyfish style.

### GIANT NUDI (*DENDRONATUS IRIS*)
SUPERPOWER: Lays eggs inside of poisonous anemones for their protection.

LATIN: Dendro (tree) / natus (back) / iris (rainbow)

### SEA LEMON (*DORIS MONTEREYENSIS*)
SUPERPOWER: Lays up to two million eggs at a time. I imagine they have a pretty hands-off parenting approach, but who knows. This NB is perhaps the cutest.

### NANAIMO DORID (*ACANTHODORIS NANAIMOENSIS*)
SUPERPOWER: Smells like cedar or sandalwood when handled. No one knows why.

## ORANGE PEEL NUDI (*TOCHUINA TETRAQUETRA*)

SUPERPOWER: Largest nude-blaster in the world—up to 50 centimetres! Can be eaten raw or cooked. A citrus addition to Fin's tide-pool soup?

## COCKERELL'S NUDIBRANCH (*LIMACIA COCKERELLI*)

SUPERPOWER: Best haircut award.

## WHITE-FROSTED NUDIST (*DIRONA ALBOLINEATA*)

SUPERPOWER: Cracks the shells of sea snails with its jaws. Ranges from white to salmon-pink to purple.

## STRIPED NUDIBRANCH (*ARMINA CALIFORNICA*)

SUPERPOWER: Hunts in packs and ambushes sea pens from under the sand. For a YouTube journey, look up "pack of hungry sea slugs ravage sea-pen colony."

## THREE-LINED AEOLID (*FLABELLINA TRILINEATA*)

SUPERPOWER: Found 0 to 50 metres deep, from Alaska to Mexico. Feeds on the polyps of the pink-mouthed hydroids.

## SHAG-RUG NUDI (*AEOLIDIA PAPILLOSA*)

SUPERPOWER: True to its name, this NB looks like a dirty shag rug.

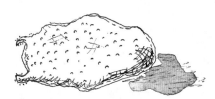

## WHITE KNIGHT DORID (*DORIS ODHNERI*)

SUPERPOWER: Looks like an old marshmallow, not exactly a knight. Eats the tasty-sounding bread-crumb sponge. And is eaten by the rose star.

### DAY 21, JUNE 25:

Wind SE 20 to SE 10. *Mist.* //
Tree Point to Foggy Islets—15 nm.

Dad and I are in sync. We don't discuss duties—
tent, fire, tarp, wood, dinner, be helpful, be
optimistic. It's so nice to have *someone*, not just
to help carry the kayak, *but* to share the *whole-
big-thing*. Someone to ensure my memories are
not a mirage of the Pacific. When this is over,
Dad and I will share a bond knit from sword ferns
and cedar bark, steeped in the smoke of camp-
fires and morning mist.

 A humpback breaches beside us while
partner-sailing. It's snotty and cold, but we make
awesome distance. The Foggy Islets live up to
their name.

### DAY 22, JUNE 26:

*No wind!* // Mary Island—10 nm.

The ocean is a mirror. Art day.

### DAY 23, JUNE 27:

Wind L to SW 10–15. //
Annette Island—Taak'w Aan—10 nm.

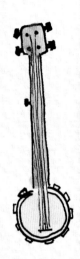

Banjos were introduced from Africa during the
slave days. The sound is twangy, playful, and,
dare I say, mesmerizing. I grew up to Dad's
"Cripple Creek" and improvised lullabies. Dad's
banjo doesn't fit in the hatches so it's wrapped
in a garbage bag, strapped to the deck. We
serenade the stars looking up from our sandy
amphitheatres.

 Surfing our way to, I lose the fishing rod and
a wetsuit boot off the back. *Chewwwy Wooeeey!*
Losing things out here makes me feel very silly.
I can't just run to Wal-Mart and pick up new
everything on a whim.

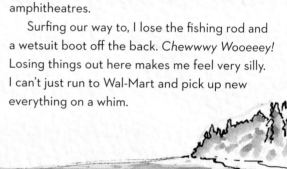

## UNSOLICITED RELATIONSHIP ADVICE

Dad has been telling me about being a dad; it turns out it wasn't easy. My parents went through everything. Four kids, one miscarriage, five cats, and three cities. "Your mother has a strong set of morals, ethics, and values; she's been important in my growth by keeping me accountable. We have matured over time, and are not the same people as when we met. Each time we survive a tough stretch, wisdom arises with expanded awareness and newfound respect... A relationship is an ongoing saga, and a model for the most intimate relationship: the relationship with ourself."

He goes on to tell me: *life is about learning, and our lovers are teachers.* It's got me looking at my partnership with Kaia, and why we haven't been able to make it work.

As a kid, I imagined my parents unfazed by the duties orbiting our family. The key: *work.* This sounds a bit lame, but maybe that's the way truth is. Dad says monogamy requires self-reflection and a deep exploration of expectations and values. He says it's a journey.

The divorce rate in Canada and the US is around 50 percent. It's comical, sad, and makes me timid. Why is everyone so bad at doing the work? Is the institution corrupt, or the people? Is this the new normal? Our purpose on Earth: to find wholeness and truth. There are different ways to experience this, and the closest I've got is in romantic relationships, and being out here.

When Kaia and I met, I was giddy, euphoric, and felt spiritual completeness. Science shows I was swimming in hormones—a serotonin-oxytocin-dopamine-norepinephrine soup that gets humans to connect and stay together. Our genes, it turns out, have their own agenda. But what about this spiritual feeling? I looked for things in Kaia I failed to find in myself. She was a symbol of wholeness and truth. But the expectation for her to supply this feeling is unrealistic. I must create my own happiness and purpose. Partners can help, but we can't depend on them and project unfair expectations. True love recognizes everyone as autonomous, beautiful, and learning. With self-awareness, a good relationship can change the world. *Hmmmm.* But how does one cultivate self-awareness, and what is love?! The Greeks had eight definitions:

1.  **SELF LOVE (PHILAUTIA):** We can't love others unless we love ourselves. Is this actually true?

2.  **FAMILIAL LOVE (STORGE):** Love for one's children and dependents.

3.  **AFFECTIONATE LOVE (PHILIA):** Platonic love, often between community and equals.

4.  **PLAYFUL LOVE (LUDUS):** The butterflies and tingles before we even know someone. A crush.

5.  **ROMANTIC LOVE (EROS):** Passionate, sexuality-based love. Or is this lust and craving?

6.  **OBSESSIVE LOVE (MANIA):** Infatuation. When everything goes haywire. Which can lead to jealousy, anger, madness.

7.  **ENDURING LOVE (PRAGMA):** After eros has burned up, what is left? This is matured love, built on mutual respect and support. Like the grandparents that make us go, "Awwwww." It is love tested by time.

8.  **BOUNDLESS LOVE (AGAPE):** Unconditional love for all beings. No strings. Just one-way traffic. Like for your dog, cat, and all living beings, without exception (even mosquitoes).

Instead of saying "I love you," we should be clearer. "Today, I love you like *this*, because of *this*, and perhaps *this* too will change."

## HOW TO LOVE BETTER

1. *Be your true self.* We are multi-sided dice, choose the sincere, humble, and clear version of yourself.

2. *Communicate your feelings* and be transparent. Speak the truth as best you can, even if you are uncertain. It's OK not to know what you're doing. Practice your words, and be careful with the power they hold.

3. *Move on.* The past holds lessons but should not strangle energy, emotion, and focus.

4. *Your meaning and purpose in this world cannot be found in another.* A profound feeling of connection exists inside of yourself, and it takes discipline and time to cultivate. Seek fulfillment *with* your partner, not *through* your partner.

5. *We are imperfect* and in a larger process. Love mistakes in others and yourself as lessons. Embrace the strange puzzle pieces in front of you. We never know exactly how things will turn out.

6. *Don't project.* See people for who they are, not the projection your mind has fabricated. Love and live in the present.

7. *Check in* with each other and yourself as things progress.

8. *Take time* to be alone, journal, and reflect. Take yourself on solo-dates *and* solo-dances.

9. *Your partner's ability to adapt is surprising.* Don't be afraid to ask for things in your relationship, even if you *think* the other person will say *"no."*

10. *True love is given without expecting anything in return.* If you expect something, it's not the big-mature-love we aspire for. It might be nice, but *not* T-Love. Hmm... It's harder to practice this than write it.

11. *Love is not the base of a relationship;* honesty, empathy, and self-reflection are. Love is just the expression dancing on top. The more solid the foundation, the bigger the love. Perhaps instead of *I love you*, we can try *I trust you.*

12. Dad also said this thing that flips everything upside-downsies: *"There's no right answer. Love is a unique process for each of us and can be pleasant, painful, ecstatic, traumatic, cosmic, and profound—all are part of being human, all are beautiful, all are an opportunity to grow."*

# DAY 25, JUNE 29:

Wind SE 10–15. *Rain.* //
Hambone Island to Ketchikan, AK—6 nm.

Last day on the water. I try to savour it, but it goes by quickly, like all good things. We pack up camp, sail into Ketchikan, and collapse in the arms of Alaskan hospitality. Interestingly, our arrival coincides with the first-place winner of this year's Race to Alaska:[5] *S/V Mad Dog.* The 30-foot hobie-dog sailed day and night, Victoria to Ketch, in three days and twenty hours. *Chowsers!* It's taken me sixty-six days (over two summers).

A monster storm is forecasted—*perfect timing.* We check into a church-hostel with beds, clean sheets, and a hot shower. There is a kitchen with a stove and sink. I turn the tap on and off, grinning.

## GOODBYE TO DAD

After 160 kilometres (100 miles) of salt water, gales, and slightly burnt food, we treat ourselves. Despite my anticipation, restaurants feel strange and unnatural, and other people seem distracted and short on love.

After two days, the ferry bound for Prince Rupert arrives. Dad heads home—back to Mom, his job, and his life. I help carry his kayak onto the ferry. He looks older (due to an unkempt beard Mom would never allow) but stronger and brighter. He gives me a bear-hug, and tells me to *take care.* He always says that.

Travelling with Dad allowed me to learn where I come from. It humanized my father. He is this normal, mortal dude, trying his best and making mistakes. Our father-son roles were thrown aside, and we established a relationship on solving

ocean-puzzles, staring at whales, and singing to the stars.

I'm lucky to have such an awesome dad.

## KETCHIKAN, ALASKA

Ketchikan is torn between wet, desolate winters and cruise-ship summers.[6] These tourist-blasters are engineering enigmas—up to 16 decks high, they withstand all conditions. They are the apex predator of the tourism industry. Mortified, I watch as thousands of bazooka-lens, selfie-stick, *lower-48ers (some Alaskans hold a slight rancor towards the softer, less rugged southern forty-eight states)* are barfed into the streets.

What's better, *access* or *autonomy*?

Many islands in Alaska are scarcely inhabited due to their remote nature, but some are money machines—fish, timber, and tourism. For better or worse, it takes its toll. I flip-flop at the confluence of conservation and access. I've come to this conclusion: our intentions matter and create feedback cycles in the fabric of humanity.

The ocean once held back all but the adventurous, colonial, and enslaved. *Now it's wide open.* This has disturbed our sense of place, and impacted cultures and environments irreversibly. We have left reverence and respect for geography behind. Kayaking isn't possible for everyone, and I don't think people *shouldn't* see these islands. But I do believe a small amount of human-powered transportation goes a long way.

## INDEPENDENCE DAY

Dad's gone. I need a couple more days' rest, and I find some wonderful hosts on Couchsurfing. Catherine is a yoga instructor and Ted works for the salmon hatcheries. They feed me crab, give me a tour of the local hatchery, and take me out on their boat! *Thank you!*

I stay for the Fourth of July (America's birthday). Four cruise-mamas are in for the event. I'm invited to play in the marching banjo band (see photo on page 200) by the local music shop. We play "Oh Susanna" and "Yankee Doodle" tromping down Main Street. It's an overload of red, blue, and booze. Is this a brainwashing tactic—promoting patriotism, bingo eating, and alcohol dependence? *I'll leave tomorrow.* Back to spruce trees, solitude, and true freedom.

# 5
# JUST DON'T DIE OUT THERE, OK?

"It is our suffering that brings us together. It's not love. Love does not obey the mind, and turns to hate when forced. The bond that binds us is beyond choice. We are brothers. We are brothers in what we share. In pain, which each of us must suffer alone, in hunger, in poverty, in hope, we know our brotherhood. We know it, because we have had to learn it. We know that there is no help for us but from one another, that no hand will save us if we do not reach out our hand. And the hand that you reach out is empty, as mine is. You have nothing. You possess nothing. You own nothing. You are free. All you have is what you are, and what you give."

ᚷ **URSULA K. LE GUIN** ᚷ
*The Dispossessed*
One of my new favs. This
quote gives me goosebumps.

*Below* Run-in with humpback in Clarence Strait. I'm not sure if this was a close one, or the most magical thing that's ever happened to me. Perhaps you need the former to create the latter.

KETCHIKAN
TO
KLAWOK

PRINCE OF WALES
ISLAND

MAURELLE
ISLANDS

KASAAN

KLAWOCK
July 6, 2016

12 MILE ARM

HOLLIS

HITCH HIKE

0   MILES   10

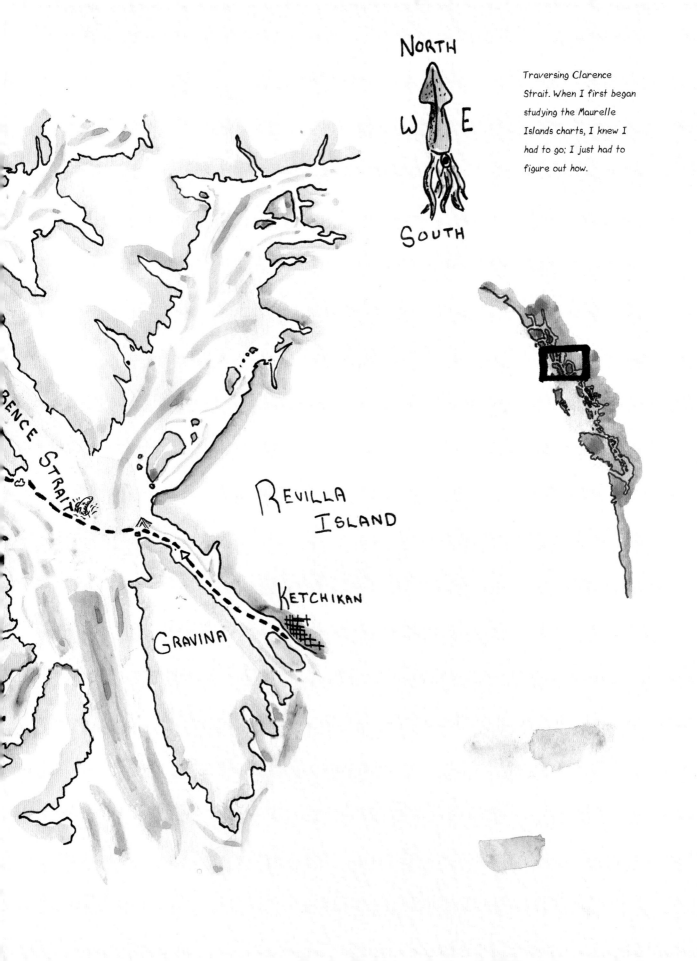

NORTH

W E

SOUTH

Traversing Clarence
Strait. When I first began
studying the Maurelle
Islands charts, I knew I
had to go; I just had to
figure out how.

RENCE STRAIT

REVILLA
ISLAND

KETCHIKAN

GRAVINA

## DAY 29, JULY 3:

Wind: S 5–10. Sun. //
Ketchikan to Gravina Island—10 nm.

*Ketch you later.* Dwarfed by cruise ships, and eventually conifers, I sail towards a new future. No one notices my departure. A couple of hours gets me to the end of Gravina. I walk in the maples and work on my fungus sketching—all hail the third kingdom. The moss is an anesthetic, and I drowse under a mama-tree.

Resurfacing, I find my stomach begging for food, and remember the one-kilogram bag of chocolate chips I bought—a lapse in judgment. My brain is left buzzing with no outlet.

The moon rises, and I struggle with sleep due to my nap-and-sug session. I listen wide-eyed to the tide crawl within inches of the tent. My senses expand to the wind sifting through the trees and the massive ocean ruling my life. A semiconscious blackness devours me.

## DAY 30, JULY 4:

Wind SE 10. Overcast. //
Kasaan Peninsula—14 nm.

Clarence Strait is an eleven-nautical-mile crossing rumoured to be dangerous and unpredictable—as though the ocean has moods.

Long crossings require calm weather, knowledge of currents, and *time*—time to wait for good conditions. Kayak accidents (and deaths) on this coast are due to groups paddling in heavy weather when they should have stayed put.[1] But mostly, people get in trouble because of too many lemons.

## LEMON (*CITRUS LIMON*)

The whole reason I'm able to *not die* in a kayak is Kate Hives and Peter Carson—legends among the west coast salts and my trainers for the Sea Kayak Guides Alliance of BC's Assistant Overnight Guide course I did before working at Camp Thunderbird. They taught me to read waves and record weather; they also explained lemon theory.

Each lemon represents a variable: strong winds, large swell, hungry, tired, low morale, tricky currents—the list goes on. While guiding, a wise leader is juggling these variables, and knows when it's too much. In short: it's never one thing leading to an accident, but the cumulative citrus squeeze.

Think about this: What makes a good leader? And how do we improve at decision-making? Is the ocean unpredictable, or are our calculators lacking?

I've heard scary stories of kayakers doing long-hauls in savage conditions. The best story:

*Nothing happened.* Either we didn't go, or we did and it was calm.

But crossing Clarence Strait, *something did happen.* A 30,000-kilogram (66,000-pound) humpback breached right beside me (see comic). Before going free-willy, I came within metres while it surfaced for air, and said, "Hello." The marine-sausage flipped its tail, dove down, and two minutes later: "KAASLOOSH!" How could I account for this sea-lemon?

The question of our time: Was it saying "hello" back?

## WEATHER

"How does weather work, and why does it change?"

The key is pressure systems. It might be helpful to imagine *two sisters and a crazy uncle*. Our first sister is *High-Pee*, or Blue-Skies. She is wonderful, consistent in the summers, and loves to blow north-westerlies, mostly in the afternoons. In the winter, she rarely comes out, and is a bit drowsy if she does.

Our second sister: *Low-Pee* or Broody-Judy. She is wet, wild, and originally from the Aleutian Islands. She migrates down to the Pacific Northwest whenever she gets big enough, and spits gale south-easterlies. For most of the winter, and a handful of times through the summer, she is queen. If you're sailing north, these lows are the key to making distance; it just means you get wet.

The crazy uncle is *Big-Blow-Joe*. He is an extra-tropical cyclone, and peels up from the equator in November and December. Every 25 to 50 years, he's strong enough to rip trees from their sockets and flood sidewalks. He is becoming more frequent. As you might imagine, it wouldn't be nice to kayak with Joe.

So that's it: Blue-eyes, Judy, and Joe. The former two are *relative* to each other, switching back and forth, looking for equilibrium—high, low, high, low, with winds *NW, SE, NW, SE*. It's not really this simple, but it's a start.

The golden rule: If pressure is dropping fast, or gnarly clouds start boiling, pull off the water. When pressure changes dramatically, you will feel it. Trust your monkey-instincts. Many mammals and birds seek refuge long before the storm.

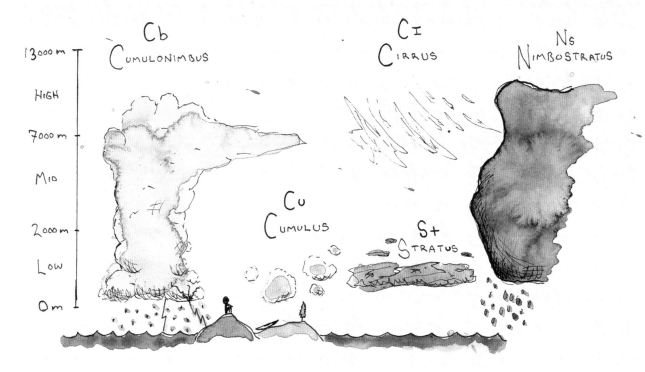

## CLOUDS

**CUMULUS (CU):** Cauliflower-puffballs. Fair-weather clouds. *Enjoy.* Cumulus = heaped.

**STRATUS (ST):** Dull grey, overcast, or fog. Stratus = spreading.

**CUMULONIMBUS (CB):** Thunder-bomb-cloud-towers. Indicate extreme weather, heavy rain, hail, snow, and thunderstorms. *Take care.* Nimbus = rainstorm. Cumulonimbus = _____

**NIMBOSTRATUS (NS):** Wet-angry-blocking-out-the-sun clouds. Indicate a frontal system. *Take care.*

Nimbus = _____ Stratus = _____

Nimbostratus = _____

*Opposite  Wind direction is determined by where you are located in relation to a pressure system. At the edge is the weather front (the transition zone between two systems), which can be volatile (erratic wind direction and speed). The centre of the system is more stable and can even be calm. Clouds are fun to learn; after a while they become friends. The Latin nomenclature is super clever.*

## OROGRAPHIC LIFT

The whole reason this coast is wild, complex, and impossible to access is the ragged coastal mountains guarding it from the tame interior. When low-pressure systems (Broody-Judy) swing down, the saturated clouds lose their weight to get up-and-over. In short: it pours. The Pacific Northwest is a temperate *rainforest*—the largest on Earth. This is why we have 100-metre (325-foot) old growth, 600-kilogram (1,320-pound) grizzlies, and the most diverse salmon-system in the universe. The landscape *creates* the weather, and the weather creates the landscape.

Shifting shadows fail to repeat
A silence filled with subtleties
Moving under feet
In the wind hides guidance
For those with open hands
A gift for those with nothing
Along the path we meet

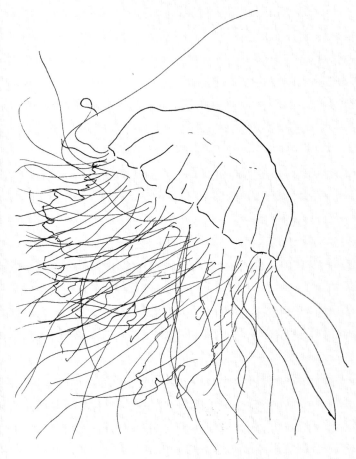

## DAY 32, JULY 6:

Wind Light to W 5. //
Kasaan to Hollis to Klawock—20 nm.

To get lost is this fundamentally human thing—*a learning process*. The most confused I ever got was in university. I wanted to study philosophy—*existentialism*. Head over heels with Kierkegaard, Nietzsche, and their independence-doctrine, I eagerly went up to my teacher: "So, how do I apply all this? How do I live out their radical-authentic theories?"

She stared blankly, *That's up to you.*

It was a mystical and philosophical answer, *perfect!* I spent the next year living out these dead-white-dudes' principles without knowing what they really were. In the end, I was lonely, depressed, and questioning the basis of reality.

Luckily I found geography—rooted in tangible, outdoor projects. It saved my mental health. More than anything, it exposed me to like-minded-open-eyes who explored rivers and secret-beaches on the weekend. I found my tribe *and* handy skills—like how to read a map.

Sailing up Kassan Inlet, the landmarks melt into one another. My disorientation dawns. *Nothing matches the chart.* The lines and symbols *hodgepodge* with the forested mountains and rocky shore. The patterns of inlets and headlands repeat themselves.

I'm eight kilometres (five miles) off course. *Mother Teresa and all that is* HOOOOLY! I curse myself until laughter emerges. So much for my *geography degree*. It costs my biceps an extra two hours. How did the Indigenous Peoples navigate this coast without maps?

I'm headed to Hollis, a community on the *east coast* of Prince of Wales Island. From there I have a weird plan. I want to hitchhike to Klawock, so I can continue on the exposed *west coast* (see page 120). I'm done with the inside passage, and

BELL PEPPER

want to investigate a rumoured sea otter population in the Maurelle Islands. After that, I'll aim for Sitka on the outside of Baranof Island—the most rugged and remote Papa in Southeast Alaska. I hope I'm ready.

## HITCHHIKING

Six years ago, I hitched across Canada with my first partner, Blakeney. We wanted to see who exactly lives in the middle. It turns out: *some really nice people*. We got picked up by wolf-loving truckers, a feminist oil rigger, single moms, an Indigenous dad, and everyone in between. There are amazing people in this country.

To conduct this technical kayak-hitch, I'll need more than my thumb. People love a story.

In front of the Hollis terminal, I wait for the Ketchikan commuters. I need a vehicle capable of carrying *Bell Pepper* and my gear. A couple folks shut me down, then I approach two Klawock locals transporting a canoe with a trailer. My elevator pitch comes out awkward: "Hi, I'm David. I kayaked here from Canada, and need to *portage* across the island so I can paddle the outside coast and do independent research on sea otters." Wayne gives me a blank look, registering my story, then a huge smile. "Sure, but

what's a *portage*?" We strap everything down and Wayne hands me a beer. Driving across, he tells his tale: logging trucks, fishnets, and tough love. One hand on the wheel, he holds the conversation easily. I gather he has driven this road thousands of times, and consumed the associated thousand beers.

## PORTAGE (VERB)

1. The carrying of boats and supplies overland between two waterways or around an obstacle to navigation.

Wayne drops me off at the edge of town—although *everywhere* in Klawock is the *edge of town*. Before unloading, he smiles and snaps a shot, saying, "My wife won't believe this."

Ridesharing should be mandatory. Our western world divides communities by class, competition, and property. What happened to cooperation? People have trouble picking up other humans because they assume it will be uncomfortable. Research shows people who talk to strangers, even for a couple minutes, have a greater sense of belonging, and are happier for the rest of the day!

Try it—being a picker-upper *and* a pick-me-up both have lessons.

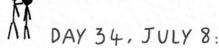

## DAY 33, JULY 7:
Wind light. // Klawock to Sea Otter Camp—14 nm.

I wake up reluctantly, and spend the morning chasing fuzzy-feelings. Right now, my family and friends are paddling their own ocean. I miss my people, and wonder if their thoughts drift *my* way. What about Kaia? Where is she? Does she miss me?

I wiggle out of Klawock and sneak up on four snoring elephant seals in the middle of the Gulf of Esquibel.[2] They bob up and down, surfacing for air. So that's how marine mammals sleep! I tempt fate and get as close as I... SPPEELOOSH! I trigger the perimeter-sensors, they dive into silence. *Sorry.*

## DAY 34, JULY 8:
Overcast. // Maurelle Islands—3 nm.

I love sea otters. When I was five I got two cuddly toys: Splashes and Splashes Junior. On my bow, Junior is strapped and salt-licked, scouting for her kin. If you are wondering if a stuffed animal has been tethered to my deck for the duration of the trip: the answer is a *soft and gentle yes.* On your own voyages, bring a friend. The Maurelles are home to super-rafts of these cuteness-machines. With binocs pressed to my sockets, I've been taking notes.

### SEA OTTER (*ENHYDRA LUTRIS*)
Sea otters are environmental engineers *and* keystone species—AKA ecosystem bosses. This

RAFT AREA / KELP FOREST

*The Maurelle Islands. This is a paddler's playground, lots of secrets to explore. There must be a Japanese Pokè-ball here somewhere!*

MAURELLE ISLANDS

MANY GROUPS OF TWO

SEA OTTER CAMP

SMALL RAFT SITE

Gulf of Esquibel

is because they eat urchins, and urchins destroy kelp forests. When otters arrive, the ecosystem shifts from urchin-barren to a kelp kingdom. This is called a trophic cascade. Kelp means more everything—primary productivity, fish habitat, biodiversity, and reduced wave action. If you're into biology, this process is fascinating to study.

OTTER FACT: They have the thickest fur on earth—up to one million hairs per square inch! Humans have about twelve hundred. No wonder we invented toques. Unfortunately, this factoid is what led to their near extinction; they were too cuddly.

In the 1700s, Russians moved into the Pacific Northwest, turning these aquatic-fuzz-bunnies into pelts. The furs were sold to China at big-ticket prices. The Russians created the first major fort on the coast, New Archangel—now Sitka, Alaska. The Spanish, who had claimed the BC coast, took this as a threat and created a fort in Nootka Sound. The rush was on, and sparked a frenzy to colonize. I'll spare the details: the otters were killed, BC ended up with the British, and thousands of Indigenous people were devastated by smallpox, syphilis, murder, rape, and other colonial tragedies. Russia eventually sold

Alaska to the Americans for 7.2 million dollars (2 cents per acre).

Not all of the otters died. Refuges remained in the Aleutians and in one colony in California.[3] A moratorium was established and populations are recovering, but industrial activity threatens. The species was smeared by the 1989 Exxon Valdez oil spill. Unlike other marine mammals, otters don't have much fat, so they depend on well-groomed haircuts; their fur traps $O_2$, creating insulation to survive the 7- to 12- degree-Celsius Pacific.

## MAURELLE OTTER OBSERVATIONS

- DIET: Wide range of invertebrates—clams, urchins, crabs, and even an octopus!

- COMPLEX SOCIAL DYNAMICS: I ponder these mega-rafts wrapped in *Egregia* (feather boa kelp), gossiping about... *what*? Do they grieve? Celebrate births? Have leaders? Otter politics? Do they take notes on *us*?

- Deadly predators! Sometimes two to three urchins in one dive! Which they smash with a rock from their armpit-locker?!

- They have culture.

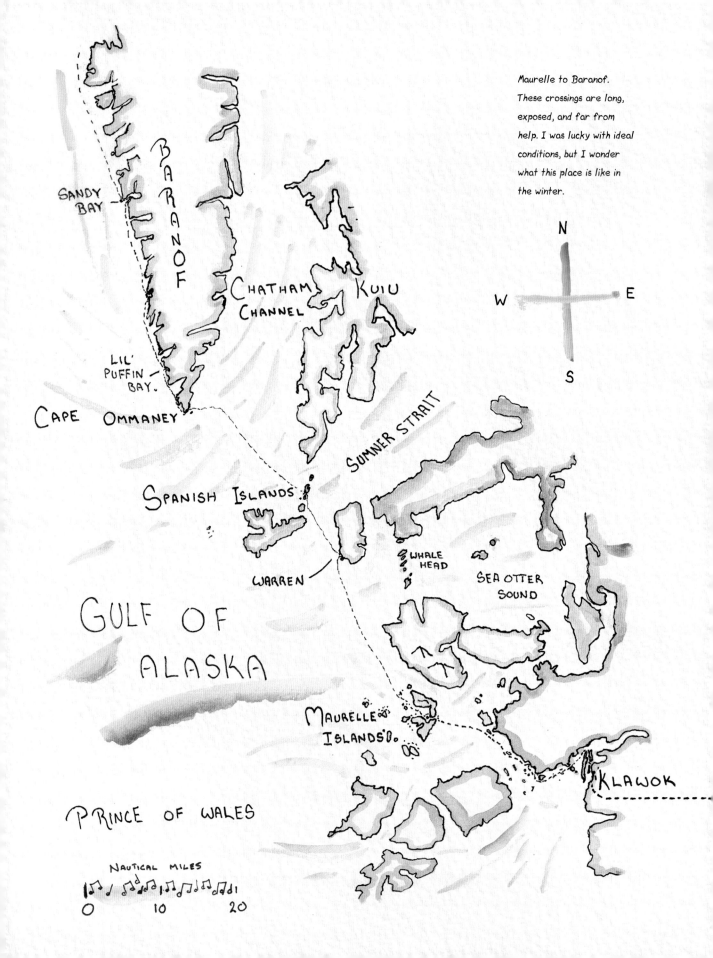

Maurelle to Baranof. These crossings are long, exposed, and far from help. I was lucky with ideal conditions, but I wonder what this place is like in the winter.

N
W    E
S

SANDY BAY

BARANOF

CHATHAM CHANNEL

KUIU

LIL' PUFFIN BAY

CAPE OMMANEY

SUMNER STRAIT

SPANISH ISLANDS

WARREN

WHALE HEAD

SEA OTTER SOUND

GULF OF ALASKA

MAURELLE ISLANDS

KLAWOK

PRINCE OF WALES

NAUTICAL MILES

0      10      20

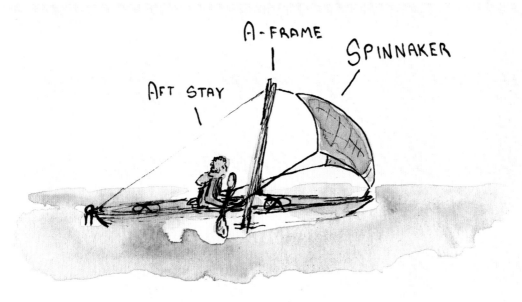

AFT STAY

A-FRAME

SPINNAKER

## DAY 35, JULY 9:

Wind SE 10 to light. // Sea otter camp to Warren Island—16 nm.

New sail tech—a spinnaker! It's like flying a kite. The wind dies after ten kilometres (six miles) of breezy cruising, and I switch to the internal Bunsen burner. Due to the calm, I redirect to Warren Island instead of the protected Whale Head Islands (although this name *has* got me curious).

Warren is chiseled by endless friction with the ocean. Scouring the chart, I find *one indent* that looks like a creek outflow. The mouths of watersheds accumulate sediment, creating beaches for safe landing. My guess is correct, but swell bombards the pebble-shore—I'll need to surf in. Timing the waves, I grind onto the tumble-shined stones and pull the boat up as fast as I can. I lose a sock in the process.

On shore, I rig a blaze and watch the lentils boil. It begins to sprinkle so I strip down and stow my clothing in the tent. Naked in the rain, I eat gruffy while a rainbow hops across

the island-ocean jungle. I feel free, lonely, and everything else. If only I could share this with *one person*. The horizon is smeared with melting watercolours. Moss-covered driftwood is wedged into the forests from whence it came. My mind expands through time and space, and joins the gazillion droplets plummeting from the heavens. *This world is seamless.* (See photo of Warren Island on page 193.)

### LIMPY

Next day. Warren disappears behind me, the sun rises, and the Spanish Islands await. On shore, I meet Limpy, a disabled mink who is searching for shore crabs and stragglers. Her paw is swollen and infected, and her back is unusually arched. She manages OK, but looks in pain.

Limpy comes within metres while migrating back and forth to the forest. She spends hours close by while I set up camp, and a relationship is kindled. I speak openly to her about my troubles and triumphs. At one point she stops, looks at me sagely, nods her head, then scurries off. I wonder if she will be alive next time I read this.

--> HOLLIS

# DAY 36, JULY 10, 2016:

Wind: L to NE 10. *Sunny.* //
Spanish Islands—10 nm.

The Spanish Islands are on the edge of protection, and my *base camp* for the crossing to Cape Ommaney—35 kilometres (22 miles) of open ocean, longer than most days I paddle. In addition to the distance and high exposure, the crossing has bizarre currents mixing from Sumner Strait and Chatham Channel.

### GREENLAND PADDLE

The first kayaks were built from stitched seal skin stretched over *whale-bone frames.* Created by the Aleuts and Inuits—Indigenous Peoples of the Arctic—these vessels were used for hunting seals, whales, and *even* caribou! Today I work on a cedar Greenland paddle with my hatchet and saw. The old salt who drew the sail-rig diagrams also gave me paddle blueprints. After five hours of sweat, and thousands of cedar shavings, I stumble and sit on the paddle. CRRAACKK! *Sweet Murphy!* I stare in disbelief… *Are you* BURGER-FLIPPIN' *me!* A good exercise in nonattachment.

I think about how many snapped paddles and faulty designs the original builders faced.

The word *kayak,* which translates to "hunter's boat," is at least 5,000 years old, meaning no hatchet, no buck knife, no YouTube tutorial. Just trial and error passed down through generations. Custom-sized for each individual, these boats were sacred to the northerners—an extension of the self.

### KAYAK HISTORY

Kayaking has new purposes and evolving designs. In 1928, a German paddler, laden with 270 kilograms (600 pounds) of canned whompers, left the Canary Islands (Spain) in a canvas kayak and reached the US Virgin Islands fifty-eight days later (5,000 kilometres / 3,100 miles across the Atlantic). Another German, Oscar Speck, took his canvas fold-boat down the Danube River to the Mediterranean, hugged the coast through the Suez Canal, and traversed Arabia, India, and Indonesia, reaching Australia *four years later* (22,000 kilometres / 13,700 miles).

In the 1940s, the first successful attempts to navigate the Grand Canyon and other gnarly whitewaters were made. *And what about the magic island-cosmos of the Pacific Northwest?*

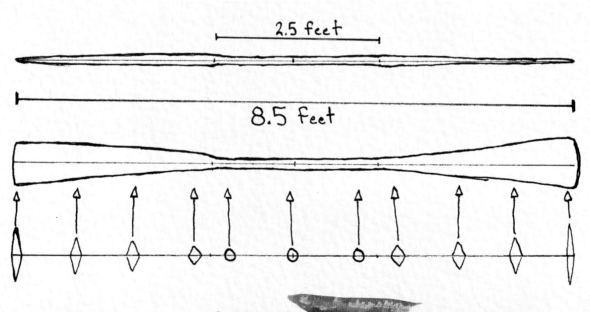

2.5 feet

8.5 feet

In the 1980s, the yak-culture we see today got its start, led by Brian Henry, Werner Furrer, John Dowd, Tom Derrer, and a paddle-full from Seattle, Vancouver, and Victoria. They formed the Trade Association of Sea Kayaking and set about developing a *culture, identity, and industry* around the sport by creating a magazine (*Sea Kayaker*), setting boat prices (so builders had a decent profit margin), and hosting the first Sea Kayak Symposium. Kayaking caught on, and soon the whole family was hauling hulls to explore remote islets and sea caves.

*Opposite* *Greenland sticks are more stable in rough water, easier to roll with (more leverage), catch less wind, splash less, and are quieter. Also fewer blisters if the wood is properly oiled. Best of all, you have a relationship with a tree, not fiberglass or plastic. You can name your paddle, just like your boat.*

Now, *everything* is possible. In 2012, Graham and Russell Henry from Victoria, BC, paddled from Brazil to Florida, taking seven months through more than 15 countries. Russell went on to set the record for fastest human-powered circumnavigation of Vancouver Island: 12 days, 23 hours, 45 mins. *Actually,* it is their tale that inspired my trip. Graham and Russell were also Camp Thunderbirders, and before leaving, Graham gave me valuable trip info and a free used paddle from his dad, Brian Henry's, shop, Ocean River Sports. *Thanks.*

Humans are creative, adventurous, and *slightly stupid,* which means kayaking will continue to evolve. Who will push the boundaries next? And *how? No one has circumnavigated the Earth yet.* It's possible, but it would take *ten years,* according to my calculations. Also, no circumnav of North and/or South America. *What about you?*

# DAY 37, JULY 11:

Winds L to SE 10. *Overcast, occasional ray of sun.* // Spanish Islands to Little Puffin Bay—*Baranof / Shee Island*—31 nm.

**01:00.** Have you ever swum in bioluminescence? Imagine kayaking in it! Startled fish dart like shooting stars under my hull, each stroke creating a boiling supernova. I leave under the eye of the moon.

**02:00.** The lighthouse on Cape Decision is my reference point, and Baranof is distinguishable only because the horizon there is void of stars.

**03:30.** The first hint of light! Tremendous sonic-booms echo over the Sound. At least 30 humpbacks are feeding on the nutrient blender of Chatham Channel. I have never been more alive.

**07:00.** A breeze is worthy of a sail, but the wind only lasts half an hour before becoming erratic.

**10:00.** A gigantic gull is flying straight at me! It's bigger than an eagle—an albatross! Good luck! So say the sailors. It comes within metres of my head and banks effortlessly, vanishing into the immense landscape. The first I have ever seen.

**12:00.** Wooden Island lays just off Cape Ommaney, and is now well defined. I can make out individual trees and a small fishing boat. As I get closer, the boat veers to investigate, "Where did you come from?!" After telling them of my crossing, they stare in disbelief. "You must be exhausted; what time did you leave? *Are you hungry?*" I paddle away with a juicy rockfish strapped to my deck. *Thank you!*

**12:40.** The rocky islets buffering Cape Ommaney are smeared with sea lions; they go bananas when I paddle by. I have been in the cockpit for nearly twelve hours, longer than most international flights, and there is no place to land. I can't feel my legs.

**13:30.** I pull off in a small cove on the west side of Baranof, devour the rockfish, then collapse face-down on sun-warmed rocks.

**16:00.** My nap leaves me disoriented. *Where am I? And what am I doing?* Then it all comes back. This cove is no place to camp; if the swell picks up, there's no escape. The tide has retreated and I drag BP down. I hope to make it to Puffin Bay by this evening.

**18:00.** A one-knot current pushes me backwards. It's infuriating and *I don't feel so good.*

**18:45.** Rockfish are surfacing. My lure dives in and attracts a bite. In five minutes, I haul aboard a biggie, the heaviest rockfish I have ever caught—*2.7 kilos (6 pounds).*

**19:10.** Little Puffin Bay lives up to its name; *Fratercula cirrhata* (tufted puffins) swoop in and out from ragged cliffs. *The landscape is severe.* Baranof has been scraped, bruised, and worn by endless waves, wind, ice, and rain.

**22:00.** I'm writing by headlamp. *My muscles relax.* The forecast on the VHF calls for 25-knot northwesterlies tomorrow. *I will sleep in.*

LITT

The Chatham Channel. On August 24, 1794, Isaac Wooden aboard the HMS Discovery fell overboard and drowned off Cape Ommaney (think Cape Ominous). To commemorate his service, ol' George Van named a desolate island after him. I'm sure his family was overjoyed. These are some of the most technical and exposed waters in all of Southeast Alaska.

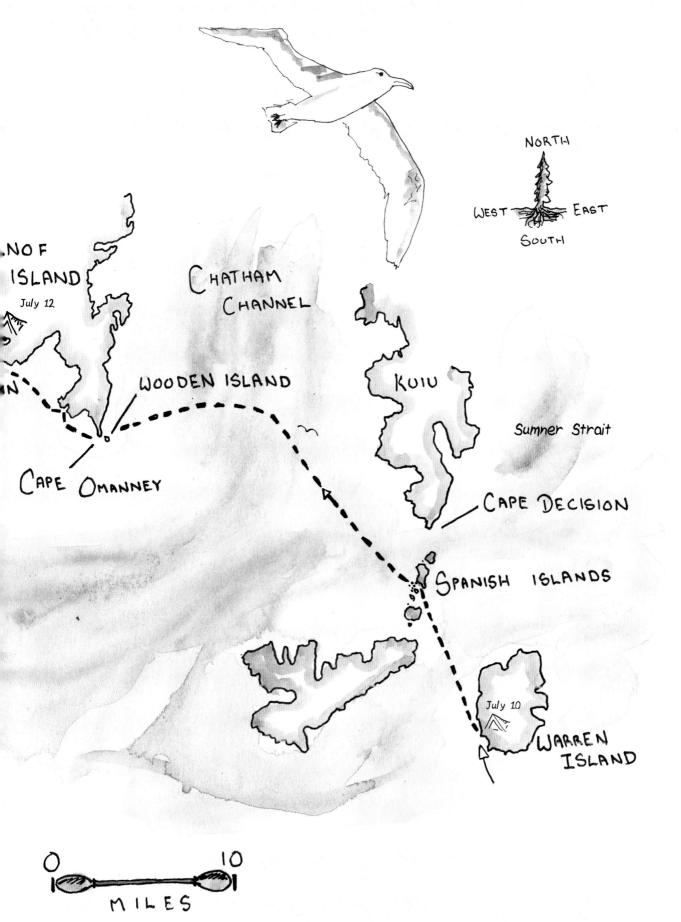

NORTH
WEST EAST
SOUTH

NOF ISLAND

July 12

CHATHAM CHANNEL

WOODEN ISLAND

CAPE OMANNEY

KUIU

Sumner Strait

CAPE DECISION

SPANISH ISLANDS

July 10

WARREN ISLAND

0          10
MILES

# DAY 38, JULY 12:

Wind NW 20-30. // Little Puffin Bay—*Day off.*

A *clicking* bounces inside my head—or is it *outside the tent?* It's early. I rustle out of the covers and slowly unzip the fly. A mother deer and fawn are *metres away. Awww.* I watch for a bit, then pass out again, in need of recovery from yesterday's odyssey.

The morning passes without me until: *Huff! Huff!* A nasal-blast jerks me to attention. *No deer this time*, a muzzle is pressing into the tent—*grizzly bear!* AHHHHH!!! I scream as loud as I can and shake the tent. The bear bolts, scrambling over driftwood and crashing into the forest. My adrenaline is thumping. I'm scared to go outside, *but need to assert my territory.*

On beach, I set up the sail so it rattles in the wind—*a scarecrow.* I'm not sure of the protocol on this one, but I light a big-smokey-fire and pee on landmarks around camp.

## WHERE IS THE BUDDHA?

In the evening I walk barefoot into the forest. My mind is *wonder-silenced*, and my heart begins to slow. Sitka spruce hold the sun in shafts, and there is a presence of... god? *Hello?* It's the golden hour, and reality seems unreal. Moss and old-man's beard tangle like spider webs. I trace my hands over lichen and river stones. The animal trail winding beside the clear-water creek could pass in a national park, worn by generations of hooves and paws. I'm drawn upstream until I arrive at a mighty hemlock—*a giant among giants.*

I sit on the roots and remember the Buddha. On his fantastic enlightenment-session, it's said he sat perfectly still the whole night. He faced temptation, pain, and the full range of human experience. And to it all: *serene equanimity.*

My emotions fluctuate and devour me. I can barely sit still for five minutes. I'm not sure if the story profoundly inspires me or deters me. Either way, I'll continue my little practice. *It's helping.*

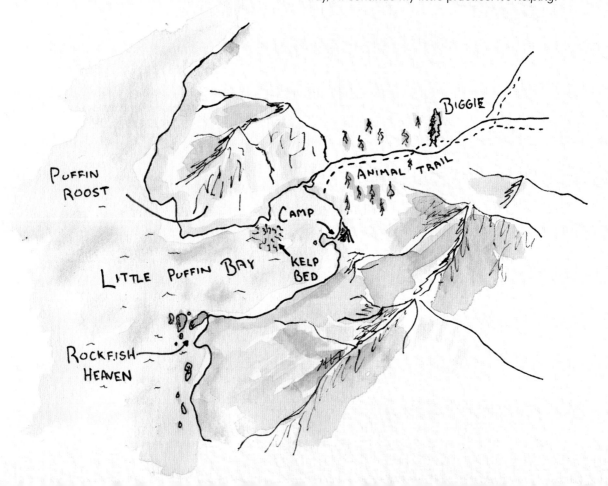

An average of 11 humans in North America are killed by bears each year. In BC, until 2018, when trophy hunting grizzlies was banned, around 350 grizzlies were killed every year. Alaska is still open for business. A guided hunt can cost USD$10,000 to $50,000. Should we condone the killing of creatures we don't eat? Should we be allowed to kill creatures in places we don't live?

## DAY 39, JULY 13:
Wind NW 20–30. // Day off.

The forecast calls for stiff NWs (20–30 knots) for three days. *I decide to stay put.* No point battling the wind and risking my biscuit.

I check my reserves: enough food to last two weeks if necessary. Lentils update: small insects present in bag, otherwise good.

Exploring my new home, I take the puffins (*Fratercula cirrhata*) as research subjects. Roosting on the south-facing cliff, they are most active at sunrise. Skimming and diving, I guess they're mostly eating fish, *but what kind*? And *what else*? If only I could get a fecal sample.

## DAY 41, JULY 15:
Wind: L to NW 15. *Overcast.* // LPB to Mystery Cove—4 nm.

I cover little distance despite my rested body. The sea is a mess from consecutive days of high winds. After an hour I feel nauseous, and a lethargic heaviness in my soul. Seasickness occurs when the body can't calibrate the *upsie-downsies.* The inner ear has fluid inside that *detects* gravity and movement. When the inner ear's perception doesn't match up with the eyes and body, which *see* and *feel* motion, the brain gets overloaded and goes vomity. A major design flaw. Or perhaps an evolutionary mechanism to scare us from adverse conditions? I guess it depends if you believe in god or biology.

Pull off in an unmarked bay. Lay down. Wooziness abates. Set up camp.

Berries are so amazing, it's unbelievable they exist at all. My mouth turns blue, and red, then purple.

## DAY 42, JULY 16:
*Night.*

02:30. *Ahhh!!* Terrible dream—chased by the boogie-man in a dark forest. *So real.* I wake up paralyzed in the sleeping bag, *in a dark forest.* A heavy force is sitting on top of my chest; my heart is *pounding*. Too scared to go out and pee. Worried my bladder might rupture.

Can't sleep. What is the evolutionary purpose of a nightmare? It is one thing to be alone. It is another to also be scared.

## DAY 42, JULY 16:

Wind: Light to NW 15. Overcast. //
Sandy Bay—10 nm.

Mighty swell marches in like soldiers only to meet its own rebellious rebound. Still shaken from nightmare.

## DAY 44, JULY 18:

Wind S 10–15. //
Sandy Bay to Goddard—29 nm.

No one in the world knows where I am. An addictive, seductive, dangerous thought.

It's hard to imagine the exposed waters ever being calm; sailing on the exposed Pacific scares me, so I stick to paddling. Today, I head for Goddard—*hot springs* on the chart. I have no idea what shape the springs are in or if they even exist. My chart atlas is from the 1970s and often shows "post office" where only moss-mangled ruins remain. This coast is not as busy as it used to be; when fish populations declined and industry centralized, many canneries and villages collapsed. The people who stayed did so not out of choice or love, but because they had become a part of the ecosystem—consumed by the organism they came to exploit.

A morning mist nulls the world and I paddle blindly with the help of magnetic north. When the mist lifts, trollers (fishing boats dragging lines) are weaving Whale Bay, looking for salmon. I sneak through the procession and tuck into the Rakof Islands—a complex group allowing enough protection to set sail.

Under the Russians, Goddard used to have a hospital and a health resort, but only two cedar shacks remain, enclosing tubs with precious, steaming spring water. My body rejoices. Three fishermen who saw me sailing earlier are anchored nearby and enjoy the evening with me. "We thought you were a buoy out there." I guess I'm pretty small compared to their big ships. It makes me think how visible and safe I am with vessel traffic. I share red huckleberries, and they share their whiskey. My face contorts into a raisin, then a grape. The salmon-men chuckle.

Eventually, they row out to their vessel and I'm left with the moon. I immerse as long as humanly possible, then saunter to my freezing ocean-lover, and slip in. Are the stars reflected in the ocean, or vice versa? Floating on my back, only my lips and nose remain above the water. My temperature plunges, my mind goes blank and blurry. Minutes or an hour? I crawl out shivering and disembodied. A deep therapy is wilding my soul; it defies psychology and western medicine.

*Opposite  Sitka Sound. These outside waters are ruled by Pacific swell. There is enough protection and refuge to wiggle north, but barely. Which bays and islands look like safe camping spots to you?*

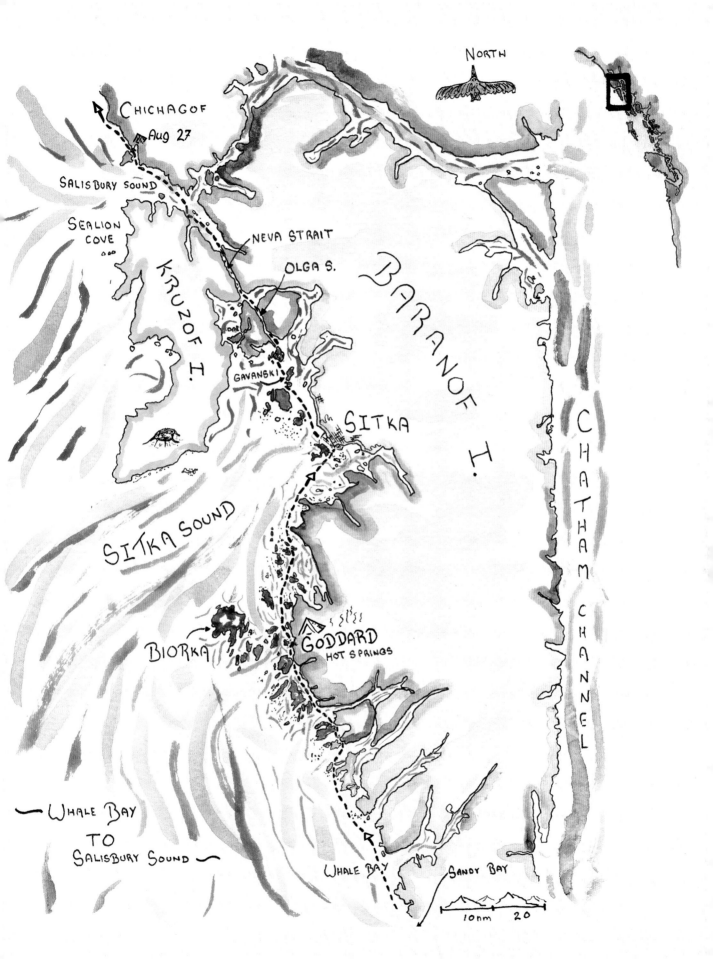

# OUR PLACE IN THE WORLD

I have been crying lately—staring at the enormous topography in disbelief, tears down my cheeks. It's the feeling of being small, yet so big, and not being able to share it with anyone. *I've discovered a secret I can never tell.*

Traveling by wind and willpower, I have caught a glimpse of how massive the world is. When you move with your own energy, in your own direction, in wild spaces, you develop an acute awareness of scale. People move too quickly these days, with planes and trains; we've lost our *relationship to the land*—what used to define our survival. What is the impact of soaring from New York to Vancouver to Tokyo in a day? To have "homes" in four different countries? To speak five languages? To never hug an old-growth tree?

What I'm getting at: it's not *all* bad. Our increased mobility and urbanization give us opportunities, just as it tears us from the deep-beating-heart of mother-earth. *Is there a balance?*

My parents took us on walks every day. Yes, *walks*. For no other reason than to get outside and be together. At the time, I thought it was bogus. But now I see value—those walks taught us to *listen*; they imbued respect and reverence for nature. Sharing family-time outside, even in the streets and forests where we lived, gave us a sense of identity linked to the landscape.

When I miss home I don't just think of my family. I imagine the Nechako River, the sticky cottonwood catkins, and the smell of ponderosa pine after a spring downpour. I remember when *Catly-Do* went missing, and Dad made *Catly-Do-where-are-you?!* posters. We marched around the neighborhood, *meowing* to see if *Catly* would hear us.

We used to be monkeys. I come back to this when I get heady and untethered. Our primate cousins are not separate from their environment, so why should we be? To believe nature is ours to exploit *and* fix is the root of our conundrum. Nature is us. If we exploit it, we exploit ourselves, and to fix it, we have to fix ourselves.

I don't *exactly* have a solution here, and in fact, *we might be screwed*. But let's take another lesson from my mom, and go for a walk.

## DAY 45, JULY 19:

Wind S 10. *Gray.* // Goddard to Sitka—15 nm.

The morning unfolds from the hot spring paradise—total relaxation. There is a storm prophesied on the VHF: *Severe precipitation warning. Sixty millimetres in the next twenty-four hours.* Yikes. A subtle but consistent southerly has crept into the trees, and seems to be doing reconnaissance for a wide-spread onslaught. Taking the hint, I set sail and begin threading towards refuge and civilization—*Sitka, Alaska.* The first *and* last fishing stronghold left to the exposed Pacific.

I'm nervous and excited to reintegrate with society. Eager to join what I was so anxious to leave.

Sitka lives in the shadow of *Mount Edgecombe*, a snow-clad, dormant volcano marking the approach for offshore vessels, and a reminder of our tectonic foundations. I wrap around a breakwater and steer past a series of trollers and seiners. *Bell Pep* is a speck compared to these creatures. I tie up to the dock—a luxury—and head into town. Smiling ear to ear, I stride through the streets, keen to interact and balance out the parts of myself that have been quiet and alone.

The Sitka Hostel will be my home until the storm passes and I figure out my next move. I need a break from the kayak and tent, at least for a bit. After checking in and being shown my bed with fresh sheets, I attend to food. The grocery store dumpster offers pleasant surprises: *four packs of low-quality cookies*, doughnuts, and assorted veg. I cook up spaghetti and gorge.

The hostel is well attended by summer students and tourists. Soon I'm sharing cookies and doughnuts. I pass around my journal and many stare in amazement: *You did all this?!* I don't know what to say, so I nod and blink. After the VHF for company since Klawock, I find it mesmerizing listening to stories and laughter.

I lie awake, buzzing from the social stimulation (and all the cookies). *I am safe and sound.* The rain held off until midnight; now it rattles the tin roof—a sound of comfort to any soul with warm sheets and a sturdy shelter.

MOUNT EDGECOMBE

SITKA ALASKA

# 6

# A CAMPFIRE STORY

Before carrying on with my fishy experience in Sitka, I want to tell a campfire story that's been on my mind. Each night, I stare into open flames and my imagination wanders. It's easy to visualize our ancestors gathered round, spinning yarns, their minds expanding. Oral traditions are cool—story evolution.

In case you never went to Camp Thunderbird, in Sooke, BC, I'll walk you through it. On the first night there is an opening campfire where new campers gather and are told the first half of this fantastic tale. On their last night, the conclusion. These story-sessions are full of drama and emotion. Every time, the tale is different, depending on the mood of the night and temperament of the teller. This is a good one to know and retell when children say: tell us a story! Here are our characters (it's set in the future when evolution and radioactive exposure have taken their toll). Enjoy.

WRENLY (SHE/HER)    LEXINGTON (SHE/HER)    PUAL (THEY/THEM)    OTTALINE (OLD)

Date: 3,000 years in the future.

Location: 48°25'2.54"N 123°38'18.33"W. Once known as Vancouver Island.

The wind howls and rain pit-pat-patters through the forest. Welcome to the future! Autumn has come early, and The Island people scramble to find sweaters, socks, and a silver-lining. The climate is still changing.

The world is not what it once was. Humans are not who they once were. *Victoria is no longer Victoria.* As oceans rose, coastal cities submerged, drowning in spite of repeated warnings of our misled ancestors. They could not listen *to themselves.*

Industrial society has fallen, they failed. Failed to adapt and mitigate problems they saw clearly. Precautions have been implemented, the New World is run by women, and education of new humans is the highest responsibility—an investment for the entire society. Population is managed carefully, so not to disturb the Natural Order.

A meeting is to be held today, and all the South Island will attend. The queen is dying, and a new leader must be found. The matriarch, Ottaline, lives in a Douglas fir forest surrounded by blackberry brambles. Figures assemble in the great forest-hall. They are soft spoken, highly sensitive, and mentally advanced, compared to the *Homo sapiens* who once thrashed around on this coast. *Like fish out of water* is the phrase to describe our ancestors—desperate and without hope. When a child acts out of greed or other primal emotions, they are scolded as such: *refrain from being a fish.*

Ottaline has been here from the beginning of the New Society. She is ancient and always sitting cross-legged practicing meditation. "My children, I'm close to death. Whoever asks me a question I cannot answer will be the next leader of our community. Be oh-so-brave in these coming months and years. *I pray for you.* May a true leader come forward, when the time is ripe."

*That is it.* Meetings are concise. Ottaline looks at them serenely, with loving-kindness, and everyone sits in meditation for some time, then slowly files out. To ask this ultimate question will take *something new.* Ottaline has been alive for 150 years, mostly in deep meditation or conducting botanical research. She knows everything, they say.

Our first candidate is Lexington,[1] a community organizer and ecosystem planner by training, but a poet by heart. She leaves South by boat, and then foot, traversing the coastal divide, pondering the ways of animals and mountains, searching for a query the queen cannot answer. After weeks alone she sits atop a cliff, and rain clouds collide with sunshine—*a double rainbow.* Her eyes widen and begin to sparkle. A question has arisen in her mind. She begins her journey home.

Upon arrival, she is greeted warmly by all, and soon the forest-hall is filled. "Great queen, I have a question. Why is it when rain and sun collide, an arch forms holding the full spectrum of colour?" The queen smiles. "Dear Lexi, that is indeed an excellent question. *But I have an answer.* Within all light, the entire spectrum is held. When water droplets intercept a sun's ray, *refraction* occurs and the light is broken into its principal parts. The arch is due to the shape of the raindrop, which bends the light. If no horizon was present, a full circle would appear. Double rainbows form when light is refracted twice within the same raindrop. That is all."

Lexington's question has been answered. As custom, she goes into exile, to live alone in the forest, to develop her mind.

Second is PuAl, a biologist, physicist, and geologist. They head East, over the Cascades, and over the Rockies. Soon immersed in an ocean of grass as far as the eye can see. *The prairies,* they used to call it. Far from the mountains, PuAl stops in the shade of a gigantic boulder. A rock so huge it would take a thousand people to lift. And no sooner have they sat down when they get up again, and begin to walk home, eyes gleaming.

As PuAl reaches The Island, the people again gather, anxious, curious, and expectant. PuAl kneels before the queen and begins to speak. "Great queen, why is it, far from the Rocky Mountains, surrounded by a field with nothing else, a massive boulder lies. *How did it get there?*" The crowd nods; a good question indeed. "*Thank you PuAl.* I commend you on your journey and observation. It is a curious question, but certainly, I have an answer. Thousands of years before even the *sapiens,* this land was covered in ice. As it receded, it carried rocks in its pockets. Even on The Island, we see the Icesheet's fingerprint. The rock you sat under was a gift from the great glacier. That is all." PuAl smiles, but their shoulders slump, and they walk off alone. They too will spend the next years in exile.

Last is Wrenly, a philosopher, storyteller, and trickster. She has the kind of smile that changes your whole day. She travels north by My-Yak into a maze of islands ruled by bears. Wren is not skilled in nature, so she suffers, often without food. She is better with company and word play than fires and wild harvesting. The journey is hard. One evening, she sits watching the flames, and a fragile red bird hops over, an injured rufous hummingbird. The next morning, she sets sail for home. She too has a question for the queen.

Wren enters the hall with her hands cupped. Everyone is nervous; Wrenly is the last of the three. "Oh, great Ottaline, I have a question which you can surely not answer. Is the bird in my hands *dead or alive?*" The people are silent. *What trick is this?* But the queen smiles. "Oh Wrenly, thank you for your courage, intellect, and hardship. You bring great value to our community. The bird in your hands is both alive *and* dead. And neither dead *nor* alive. For every moment all beings are continually dying and born again. At the particle-level we are in a constant flux. Nothing solid. Nothing stable. No self. Only change. When we investigate deeply, we can experience this for ourselves. It is a matter of sensitivity. That is all."

*KAABOOOMM!* Thunder blasts from the heavens, and from between Wrenly's fingers a beautiful light-bird flies up into the sky. *It begins to rain.* Wrenly opens her hands to find them empty. Her question has been answered. She too leaves for exile.

## CLOSING CAMPFIRE

Waves explode off the rocks and trees bend sideways in the gale. The night is black, punctuated by thunder and breaking branches. It is winter and Wrenly huddles in a cave. Alone, cold, hungry and scared. It has been three months since she left home, surviving off grubs, wild fruit, and willpower.

When spring emerges, her features are inverted—skin and bone. She needs help, and ventures in the direction of PuAl. They are better off and have built a cabin from river stones. The two embrace, thankful for the presence of another. For months they live together: content, supportive, friends. Wrenly is good at talking with animals and begins taming wild chickens. PuAl is good with plants, and together they make a garden. They smile often, in spite of days without food.

One day, they hear a scream. It is Lexington. While trying to find them she has fallen and broken her leg. PuAl and Wrenly create a stretcher from sticks and carry her to camp. They nurse Lexi to health and soon she is walking again. United, the exiles rejoice. All three are soon telling tales, and laughter drifts through the forest. Lexi had worked on The Island as a community organizer and ecosystem planner. Her knowledge helps them design raised beds and irrigation canals. They increase the hen population and begin selecting for certain egg characteristics. In the summers, they eat omelettes. In the winters, they hunt large game and kill some of the chickens. They survive, *together*.

After three years, they are thriving, with time to dance, sing, and tell stories. Time to explore nature and be happy. One night, sitting around the fire, with no words spoken, they share a special moment. Just joy and tranquility. Then smiles. *Then laughter.* And soon all three are giggling and beaming with joy. They have a question the queen cannot answer.

They march back to The Island hand-in-hand. The people are full of joy and relief. No one has asked any questions since they left, and the queen is now spending almost all her time in deep mental absorption, conserving energy. The great hall fills and Ottaline beams at the exiles. *Welcome home!*

The friends take turns speaking: "Dear queen and people of The Island. We have spent time alone, and we have spent time together. We have gone without food, and we have had great feasts. We have lived in hardship and happiness. And now we, *together,* have a question for the queen."

"Why is it, great queen, only one of us can rule? Why can we not rule together—the story-teller, the organizer, and the scientist, as one? *That is our question.*"

Queen Ottaline grows bright, illuminating the whole forest. "Dear Wren, PuAl, and Lexi, that is indeed a wonderful question. And one for which *I have no answer.*" With that, a thunder clap booms above, and from the queen's body a lightning bird flies through the canopy and disappears. The people cheer for their new leaders, and celebrate the life of the queen. Tears of all kinds are shed, spread, and shared.

And they all live *realistically* after.

*Fin.*

# 7

# SPAWNING SALMON

"Whenever I find myself growing grim about the mouth;
whenever it is a damp, drizzly November in my soul; whenever
I find myself involuntarily pausing before coffin warehouses,
and bringing up the rear of every funeral I meet; and
especially whenever my hypos get such an upper hand of
me, that it requires a strong moral principle to prevent me
from deliberately stepping into the street, and methodically
knocking people's hats off—then, I account it high
time to get to sea as soon as I can."

**✄ HERMAN MELVILLE ✄**
*Moby Dick*
Dave makes all his deckhands read *Moby Dick*.
This book is a life-changer for ocean lovers.

E ROSE

Above This is a cutter-rig ketch—ketch, meaning it has two masts, and the mizzen (aft mast) is shorter. "Cutter" means it has two headsails: note the furled genoa and the jib up front. The lines holding up the masts are stays and shrouds. The ropes to pull up the sails are halyards.

The two big poles near the back are for trolling (dragging fishing lines) and hinge down to forty-five degrees, like wings. Note the aft bucket, where salmon are hauled in and gutted. The cabin is roomy and has a kitchen with stove and fridge! I stay in the fore cabin, down the hatch. Could you call this boat home?

TRUCK DOGS IN SITKA

## SITKA, ALASKA

I spend the next week in Sitka while the sky detoxes. What should I do?

Two options:

1.  *Kayak.* I want to continue to Skagway, or even Yakutat, but I need a break from the cockpit.

2.  *Salmon fishing.* I could get a job in the fleet as a deckhand. My hot-spring friends told me boats are looking for help due to mid-season turnover.

I might as well walk the planks and ask around. Immediately I'm directed to the *Albee Rose*—a skookum fifty-three-foot *ketch*—a sailboat converted into a salmon troller. I have pancakes with me and bring them on board as a gift. The crew: *Captain Dave* and *Huckleberry-the-dog.* Huck is an ancient-thing and Dave helps him on and off the boat due to his wobbly legs.

I tell my kayak-story and how I'm keen to catch fish. Dave nods ponderously and tells me he's doing maintenance and will need a *hand* when he sets out next week. *We get along.* He's a crafty intellect, quoting Shakespeare and other classics. I spend three hours getting a tour of the boat and how everything works. Dave thinks it over for a couple days and offers me on. *Yahoo! I can't believe it.*

GAFF HOOK

**Left** *Dave uses a gaff hook to haul in a silver/coho. To get the fish into the boat is tricky, and some fish are lost in this last maneuver (especially by me). It requires piercing the fish in the gills and swinging it on board. To say the fish puts up a fight is an understatement. Blood is squirting everywhere, and if the fish doesn't land in the bucket, it gets messy, quick. I lost one gaff hook overboard already. Sorry.*

## DAVE

Our first voyage takes us south, and we troll under sail—Captain Dave's dream. We drift the nights in the open ocean, guessing which way the current will take us and where we will awake.

Dave has carved a philosophy from his fascinating life, and I really look up to him. His story was always linked to fishin' and writing. His dad took him out on lakes when he was a kid, and once he grew up he began writing for a fishing magazine. This allowed him to connect with fisherpeople all over North America and travel. Through the mag he also met Rose.

Dave's picture appeared in a section of the magazine, and Rose, who had never met him, was dared by a friend to write a letter. Dave wrote back, and soon they met. And married.

I guess before the Internet, this was common, but to me it sounds remarkable. Love ties lives together in mysterious ways.

His story goes on and becomes tricky. *Rose died.* "She swerved in a pelting rainstorm, alone, at night, off a highway in Florida. Knowing her tender soul, she was probably trying to dodge a possum. Lost control, collided head-on with the only hardwood for miles." The *Albee Rose* is named for her and for a loyal dog, Albee, who also passed.

Dave began spending more time at sea, and for the last ten summers he's been in Sitka dragging lines. I ask him if he relates more to fish than people and he smiles. In the moments we aren't fishing, our conversation traces love, life, politics, and death. He jokes—*but not really*—that I'm too absorbed philosophizing to ever be a good fisherman. It's true. I also don't like killing these wild ocean eyes.

## TROLL (VERB)

1. To carefully and systematically search an area.

2. To fish by trailing a baited line behind a boat.

3. To deliberately antagonize others online.

4. A not-so-clever humanoid monster, often living in caves and eating children. They turn to stone when exposed to sunlight.

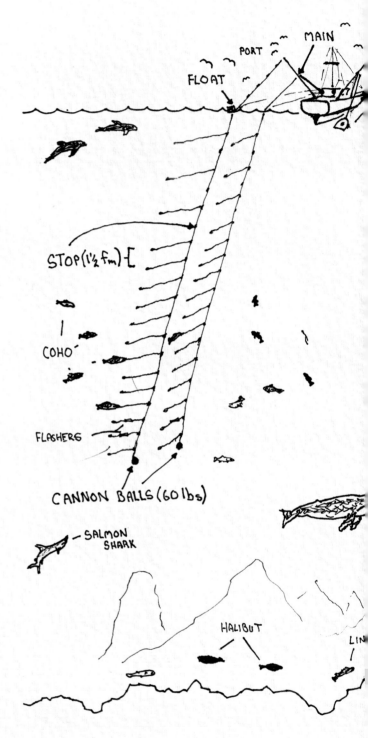

Typically, four lines are dragged with ten to twenty hooks each, at a speed of two to three knots. Different lures and flashers are used depending on the target species. On a good day we would catch over a hundred fish, some days only a dozen. Coho sells for two dollars a pound, and each fish averages four and a half kilos (ten pounds). So, on a good day we bring in USD$2,000, of which I'm paid 10 percent (15 if I stay till the end of season). All considered, it's a good summer job, if you don't mind waking up at 04:00, weathering traumatic storms, and killing fish.

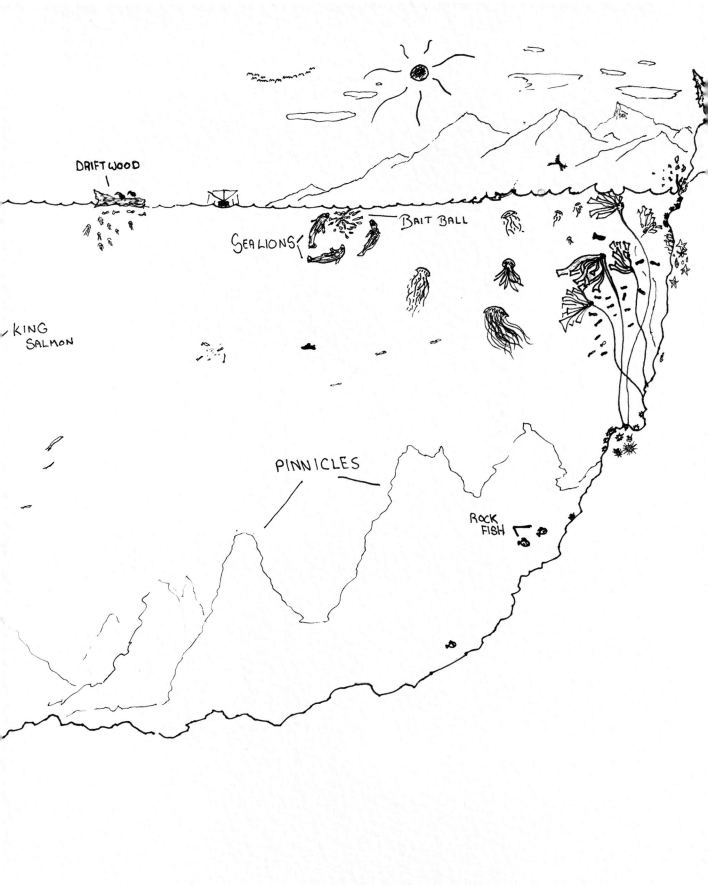

## ON DEATH

In the ocean, animals eat each other. Death is this normal thing permeating the ecosystem. Sailors are also lost to the sea—sometimes instantaneously, sometimes slowly. Every salt in Sitka knows someone sent to Davey Jones. Death can be the consequence of incompetence, bad luck, and perhaps, fate.

My grampa died last year. He was old and losing bodily function. His last serene words: *I'm going home.* What did he mean? Home? I guess he was *ready* to die. And perhaps he could see something we can't.

We spend our lives insulating ourselves from death—collecting comforts and preventing pain. What is the cost of our fear of death? Do we hold on and suffer while the world decomposes and devours itself? Why only at old age should we embrace nature's inevitability?

I like the idea of Death as a friend, patiently accompanying us through life's mysteries. The image helps wash away trivialities. If I were to die at the end of today, what would I do different? Perhaps I would live more like a fish. In a weird way, I look forward to death. Curious to answer the ultimate question: what's next?

## FISHES OF THE PACIFIC NORTHWEST

### CHINOOK | KING
### (*ONCORHYNCHUS TSHAWYTSCHA*)
**WEIGHT:** 15–22 kg (30–50 lbs)
**AGE:** 3–4 years

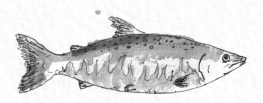

### CHUM | DOG
### (*ONCORHYNCHUS KETA*)
**WEIGHT:** 7–15 kg (15–30 lbs)
**AGE:** 1–3 years

### COHO | SILVER
### (*ONCORHYNCHUS KISUTCH*)
**WEIGHT:** 7–15 kg (15–30 lbs)
**AGE:** 3–4 years

*This is the ocean phase of salmon. When they spawn in freshwater natal streams their bodies change dramatically: curved jaws, bright colours, and pronounced humps. This is to attract mates. The longest salmon migration on earth is the Yukon Chinook run, at 3,000 km (1,864 miles).*

## SOCKEYE / RED
### (ONCORHYNCHUS NERKA)
WEIGHT: 4–8 kg (10–20 lbs)

AGE: 3–5 years

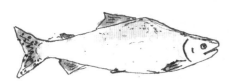

## PINK / HUMPY
### (ONCORHYNCHUS GORBUSCHA)
WEIGHT: 1–4 kg (2–10 lbs)

AGE: 2 years

## ROUGHEYE ROCKFISH
### (SEBASTES ALEUTIANUS)
WEIGHT: 2–7 kg (5–15 lbs)

AGE: 100–205 years

## QUILLBACK ROCKFISH
### (SEBASTES MALIGER)
WEIGHT: 1–3 kg (2–8 lbs)

AGE: 50–95 years

## BLACK BASS
### (SEBASTES MELANOPS)
WEIGHT: 2–5 kg (2–12 lbs)

AGE: 20–40 years

## STARRY FLOUNDER
### (PLATICHTHYS STELLATUS)
WEIGHT: 2–9 kg (5–20 lbs)

AGE: 10–22 years

## HALIBUT
### (HIPPOGLOSSUS STENOLEPIS)
WEIGHT: 50–230 kg (110–510 lbs)

AGE: 20–55 years

## LINGCOD
### (OPHIODON ELONGATUS)
WEIGHT: 10–60 kg (20–130 lbs)

AGE: 10–35 years

# AUGUST 14:
Winds S 10 to light. *Sunny.* //
Lisianski Strait

**04:14.** The engine rips me from my slumber. It has been my alarm clock for over a month. Where's my headlamp? I crawl up the ladder and push open the hatch with my head. Still dark. Dave and I listen to *Moby Dick* on audio tape, drinking coffee until there's enough light to see out of the anchorage.

**05:32.** We try the hooks close to shore. Finding more rockfish than salmon, so we head to the 50-fathom edge.

**10:28.** Twelve coho and two kings on board. The wind has died and Mount Fairweather slices the skyline. A sea lion chases our lines and Dave shoots at it with his shotgun to scare it off. "Don't worry, it's just bird shot." Some captains aren't so kind, and use jury-rigged dynamite grenades called *seal bombs.*

**12:00.** Twenty-five coho. Three kings. *Not bad.*

**14:10.** The lines get mangled. Dave is furious as lures and flashers require cutting. At the bottom of the line, a potential culprit—a massive king that might have crossed the lines. Dave doesn't think so and blames my *blithering-sissy-incompetence.* He's a wild-fire when things go wrong, *but in a good and practical way.* To be honest, I've been making mistakes; it's tricky work and requires focus, all day long.

**16:15.** Forty-five-minute nap. I awake to a stow-away. A storm petrel has landed on the ship to take refuge. It's exhausted and accepts my handling—interesting how desperation can lead to faith and surrender.

**18:34.** We listen to National Public Radio (NPR) while lines span the water column. I wish I had a radio on the kayak.

**19:45.** Humpbacks flop on the horizon.

Leach's *Storm Petrel*
(*Hydrobates leucorhous*),
the stowaway.

**20:06.** *Fish ho!* The wires are packed with coho. Nine on one wire, three to go. The sun dives into the Gulf of Alaska and sets the mountains ablaze.

**21:10.** Dinner! Exclusively eating wild salmon is the keto-dream; my body has never felt better.

**22:00.** Cutting the engines and pulling up the lines, we drift the night. The full moon rises over Yakobi Island, and we gut the bounty in silence.

**23:00.** Throwing the last innards overboard, we watch salmon sharks swarm and circle. I get shivers watching them gobble our leftovers.

**23:15.** Total: 101 coho, 4 kings (a single king salmon can sell for USD$50–300, *coho sell for USD$10–60*). We pack them on ice. We caught 50 salmon in the span of two hours. *Holy smokes.* "They like tide changes," Dave explains. "Salmon capitalize on currents mixin' up the nutrients, which attracts forage fish." Sounds similar to humans.

**23:30.** I'm exhausted.

**23:45.** I brush my teeth while writing the above by headlamp. *Jesus-murphy*, what a day.

**00:00.** I fall asleep reading Alfred Lansing's *Endurance: Shackleton's Incredible Journey.* I awake at 04:00 to the engine's roar, my thumb still between the pages. Sleep, fish, eat fish, repeat.

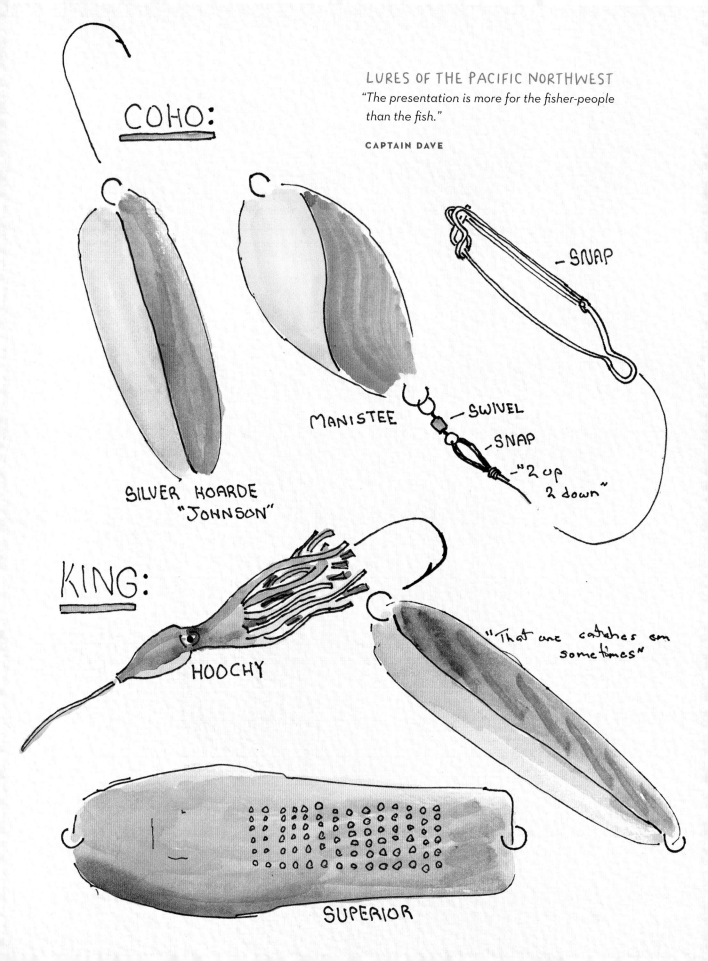

LURES OF THE PACIFIC NORTHWEST
*"The presentation is more for the fisher-people than the fish."*

CAPTAIN DAVE

COHO:

MANISTEE

— SNAP

— SWIVEL

— SNAP

"2 up 2 down"

SILVER HOARDE "JOHNSON"

KING:

HOOCHY

"That one catches 'em sometimes"

SUPERIOR

## AUGUST 24:

Winds SE 30-40. *Bonkers out.* // Sitka

Time has passed. I've been so busy I've hardly written. The *Albee* is tied up while a storm rifles down from the Aleutians. Fifty-knot winds invert umbrellas and turn raindrops into bullets.

I post-up in the library and call Kaia. We've been talking. She bought a plane ticket to visit, but tells me she's not coming. *"I just can't."* She has a life in Victoria and a wooden sailboat to fix. Her community is there. *I'm an idea to her*—a lover lost at sea—and our relationship is teetering on the edge. It's hard to be together when you're not together; even harder when I'm relatively unreachable and thought not to return.

*I cry.* I write. I feel as though part of me is being surgically removed. I long to be alone, but my heart is in rhythm with another. The only thing cheering me up is the dock-cat I name Couscous, impervious to long-distance-young-love earthquakes. Cats are the origin of cuddles, comfort, *and* independence.

## THE END OF SITKA

In one week it will be September. Fall is here. Still 480 kilometres (300 miles) to Skagway, and I'm warned of the monotony of Lynn Canal—the final stretch. I change my destination, which requires swallowing my pride. This whole trip, I imagined pulling up to Skagway as a hero and returning home to tell *my* grand-fantastic journey. It's insane how many times I've visualized telling this narrative to others upon return. *Why?* I'm not here to boost my ego! *Am I?!* Isn't this process supposed to whittle away my conceit and attachment?

I turn my attention to Gustavus, the toe of Glacier Bay. I could continue fishing with Dave into September, but I tell him I plan to move on. I feel I've let him down, but he understands, bids me fair tides, and gives me a cabbage for the road. He also leaves me with a Latin line from Nietzsche: *Amor fati.*

Gustavus is 140 nautical miles, I need to move. My time on the *Albee* was an opportunity of a lifetime, but it consumed the tail of summer. The leaves are changing, and the fishermen tell me September storms can be devastating. *I hope I'm not too late.*

*Opposite* A lure is designed to attract predatory fish with its prey-like appearance and movement. It is an imitation-tool. Egyptians and Chinese people as early as 2,000 BCE used hooks and lures made of bone, wood, or bronze. Now we have infinite variations and materials, some even implanted with flashing LEDs.

Sitka Dock Cat

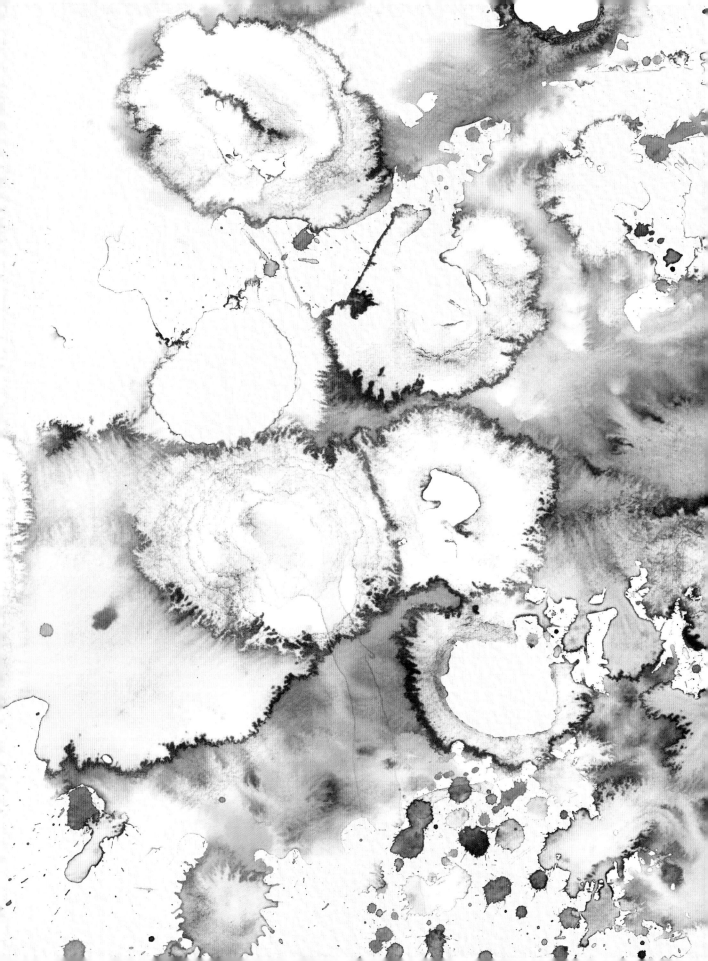

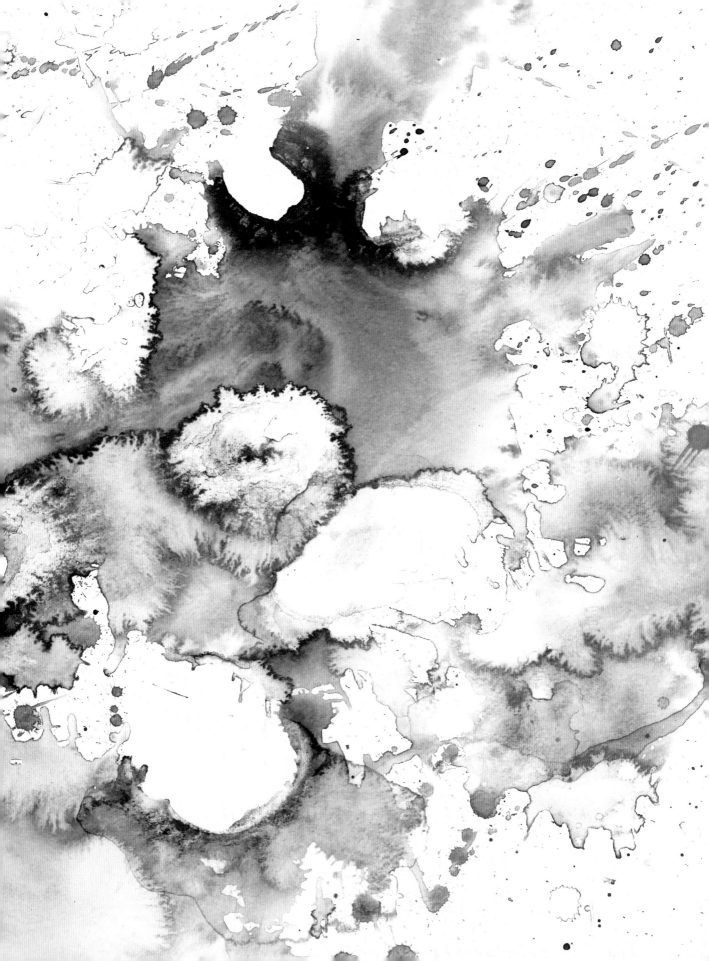

# 8

# SEPTEMBER STORMS

"You can either see yourself as a wave...
or you can see yourself as the ocean."

~ OPRAH WINFREY* ~

*My sister Lexi and I used to watch Oprah every day
after school, mostly because we only had two channels,
but also, Oprah's awesome, honest, and has empowered
a lot of people.

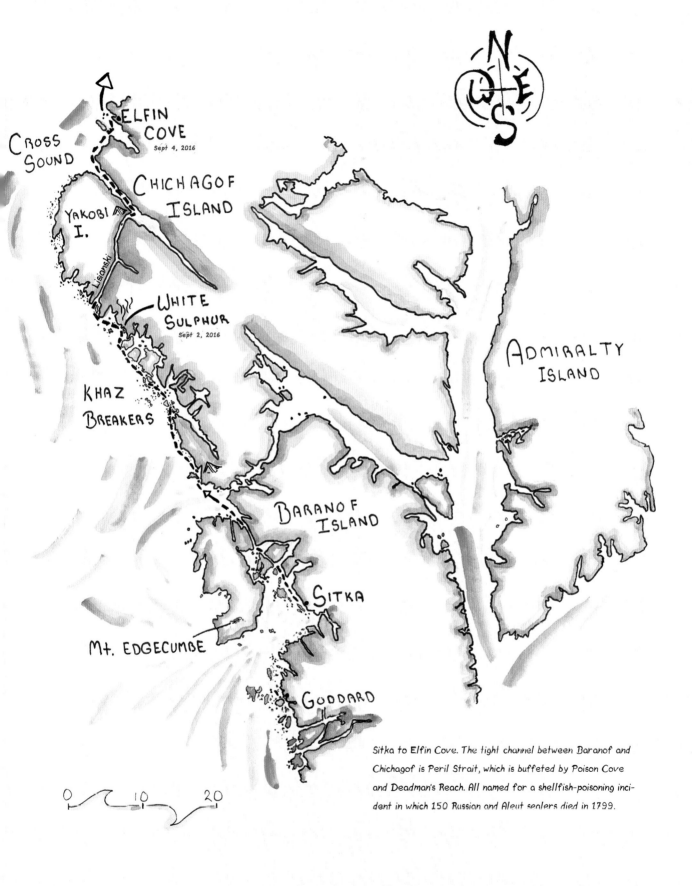

N

E
W
S

ELFIN
COVE
Sept 4, 2016

CROSS
SOUND

CHICHAGOF
ISLAND

YAKOBI
I.

Lisianski

WHITE
SULPHUR
Sept 2, 2016

KHAZ
BREAKERS

ADMIRALTY
ISLAND

BARANOF
ISLAND

SITKA

Mt. EDGECUMBE

GODDARD

0    10    20

Sitka to Elfin Cove. The tight channel between Baranof and Chichagof is Peril Strait, which is buffeted by Poison Cove and Deadman's Reach. All named for a shellfish-poisoning incident in which 150 Russian and Aleut sealers died in 1799.

# DAY 46, AUGUST 26:

Winds L to NE 10. *Sun.* // Sitka to Little Gavanski Island—6 nm.

I hit the post office to send a love letter to Kaia and an *Iditarod* sweater to my dad (he likes dogs). I got to know wonderful folks in Sitka, and now I say my goodbyes. *Why am I always leaving?*

Hoping to feed on fish, I restock with the essentials (potatoes, carrots, onions, peanut butter, oats, and salt to preserve scalies). My dream is to catch a lingcod or a salmon from the kayak.

## KAYAK FISHING

On the *Albee* I killed and gutted *over a thousand fish*, and have become versed in their wiggly ways. There are three main strategies: 1. *Trolling* (as discussed previously) 2. *Seining* (using nets to surround the fishies) 3. *Jigging* or longlining (my fav).

*Jigging* is about *location, location, location.* I pick headlands, channels, and back eddies—places where water is moving. To stay off the bottom, I reel up two or three metres once I feel the line go slack; this prevents getting hooked on rocks or kelp. But getting stuck happens, like,

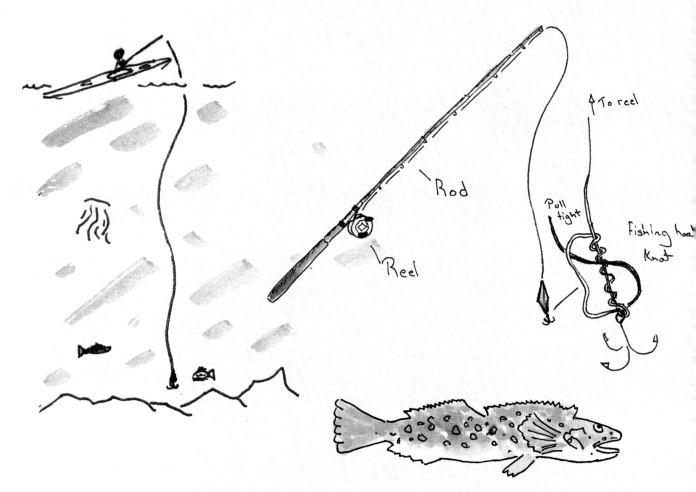

Ling cod (*Ophiodon elongatus*)

*all the time.* It's actually *the reason* we go fishing: to learn patience, and attach ourselves with an umbilical cord to the unknown.

The hardest part is what to do once I've got one. I usually stuff it in the cockpit, then go to shore and bludgeon it. I've lost a few slippery-jacks whacking them on deck. But having a live fish in your cockpit comes with its own crotch-related punctuation marks. Remember, rockfish have toxins in their quills.

*The Khaz Breakers are beyond words and wonder. They're the most complex and remote islands I've encountered, and extremely difficult to access. If you're looking for a real kayak adventure, this is it. At the least, do a Google Earth tour.*

# DAY 49, AUGUST 29:
Winds light to N 10. *Super sunny.* //
Klokachef Island to Khaz Breakers—14 nm.

The Khaz Breakers were crafted by a drunk architect with a background in abstract art. After frying up a brown bomber (*Sebastes sp.*), I walk between the timbers. An amber light saturates *everything*, and I watch the landscape transform. I visualize the sprouting seeds from which these mamas came, and the gale force winds that will knock them over. Every ice sheet, storm, bird, wolf, and fungus has played its role. The past whirls and melds itself with the present, and I'm left barefoot on thick moss, *alone*. Riveted by a nameless magnet.[1] A sliver in me begins to grasp the time scale in which this world works.

KHAZ BREAKERS

## ON INTELLIGENCE

*Thud... thud... thud... shmack*—I'm under attack! In the morning light, squirrels are trouble, dropping spruce cones on the tent. *Sciurus vulgaris* (red squirrels) store up to 4,000 cones every summer in preparation for the winter. Think *apocalypse hoarding*.

Dancing between boughs, taking time they could be foraging, *they are playing*. Anthropomorphizing animals can lead to a misunderstanding of biological processes, but we can't only view animals through evolution. Sea lions have accompanied me for miles, dolphins have surfed my wake, and sea otters have, well, sophisticated culture.

In university, we had a lecture dedicated to whales breaching. There is no decent evolutionary reason for them to hurl through the sea-sky barrier. Are they scratching off barnacles, communicating predator proximity, aiding digestion, or exercising? *Mother Teresa* (forehead slap)... could it be they are just having fun and probing the boundaries of reality?

When I was 12, I crashed my mountain bike regularly, almost always in the name of untethering from gravity's pull. I wanted to know if it was possible to fly. Whales have as much, and more, brain than us; perhaps they too are scientists, and experimental children, searching for the meaning of life.

One of my best friends, Justin Ming, had his own theory: "Maybe they just really need air."

Every organism has an intelligence that, at times, defies evolutionary theory. Animals have personalities; *they are people too*. At the Hakai Beach Institute, we put creatures and their behaviours into *tidy-measurable-boxes*. From what I've seen, ecosystems are mind-bendingly complex and messy. Is it possible to quantify something we can only partially grasp? And if we choose to use the scientific lens and call it god, *do we limit our perspective?*

What do you think?

## DAY 53, AUGUST 31:
Winds light. *Sunny.* // Myriad Islands to White Sulphur Hot Springs—11 nm.

I wiggle out of the Khaz Breakers through Tawak Passage and set up camp in the Myriad Islands. The next morning the lions at *White Sisters* (a barren set of islets) howl constantly. *What secrets are they divulging? What sermons do they preach?* At breakfast, black flies invade my camp, and I'm pursued for over a mile on windless water. Swinging my head and hands to parry off the bombers, *I lose my mind*, then my sunglasses. They descend into the abyss. I love insects, but do they have to be so good at what they do?

I heard about White Sulphur Hot Springs from the Sitka locals, but never got a chance to visit due to its poor anchorage. The only safe way to access is by kayak.

Before finding the springs (an *"X"* marked by Captain Dave), I try my luck for coho. An estuary three kilometres (two miles) south might be prime salmon-hab. Towering trees dip their roots on either side of the bank; this forest is pumped by nutrients and fertile soil. I wind upstream, battling the tidal outflow, eventually coming to a bottleneck with stone inuksuks (piled stones). Past the narrows, I see the water is alive and wriggling. Shapes move under the surface like starlings. *Coho!*

There are thousands. I dip my paddle down to disturb the mass and they move in synchronized formation—an army on the march. I beach *Pep* and begin casting from shore. A couple jump on the hook, but are so powerful they break the line. They are so close to their evolutionary climax.

Two kayaks morph into my periphery, making strokes upstream. It takes me a moment to register—other kayakers! *Humans!* I haven't met any paddlers this whole trip. *Hello!*

Kelly, an old grizzly-bear of a human being, is smiling. "I thought they might be here." It turns out he has been fishing this stream every fall for the last five years. He unloads, taking out his own fishing rod and a *gaff hook*. He is accompanied by a young Canadian named Simon Behman, who completed a similar summer traverse as myself, except he paddled the *outside* of Vancouver

Island! Kelly, who is in his forties, has taken Simon under his wing for a couple days, and they are exploring the area around Elfin Cove.

Kelly has two coho on shore and gutted in fifteen minutes. *Wowzers.* He tells me last autumn he camped here and smoked over twenty fish under a tarp-rigged tripod, burning river alder. Also, his camp got flooded in the middle of the night by a September storm surge.

We paddle out, two coho on Kelly's deck. Simon and I never did get one. As we approach White Sulphur Hot Springs, he tells me, "This is where I spend my winters." *Winters?* From October on, this coastline contends with sixty-knot gales and fifteen-foot seas. I look around and can't find a spot to land. Kelly steers into a secret cove twenty feet wide. *Welcome to paradise.*

## KAYAK KELLY

*It's not what people think of you, it's what you do.* Kelly was a registered nurse in the Lower-48 until a crisis of identity sent him to Southeast. "The first year was the hardest, I had no idea what I was doing." Kelly was sick of American culture, and has spent the last ten years living out of his kayak, *Bruiser,* in remote areas of the Alaskan Panhandle. In towns like Elfin Cove, Pelican, and Sitka, he has a reputation, earning the nickname *Kayak Kelly.*

One winter on the outside of Chichagof Island, he had eaten nothing but seaweed and bone broth for a week. "I was getting worried, until I came across deer tracks." The buck was on the beach, and Kelly didn't want to scare it, so he got in his kayak and crept up the coast. Kelly took aim and shot the deer with his *shotgun* from the boat. He camped beside the carcass for the next week, sucking marrow from the bones. *Shotgun? Bone marrow? Winter?* What the blaster-caster! I'm still having trouble lighting fires.

By drying meat with salt, dehydrating seaweed, and smoking fish, Kelly preserves enough food to survive in isolation through the snowtime. "*Spring is full of seaweed, the summers are easy, and in autumn I eat salmon—December is when it gets tricky.*" Kelly tells me this while showing me photos of paddling in a February blizzard. *What is he saying?* I can't imagine this level of removal.

KK is in this for life—he's been permanently transformed, absorbed into the ecosystem. It puts my trip in perspective; I'm just a tourist. He too sought a leave from Western culture—but *he stayed.* A part of me longs for this, but a part of me knows Kelly is lonely. I ask him over a sizzling coho. "Sure I'm lonely! Who the hell isn't? At least I'm honest about it."

*Above* Going to Alaska to escape and test capacity is kind of a thing (think Into the Wild). And here I am too. There is something seductive about a secret corner of the world where city lights can't penetrate. But it's a very colonial narrative, and there is something superficial about it. Am I any better than ol' George Van or Cap'n Cook and his band of Indigenous killers? This line of questioning makes me a little queasy, as it undermines my entire project and the privileged foundation on which I stand. Which is good.

## WHITE SULPHUR HOT SPRINGS

Kelly and Simon leave for Pelican the next day and I spend three nights at the springs, *indulging.* A cedar structure encloses one main tub, and there are paths leading to crabapple trees and outdoor pools.

The routine: *Wake up, tub-time, read, breakfast of leftover coho, explore, tub-time, split wood, late lunch, tub-time, ocean swim, read, tub-time, bed, repeat.* It's my reward for all the damp sleeps, endless crossings, surprise storms, and infected toes. *This moment right now as I write could be the happiest I've ever been.*

The weather *is* dismal—although I'm treated to one mighty sunset. I walk around naked to not get my layers wet. To warm up, I jump in the tub.

## SEXUALITY

OK, share time. I've struggled with an addiction to pornography since I was 17. There, it's out. The potent images have mucked up my romantic life and sexual expectations. Being here offers time for reflection, and prevents me from indulging in my tricky habit. This is part of the reason I left in the first place, but I wasn't ready to tell you until now.

Our society has mangled sex. On TV, it's glorified, exaggerated, and encouraged. At home and in religion, it is hidden, stigmatized, and forbidden. *I'm confused.*

I learned to put condoms on bananas in gender-segregated sex-ed classes, and wrote anonymous queries in the "sex-question-box." Then the Internet arrived and no one warned me of its contents. I remember watching porn with friends in high school and, more and more, by myself—mesmerized by the shapes, sounds, and ease of access. *Are women so easy? Are men so dominating?* It's unrealistic, dangerous, and disgusting.

ᨆᨆᨆᨆᨆᨆᨆᨆᨆᨆᨆᨆᨆᨆᨆᨆᨆᨆᨆᨆᨆᨆᨆᨆᨆᨆᨆᨆᨆᨆ

We are born from sperm + egg, and the instinct to reproduce is embedded in our genes and driven by hormones. We are survival-machines, but the system can go haywire when exposed to a fictitious fantasy world.

Miscommunication, failed expectations, and power imbalances are already cropping up in my young sex life. I feel our generation was abandoned to behaviour promoting pain and trauma. Sex, in a moment, can give you the highest high or the deepest psychological scar.

I want to embrace sexuality with true self-less love. But my selfish habits are hard to break. When making love I have profound feelings—a full-body meditation beyond the rational monkey-mind. Along with being in nature, it's the closest thing to a *spiritual experience* I've had.

I wish sexuality was celebrated. The discourse in high-school: "How many notches you got in the belt, bro?" I wish men would talk about this, and support each other. I wish our culture hadn't created such destructive habits. I hate porn and what it's done to me, I hate what *I've* done to me. I wish I hadn't made so many mistakes. *Somebody help me.*

The good news is I'm not alone. Sixty-eight million search queries related to pornography are generated per day. That's buck-wild. Imagine all the people right now sneaking away from spouses and loved ones to indulge in sex-fantasy-land. It's not just me who needs an intervention.

PS: It feels so good to come out with this.[2] *What a relief.* For so long I thought I was hiding from others, but really, I was hiding from myself. Honesty is therapy. I think this is the first step for many men. Just start talking about it: "Hey, I'm addicted to porn, and I feel _____ about it." Especially if you have a partner, because they are directly affected.

## NUDISM

I spend sunny days on the beach completely naked. It's liberating and sensual, and it's healing trauma I never knew I had. At first I looked around as if a journalist would stumble out of the cedars; I was conditioned to cover up. Confidence increased, and sometimes I undress before unpacking *Bell* and setting up camp. It's comfortable, that's all. Nothing weird.

I also have no mirror, or anyone to look good for. My self-confidence is increasing, and I realize how silly it was in university to cultivate a certain style—which for me was: disheveled-thrift-shop hipster. I'm not saying we should all stop grooming and go nude, but at least we should pay attention to the mega-self-image market bidding for (and instigating) our insecurity.

One more sex-secret: I still masturbate, *but it's different.* There are no external images fueling my instincts, it's just body sensations and imagination. Kind of amazing, actually. I won't go into details, but my experience with sexuality alone out here is beautifully new and refreshing. My old habits were motivated by MTV and male peer pressure; now I can see what's deeper down.

OK that's it. *Thanks for listening.*

*It's embarrassing how few resources there are for porn addicts. Usually it's a tag-along on alcohol and substance abuse websites. Porn is not booze, though I think there are neat lessons from the famous 12 steps: (1) Admit our power-lessness or difficulty with addiction. (2/3) Ask for help from others. (4) Deeply analyze our behaviour. (5) Admit to others and create public accountability. (6/7) Believe we can change, and make a plan. (8/9) Ask for forgiveness from those we've harmed. (10) Work with mentors to analyze ourselves deeply and hold ourselves accountable to our goals. (11) Meditate and cultivate better habits. 12) Share our journey / help others. (This is my personal, non-religious version.)*

*That said, I think we have to tackle porn addiction head on, through open conversation, research, education, and regu-lation. I'm not totally against porn; I think many people might have healthy relationships with it, and now there is discourse around ethical porn. But, we need to talk about it.*

# DAY 54, SEPTEMBER 3:

Winds N 10. *Sun and clouds.* // Lisianski
Strait—13.5 nm.

River otters bid me adieu as I paddle away from
the springs. The wind is against me for two hours
until Lisianski. The light shifts until the ocean
turns a black, slippery mass. *What time is it?* I just
left the hot springs, but it's dark already. Time on
the water melts in mysterious ways. September
also means shorter days.

I spend the night at a storm shelter at
Lisianski Junction. My VHF has been acting
up, and no one replies to my radio checks. The
antenna is split and leaking rusty goo. I finally
get patchy reception: *Winds east 60 knots with
13 foot seas in Cross Sound tomorrow.* Chewy-
wooey! Also a heavy precipitation warning. This is
what I get for paddling in September. *60 knots!*
Sweet Suzan! If I'm to make Gustavus, I'll have to
make wise decisions. No ego allowed.

Note to self: get up early.

MN POINT

## DAY 55, SEPTEMBER 4:

Wind S 15 to E 15. *Wild dark clouds.* //
Lisianski to Elfin Cove—16 nm.

05:00. Rockfish preserved with salt and
flame-blasted-bannock (batter made from flour
and water, cooked like a marshmallow) for breakfast. Foreboding skies. The sail pulls me into
Cross Sound—one of the gnarliest water bodies
on earth. Clouds churn and push past glacial
mountains; the waves can't make up their mind;
the potential is tangible. *A storm is coming.*

I turn at Column Point, and eight kilometres
(five miles) later I see no trace of what should
be *Elfin Cove.* Hidden from offshore waters by a
tight inlet engraved into a corner of the sound, I
must trust the chart.

It's truly unruly when the colourful roofs of
Elfin emerge. I'm astounded a town can exist in
such remote austerity. The buildings are about to
fall over, hanging onto life by stilts and willpower.
The docks are abuzz with the entire Elfin fleet,
clamouring in preparation for the blow. *Where
are all the elves?*

I creep in unnoticed and dog-tired.

## ELFIN COVE

People here smell like salmon and talk about them with equal potency. Everyone wears brown rubber boots called *Ketchikan kicks* or *Sitka sneakers*. The town shows the length humans will go to acquire fish. Twenty tender souls live here in winter; the northern waters are too volatile and unforgiving for transportation or fishing during those months.

Even September seems unpredictable.

Rain falls and wind begins to whisper. I'm invited to stay in a room above the grocery store by the folks who run the salmon barge. I will hole up for two days while the storm passes.

*The sky turns black.* I huddle, looking out the window, watching the raw power of Neptune, Zeus, and the Gulf of Alaska. Salt-licked trollers grasp with coarse ropes to questionable docks as amber light searches from portholes. A constant howl whistles through every needle on every tree. Thank god I'm not in the tent.

With my day off, I study the mysterious fallen stars: Echinoderms.

*Elfin Cove has an average temp of 6 degrees Celsius (43 degrees Fahrenheit); in the winters, down to minus 17. Average annual precipitation: 1,240 millimetres (50 inches) over 241 days a year. Average snowfall: 291 centimetres (115 inches) over 47 days a year. This place is gnarly; look it up on Google Earth.*

## ECHINODERMS OF THE PACIFIC NORTHWEST

The phylum *Echinodermata* ("spiny skinned") includes cucs, sand dollars, and urchins. The take-home from these cosmic lovers? Well, there's loads. First, Echino-blasters are radially symmetric (usually fivefold) and they have calcium carbonate *endoskeletons*, not exoskeletons like crustaceans. And yes, most Echinos regenerate limbs, *and* can also reproduce through dividing themselves (multiply by dividing!). Last but not least, to eat shelled crustaceans, starfish vomit their stomachs into the shell, pre-digest the prey, then slurp it up. Yum, and yuck, and coo*ool*.

## SUNFLOWER STAR[3] (*PYCNOPODIA HELIANTHOIDES*)

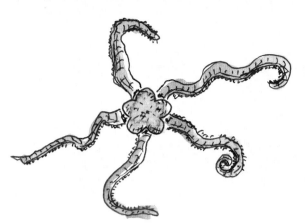

DAISY BRITTLE STAR
(*OPHIOPHOLIS ACULEATA*)

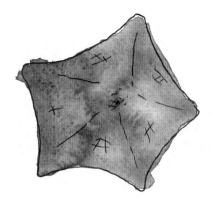

BAT STAR
(*ASTERINA MINIATA*)

ROSE STAR
(*CROSSASTER PAPPOSUS*)

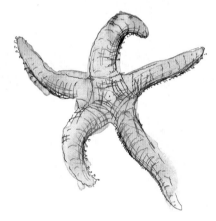

OCHRE STAR
(*PISASTER OCHRACEUS*)

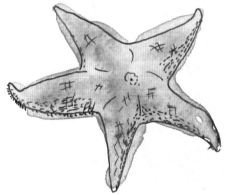

LEATHER STAR
(*DERMASTERIAS IMBRICATA*)

Cross Sound. This is the land of tidewater glaciers, where icebergs float haphazard. In the 1750s, a unified glacier came all the way out to Lemesurier Island. Now we must travel 105 km (65 miles) into Glacier Bay to touch solid ice. Where will we be in another hundred years?

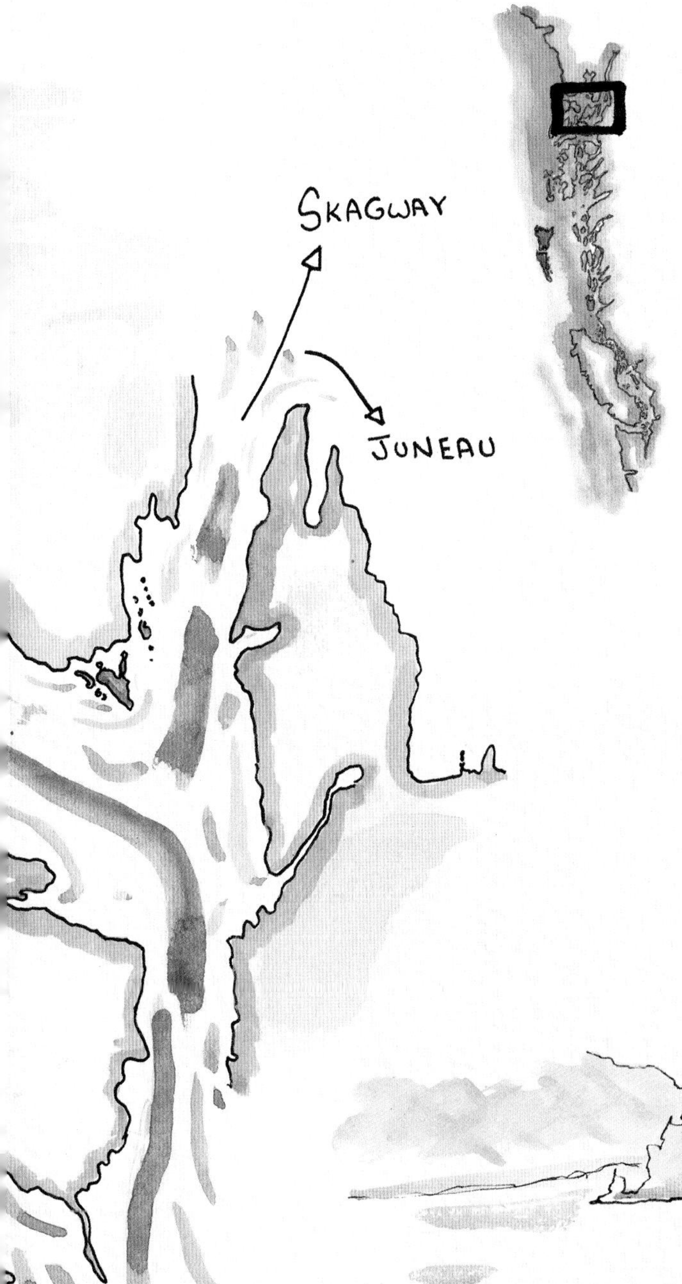

SKAGWAY

JUNEAU

# DAY 57, SEPTEMBER 6:

Wind E 15 to light. *Sunny.* //
Inian Islands—6 nm.

Elfin offered refuge when I needed it most. Now, the last leg—48 kilometres (30 miles) to Gustavus. *Home stretch.* Today is beautiful and clear, but the forecast is not encouraging—30-knot easterlies tomorrow.

Mount Fairweather is staggering, marking the beginning of a land ruled by granite and glaciers. I slip under its shadow and into a maze of islands. Rockfish for dinner.

With the end in sight, I'm nervous and uncertain. What does it mean to reach a destination? I have spent so long immersed in the process of getting somewhere, I can't fathom life afterwards. *Please let everything work out.*

# DAY 58, SEPTEMBER 7:

W 15. *Foreboding skies.* //
Lemesurier Island—9 nm.

The weather is turning. I'm so close, *but to what?* Be patient. Tomorrow I could reach Gustavus and end this whole-big-thing, but only if the weather doesn't go full-squirrely. Only if I don't flip.

I sleep without the tent, but set up around midnight once it starts raining. I lie awake rereading the journal by headlamp and reflecting on how far I've come. My nomadic life threaded together by islands, bull kelp, and breaths of wind. It all seems so normal.

# DAY 59, SEPTEMBER 8:

Wind SE 20-30. *Thick rolling clouds.* //
Gustavus, Alaska mainland—14 nm.

Waves are breaking up to my chest, engulfing
the entire boat. *It's ferocious out.* No one
should paddle in this. As I struggle past the
entrance to Glacier Bay, I begin to get sucked
in. CHOWSSERR! How did I not expect currents?
Hundreds of porpoises are coursing the whirlpools. *Bell* does a full 360 and I lock eyes with a
sea otter. It plunges. *So much life*—indifferent to
my cause.

What is everyone else in the world doing
right now?

Finally I scrape *Bell* up to sandy safety. *Six
kilometres (four miles) to Gustavus,* but the afternoon wind is peaking and the forecast calls for a
three-day storm. *I'm frozen.*

White water smashes the beach, rearranging
sand grains. I'm so close—to *something.* My mind
is anxious: *just get it over with.* A part of me
wants to never return, *the wind* is pushing me
sideways. *There is no fear when you let go of
everything you know.* I push *Pep* back in, reacting
out of habit and faith rather than logic. Cresting
waves launch over starboard. The next miles are
the most difficult of the entire trip. When you are
closest to completion, you are challenged the
most—to see if you have learned your lesson, and
if you truly want the buried treasure.

My mind calms in the madness. *Breathe and
paddle.* Don't flip. *Each stroke is the destination.*

The Salmon River is the entrance to Gustavus,
and best traversed on an incoming tide (otherwise you battle the river's current). Paddling out
of the chaos, I head upstream towards *civilization* and the end of my kayak odyssey.

There is no warm welcome. No crowd
cheering my final strokes. *No hot soup.* I pull
up *BP* on a muddy bank in a downpour. Three
retired fish boats loom above, decomposing. I
set up tent under the failing roof of a dilapidated
gazebo beside an abandoned field, strip naked,
and change into my last dry pants. I collapse in
the sleeping bag, defeated.

## GUSTAVUS, ALASKA:

*Sun and clouds. //* Total distance
from Victoria: 928 nm / 1,720 km
(total days from Victoria: 92)

I'm not sure what I expected upon ending the
journey, but *this* seems appropriate. I struggle
and swim in the same ocean. My mind still wavers
and consumes me, and I still make mistakes. I'm
still human, still me. Growth has taken place, but
seems too integrated to define.

Standing on the edge, I watch the Salmon
River wiggle its way to sea. *This landscape is
massive.* Jagged mountains cradle glaciers
like babies; clouds move like freight trains; an
eagle sits on a worn piling staring back at me.
*I begin to cry.* I've paddled 1,700 kilometres
(1,000 miles) to sleep in a shack beside an over-
grown golf course; to watch storms peel by in
September air; to write this journal you now read.
My tears are joy, grief, and every other emotion
on the spectrum. *It's hard to translate.*

## KAIA

Her voice sounds so close. I call from a bakery and tell her I will come. *I miss you. I love you.* My thoughts drifted her way too often not to try things *one more time.*

I hope I can put the insights from this trip into our relationship—*into my life*. Otherwise, what's the point of going through such turmoil, loneliness, and challenge?

*Gustavus is headquarters for Glacier Bay National Park, and home to talented naturalists and scientists. John Muir first explored the bay in 1879. An amazing journal of his escapades "discovering" the area is available online, with sketches.*

## COMING HOME

I spend the next week in Gustavus waiting for the ferry. Walking through town, I'm treated with a friendly tone—but as a tourist. No one knows my hardship, my transformation, how far I've come. My ego implodes.

*Breathe.* The pride dissolves (a bit), and I go back to writing. I'm in the bakery with an old local named Bobby Lee Daniels. "Nice journal," he says, and scootches over.

"Thanks." I show my paintings, *my story.* He's in awe, and again I ponder how to share my wild-wide eyes and dotted ink lines.

The next morning, I board the Gustavus-Juneau ferry, then on to Skagway. These vessels are spaceships, unperturbed by the waves and wind that held me anxious and alone for months. Darkness falls as the vessel traverses Lynn Canal. The stars shiver, reflected in the ocean—my great teacher.

I'm going home to Victoria and an uncertain future. It scares me, but if there is anything I've learned: *life tends to work out, sometimes just not how you expect.*

*Yes, I still have questions, if not more. But perhaps I'm no longer looking for answers.*

THE FERRY HOME

# EPILOGUE: OCTOBER, 2016.

My thumb is cold; it's minus 10 Celsius (14 Fahrenheit). The last of the leaves hold on by a frosty thread. I'm hitching back to Victoria to see Kaia and start a new chapter. *Bell* is left behind at a friend's, in the Yukon.

I write from the outskirts of Dawson's Creek—mile zero on the Alaska Highway. There are signs of industry everywhere: a landscape pock-marked with oil and gas development, fracking for deposits locked 2,000 metres underground. Residents worry about sour gas leaks, habitat loss, and most of all, *water contamination*.

Thinking back to Lelu Island, I begin to realize the scale of the issue. This is where the proposed Petronas pipeline begins. This is more than the Lax Kw'alaams opposing oil and gas being shoveled through their territory, *this is about cultural momentum*. In my journey, it was impossible not to be moved by the raw, intricate beauty of the

Pacific Northwest. The impulse to protect it is powerful.

As a member of society, I'm linked to extraction and complicit in its environmental impact. We depend on resources, as we depend on the ecosystems holding them. The coastal rainforest is beyond economic quantification; to communicate its true value we need to tell stories. Our collective narrative matters, and is built by the perspectives we have about places, people, and politics. *Ideas are contagious.* Not everyone will be able to witness what I have, so I want to share my experience. This propels me to write.

This adventure taught me the value of solitude, the intricacy of the human mind, and the time scale we walk. It also showed me I am vulnerable, emotional, and prone to poor decision-making. *Everyone is*, and if we do nothing in return for the things we care about, they tend to disappear.

A truck pulls over and asks where I'm headed. *Home,* I say.

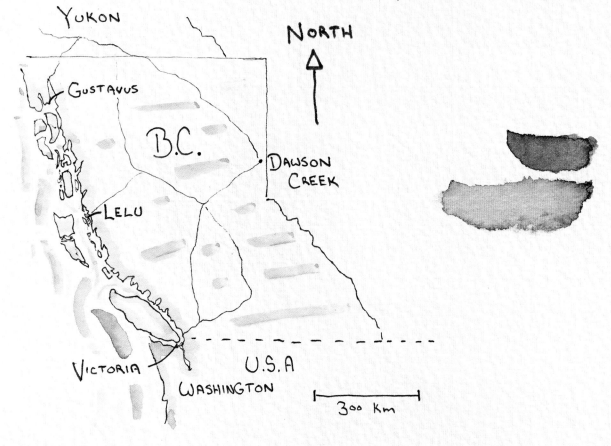

## KAIA

The awaited embrace. To spend months away from someone you love and finally hold them is a remarkable human experience. *I'm nervous as a puffin before first flight*. My sailing from Vancouver to Victoria is almost cancelled due to high winds; the ocean continues its symphony.

*And there she is*. We clutch together like old friends reunited after a war. Her body presses against my own and her hair tangles on my wool sweater.

Her new-old sailboat, *Cinzano*, is tied under the bright lights of downtown Victoria. We ignore everything but each other. My head ducks into the cramped cabin, and with a couple candles, it's a suitable nest. We have much to talk about, catch up on, and *work* through. But we are silent and shy.

Tomorrow, I will figure it all out—what I'm doing with my life, and how to do it. How *we* are going to do it. Right now, I want the sea that stretched me thousands of miles, to the edge of survival, and served as my ultimate mentor, to support and contain us in this small wooden boat.

Waves lick the bow like inchworms. And somewhere, out there, past the city lights, bull kelp dances in the swell of the Mighty Pacific; nudibranchs reign over tidal kingdoms; and salmon march into the jaws of grizzlies, orcas, and wolves. Somewhere, out there, past the city lights, is forest so dense it feels like dawn at midday; where old cedars wear tattoos from bark stripped for baskets and boxes; where people still know the names of plants and what they are for. Somewhere, out there, past the city lights, lies an invitation—an opportunity—to grow and be humbled. When we go into wild spaces the curriculum is not up to us, the lessons depend on *our capacity and willingness to learn*. If we enter open, and empty, we will return fulfilled and whole.

# 9
# APPENDIX

"And is it possible for something
to ever end? Or do all our
choices and actions simply
spiral, domino, and combine?
Like tributaries moving
toward the ocean."

⌒ **ME** ⌒
*I said this.* While crying
on the way home.

BEADED LANCE TOOTH

## NUMBERS

**TOTAL DISTANCE COVERED:** 928 nautical miles (nm) or 1,720 km (1,070 miles)

**TOTAL DAYS KAYAKING (BOTH SUMMERS):** 92

**LONGEST DAY PADDLED:** 28.5 nm

**SHORTEST DAY ON THE WATER:** 1.5 nm

**DISTANCE HITCHHIKED WITH KAYAK:** 32 nm

**DISTANCE SAILED:** 132 nm (14 percent of trip)

**LONGEST EXPOSED CROSSING:** 21.3 nm (Spanish Islands to Baranof)

**FASTEST SPEED (WITH CURRENT):** 8 knots

**AVERAGE DISTANCE PER DAY:** 10.2 nm

## OF INTEREST

**COMMUNITIES VISITED:** 9

**OTHER KAYAKERS MET:** 3

**FLIPPINGS:** 6

**FISH CAUGHT WHILE KAYAKING:** 24

**FISH CAUGHT ON THE ALBEE ROSE:** 1,165 (1,004 coho, 16 kings, 53 pinks, 4 sockeye, 47 rockfish, 20 halibut, 16 lingcod, 5 mystery-fish)

**ITEMS LOST:** 2.5 flip-flops, one wet suit boot, a fishing rod, a water dromedary, two sunglasses, and lots of other bits and bobs.

**ITEMS FOUND/GIFTED:** 2.5 flip-flops (actually there was loads), a fishing rod, unlimited water

bottles, sunglasses, and lots of other bits and bobs.

WEIGHT BEFORE: 80 kg (176lb); after: 63 kg (152 lb)

## WEATHER CONDITIONS

MORNINGS WITH LIGHT WIND: 44
AFTERNOONS WITH LIGHT WIND: 14
NUMBER OF WEATHER DAYS: 6
HIGHEST WINDS ON THE WATER: 30 knots
DAYS WITH PRECIPITATION: 23
HIGHEST WINDS ON WEATHER DAY: 60 knots

*Opposite, top left* Tent setup. First night in Alaska with Dad.

*Opposite, top right* Bell Pepper in the Rendezvous Islands.

*Opposite, bottom left* Just Jen and me on the dock of her post office.

*Opposite, bottom right* The Collapse of Minstrel Island.

*Top, left* Kaia on the dock, Victoria, BC.

*Top, right* Sailing beside Hambone Island, AK. Photo by Dad.

*Bottom, left* Surf landing beach on Warren Island. Sunset watercolours.

*Bottom, right* Kaia and I on the Sidney wharf (June 3, 2016).

NORTHERN RICE ROOT.

BLACK LILY

fruit: Narie camchatunsis

# THE PACIFIC NORTHWEST CROSSWORD

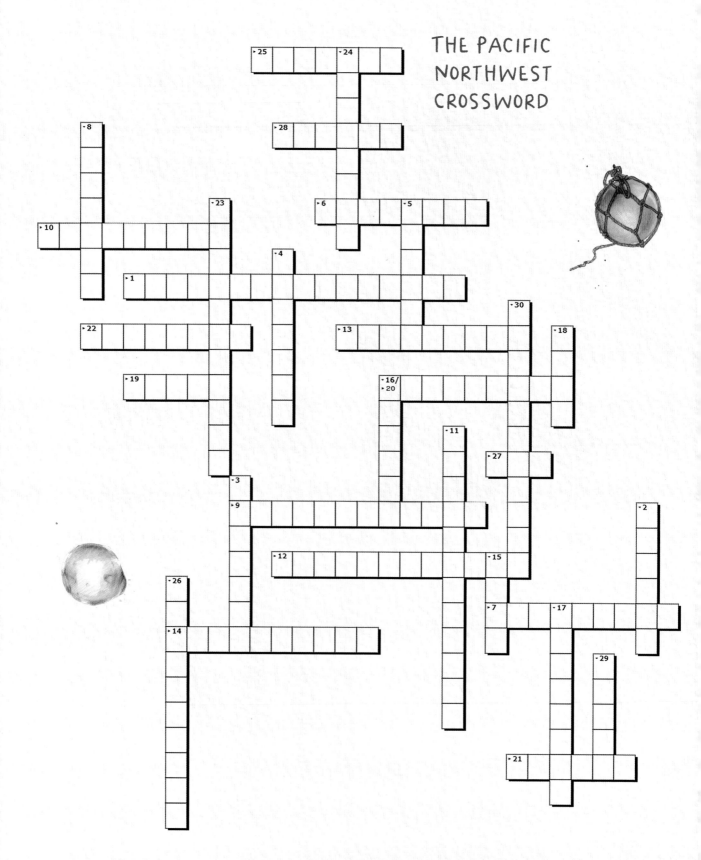

## QUESTIONS AND CLUES

Write in the book, don't worry. For species we are looking for the Latin genus.

1. To study time, space, and trees. (page 41)

2. Algae + fungus = (page 39)

3. An island that's not quite an island. (page 70)

4. Chow + Wowsers = (many pages)

5. Sandstone eroded by saltwater and time. (page 22)

6. A medieval entertainer travelling to sing and recite poetry. (page 40)

7. Ol' George _____ seemed to think he owned all the islands. (page 134)

8. The First Nation spanning most of Southeast Alaska. (page 108)

9. The most important genus on this coast. (page 156)

10. Underwater opera singers. (page 20)

11. *Heaped rainstorm.* (page 125)

12. The most intelligent invertebrate. (page 20)

13. Your best friends / teachers while camping. From June to August. Buzz. (page 79)

14. To live by the ocean as a terrestrial plant requires this superpower. (page 77)

15. A genus of algae with a flat, membranaceous, bright-green frond. Tasty. Rhymes with vulva. (page 70)

16. A deposit containing shells, bones, and other refuse that indicates human settlement. (page 32)

17. The pattern of deflection by objects (like ocean currents) as they traverse the Earth. (Chapter 2 endnotes)

18. After the first- and third-quarter moon, when high and low tide heights are closest. (page 34)

19. The jam-genus. (page 34)

20. Shucks, that's one slimy bivalve. (page 29)

21. A wading bird in the family Ardeidae, near shorelines and wetlands in North America. Also "old man" in Japanese. (page 24)

22. A green leafy kitchen lobotomy. The most efficient vegetable. (page 17)

23. Inside-out sushi. (page 72)

24. The Easter egg current. (page 48)

25. The highway knot. (page 67)

26. Radial symmetry. Outside stomach digestion. (page 178)

27. My (slightly robotic) company on the water. Prophet of the wind and rain. (page 23)

28. The mustache island. Spelled as if the island was edible. (pages 23, 27)

29. The other most important genus on this coast. The *real* Giving Tree. (page 41)

30. The longest bird migration, in proportion to body size. (page 51)

# JULY 2017

The pipeline was abandoned; Petronas backed out at Lelu. They cite "changes in market conditions." I'm not sure what that's code for, but active resistance from Indigenous Peoples and environmentalists had *something* to do with it. I should be happy, right? An irksome feeling lingers. The Pacific Northwest is full of "resources," and remains relatively unprotected. These pipelines and poorly planned resource-hauls are symptoms of a faulty foundation. Unless a deep-level-system change occurs, more threats will come.

Again, I'm not opposed to development—we rely on energy to power society. But is a marriage between our capacity *and* consumption possible? Is our comfort negotiable? What is the cost of capitalism, conformity, and short-term vision?

It seems there is a block in our creativity. This isn't an environmental problem, it's a *values issue*. What do we put first: luxuries or whales? Compassion or corruption? Greed or generosity? Humility or arrogance? *You choose.*

I caught a glimpse of my instability and patterns of self-gratification while drifting the islands. I fail to think about tomorrow, let alone seven generations. How do *we* decide what's good for *our* future, when I don't even know for myself?

PRECAUTIONARY PRINCIPLE (NOUN)

1. To account for the unknown unknowns in decision making. Instead of *shoot first, question later,* let's go slowly when deciding about shared landscapes and resources.

*History will repeat itself.* I will become a father. And my children will march into the collective cosmos. I must be brave, ethical, *and not get distracted.* I must have the commitment of an old-growth tree, *steady in storm winds.* I must, I must, *I must…* be gentle and patient. This process of cultural evolution is bigger than me.

*I love the Pacific Northwest.* It's my passion to explore, protect, and share its complexity. It's an organism—a whole—not to be reduced, divided, and sold to short-term pill-poppers. There's a *seamlessness* out there that transcends science, economics, and humanity. I hope with this story, you can taste it.

- Dear reader, *I love you too.* Thanks for taking the *time and space* to travel with me. Keep it humble, be true, and take it easy, *alright.*

- Keep watering the plants. Do one thing at a time. Breathe deep, seek peace.

- *Fall asleep in weird places.*

*Top, left*  My field school classmates on Calvert Island. Hakai Beach Institute, BC.

*Bottom, left*  Rick Wilson of the Heiltsuk First Nation holding a coho at Koeye River.

*Top, right*  The mesmerizing Lions Mane Jellyfish (*Cyanea capillata*). I almost fell in taking this photo.

*Bottom, right*  Licorice fern (*Polypodium glycyrrhiza*) spores in spring. The roots can be eaten raw or made into tea.

Top, left  The magical opalescent nudibranch (Hermissenda opalescens).

Bottom, left  Intertidal gooey-wooeys, Calvert Island.

Top, right  Eagle talon in the forest. Cause of death unknown.

Middle, right  The endangered Northerm abalone (Haliotis kamtschatkana).

Bottom, right  Insect-eating Sundews! (Drosera anglica). Don't get stuck.

## A NOTE ON THE MAKING OF THIS BOOK

I had no idea what this project was going to be, and almost no skills in illustration, writing, design, or publishing. After returning, I knew I had to do something, so I started transcribing the journals and scanning my paintings. Kaia and I were living on *Cinzano* in downtown Victoria. It was a change in pace. I picked up a part-time job at the Victoria Bug Zoo and spent the rest of my hours on the "kayak book." The learning curve was steep. Even though I had graduated from UVic, I used the Fine Arts computer lab, where there was always someone to help with InDesign and Photoshop. I also spent hundreds of hours in the Victoria Public Library, where charts of the entire Pacific Northwest are available.

The one vision I held was a story that could communicate science *and* magic. Science is trapped in the ivory bubble, often failing to communicate its findings with government and the public. And magic—the beautiful parts of the universe we have no words for—often has trouble being explained at all. Pictures help, and so does a relatable human experience.

This was my take-home: To change the world, yes, we must change ourselves, and then translate and share the experience. We live in the age of information. All this content blasting around is dizzying. To effectively access someone's heart takes a certain kind of story—a certain kind of honesty. I'm not sure if this book will do much, but if one person sets out up the coast, that's enough. If you are thinking to go out on your own, to find something worth holding on to: be oh-so-brave and know that what you are doing has value that transcends the doubts, dangers, and dragons you will face. *I wish you fair tides.*

## TIME TRAVEL AND MISTY MEADOWS

It's 2022, eight years since my first trip with *Bell*. I'm in Thailand after living in India for the last two and a half years. Kaia and I broke up a year after my return; I still had itchy feet. We are friends and I value the connection we maintain. She lives with her emotionally intelligent, musically gifted, and compassionate partner in the Strait of Georgia.

Young love is important and I wish I'd cherished it more. But there are many ways to live; being in a relationship is one. I'm content in my solitude and the path I walk. I think we need alternatives, and I'm still exploring.

Left  *Sailing and fishing on the Alboa Rosa.*

Right  *Sky under sail.*

*Top left*  Reading through the plant-bible on Calvert Island. "Learn one new species a day." Note the disheveled hipster vibe. Photo by Kalina Hunter.

*Middle left*  Dad in Ketchikan, AK.

*Bottom left*  The irresistible black matchstick lichen (*Cladonia sp.*).

*Top right*  Playing banjo in the parade, Ketchikan, AK. Yikes.

*Middle right*  Black Bomber, Baranof, AK.

*Bottom right*  Bell Pepper and wet gear drying in the sun (date unknown).

## THE DAVIDISM DICTIONARY

My mom has little to no boundaries when it comes to the English language. Growing up, I was bombarded by made-up words, Christmas carol mom-remixes, and mysterious grammar overrides. She's actually a super strong writer and taught me much of what I know, including how to make up new blasters (expressions). As she might say (but never has), *to truly access* someone's *heart with your words, you must first confuse them a little bit.* It's psychology, that's all.

Please try some of these out, and more than anything, make up your own combo-jombos (my mom really says this, usually about elaborate sandwich inventions—*nice combo-jombo*). I should note most of these are real words, they are just on the outskirts of society, and I sometimes use them in slightly different ways. Enjoy, and use with care.

### "ARE YOU BURGER FLIPPING ME?"
1. When you are mad but don't want to swear.
2. If someone is backseat driving.

### BLASTERS (ADJECTIVE)
1. Could be anything really. Mostly I hyphenate it with nouns to make something sound more dangerous / appealing / interesting. For example: nudibranchs can now be *nude-blasters*.

### (TOTALLY) BONKERS (ADJECTIVE)
1. An expression of awe and disbelief.
2. An expression to note something irregular or unnatural.
3. Adverse or poor weather conditions.
4. To describe an intoxicated person.

### BUCK-WILD (ADJECTIVE)
1. Out of control and unrestrained. (Sea lions are often buck-wild)
2. Gale-force weather conditions.

### CHOWSER (ADJECTIVE, NOUN)
1. An expression of profound inspiration and wonder. Imagine you see a whale breach, *"holy-chowser."*
2. An expression of frustration and/or pain. You step on a barnacle, *"chowser-yaowzer!"*
3. A person whose moral compass is poorly calibrated. Selfish, greedy. *"Wow, that person is a bit of a chowser today."*
4. A cute and cuddly animal. *"Awww, what a little chowser."*

### DOOZY (NOUN)
1. *Something extraordinary and/or troublesome and problematic.*
2. *A headache.*

### HIGGLEDY-PIGGLEDY (ADVERB)
1. My mom uses this daily. It means to do something in a disorganized, random manner. (A real word.)

### HODGEPODGE (NOUN)
1. A heterogeneous jumble or mess. (Also a real word.)

### "HOLY MACARONI AND CHEEEEEESE!"
1. To be used when going really fast. Try it next time you go surfing, or riding a bicycle.

### MAMAS (NOUN)
1. A unit. Of distance, time, or something along those lines. I've paddled 20 nautical-mamas today.

### WHAT THE MEGA-MURPHY!? / SWEET MURPHY! / SWEET DYNA! / SWEET SUZAN! / MOTHER TERESA!
1. An expression of confusion and appreciation, at the same time
2. They all pretty much mean the same thing and can be used interchangeably.

### WHAMMIES/RAMMERS (NOUN)
1. Calories.
2. Cookies.
3. Sandwiches cooked in a panini-press.
4. A group of kittens.

# THE DAYS:

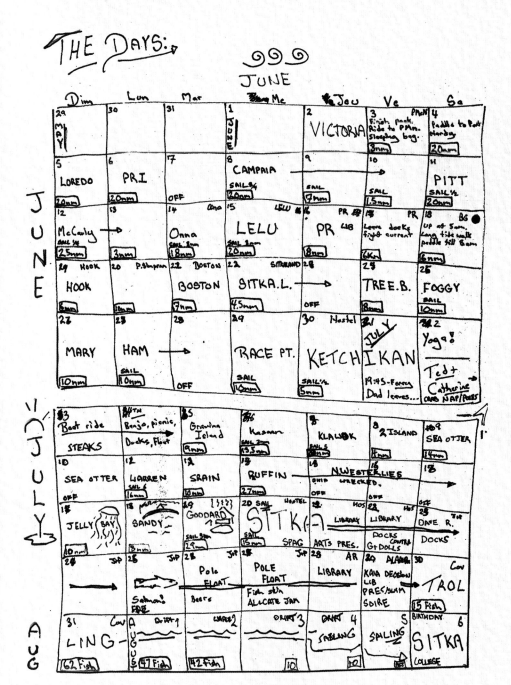

## JUNE

| Dim | Lun | Mar | Me | Jeu | Ve | Sa |
|---|---|---|---|---|---|---|
| 29 MAY | 30 | 31 | 1 JUNE | 2 VICTORIA | 3 Finish pack. Ride to P.Mm. Sleeping bag. 3nm | 4 Paddle to Port Hardey 20nm |
| 5 LOREDO 20nm | 6 PRI 20nm | 7 OFF | 8 CAMPAIA SAILS4 20nm → | 9 SAIL 7nm | 10 SAIL 1.5nm | 11 PITT SAIL 1/2 20nm |
| 12 McCauly SAIL 1/4 25nm → | 13 3nm | 14 Onna Onna SAIL 3nm 18nm | 15 LELU LELU SAIL 2nm 20nm | 16 PR PR 8nm | 17 PR Leave docks fight current 6Kn | 18 BG Up at 5am. Long tide walk paddle till 8am 6nm |
| 19 HOOK HOOK 8nm | 20 P.Simpson 18nm | 22 BOSTON BOSTON 7nm | 22 SITKA.L. 4.5nm → | SITKLAND 23 TREE.B. OFF | 24 8nm | 25 FOGGY SAIL 10nm |
| 27 MARY 10nm | 28 HAM SAIL 10nm → | 28 OFF | 29 RACE PT. SAIL 10nm | 30 Hostel KETCHIKAN SAIL1/2 5nm | 31 JULY JULY 19:45-Ferry Dad leaves... | 2 Yoga! Ted + Catherine CRAB NAP/PIZES |

## JULY / AUG

| | | | | | | |
|---|---|---|---|---|---|---|
| 3 Boat ride STEAKS | 4TH Banjo, picnic, Docks, Float | 5 Grandma Island 9nm | 6 Kasaan SAIL 2nm 13.5nm | 8 KLAWOK SAIL 5 3nm | 8 2 ISLAND 4nm | 8 9 SEA OTTER 14nm |
| 10 SEA OTTER OFF | 11 WARREN SAIL 6 16nm | 12 SRAIN 10nm | 13 RUFFIN 27nm | 14 N.WESTERLIES SHIP WRECKED. OFF | 15 OFF | 16 OFF → |
| 17 JELLY BAY 10nm | 18 SANDY 3nm | 19 GODDARD SAIL 5nm 29nm | 20 SAIL Hostel SAIL 15nm SPAG | 21 HOS LIBRARY ARTS PRES. AR | 22 HOS LIBRARY DOCKS CONTRA Gt DOLLS | 23 DAVE R. 3rd DOCKS → |
| 24 Jap 25 → | Jap 25 Salmon! FEE | Jap 25 Pole FLOAT Beers | Jap 25 POLE FLOAT Fish stA ALLCATE JAM | Jap 28 LIBRARY | 29 ALASKA KAIA DECISION LIB PRES/SUM SOIRE | 30 Cov TROL 15 Fish |
| 31 LING- 62 Fish | Cov A U G U S T Drift 1 47 Fish | WARES 2 42 Fish | DRIFT 3 10 | DRIFT 4 SABLING 10 | 5 SAILING | 6 BIRTHDAY SITKA COLLEGE |

Original calendar from the second ocean-journal. Note the distance dates for each day, including distance sailed. Also number of fish caught per day while on the Albee Rose. I collected a lot of data while paddling, mostly about the weather and sea state. Also, note what a mess it is.

## SKINNY DIP.
AUDREY LANE COCKETT

*Dedicated to the salt water, written in
Heiltsuk Territory.*

*I cut my feet on jagged rock barnacles.
It is cold today, rain is hung in the air.
My body is heavy, nothing I do is graceful.
Naked, huddled, and small—against a cliff.
The sea has no tolerance for my insecurities.
I try apologizing for not coming yesterday…
the sea is like "What?"
I made the commitment to dip every morning.
So I am here, bleeding ribbons into kelp.
I steel myself for the plunge.
Awkwardly, I fling myself into the Pacific Ocean.
Displacing the space of me onto shores
everywhere.
Intestines jump—bones relax.
I submerge.
This water holds me. It holds my toes, my knee-
caps, bellybutton, breasts,
collarbones, freckles, moles, scars and asshole. It
holds me.
I breach.
Half in half out, surrendering and escaping.
The waves do not give me special treatment.
No judgment or respite.
I am not the first to striptease these seas.
I will not be the last to jump in, swim
Feel small, and vast.
Strong, powerless, and held.
I clamber out into the misty morning.
It is a change of state.
Dipped in and dripping tremendous unrelenting
grace.
We evaporate.
My cut is salt stung, and cleaned.
Naked. New. Awake.
On these rocky shores.*

## SALTY FINGERS.
KAIA BRYCE

*Lick the salty fingers
of the trees where the breeze lingers
and the sea flings itself up to the sky.*

*Why should we earthlings bring
more than the senses we possess
our five defences, to the scene.*

*The immediacy of the seaward careen
of the eagle—life collides
with life behold
a fish in flight.*

*And last light making prisms
of last waves arcing steel lavender cold grey
and yellow
A harbinger of mellowing night.*

*We can offer nothing but a witness signature
Eye for an I. Guided by sight, smell, sound,
touch and taste.*

*Lick the salty fingers
of the trees where the breeze lingers
and the sea flings itself up to the sky.*

These poems are from two ocean friends, and this whale was
painted by children in Thailand under the sage guidance of
Kru Baz (Maturot Intarabutra). Thank you.

# ACKNOWLEDGEMENTS

Thank you. This book (and perhaps my life) is the inevitable result of many lives, and stories, seamlessly coming together, like a braided river working towards the delta.

## DAVID MILLAR NORWELL AND JANE INGLIS BERRY

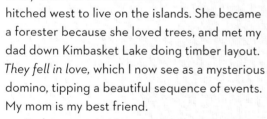

My grandparents immigrated to Vancouver after the Second World War. Grampa was a gregarious doctor who actually wanted to be a concert pianist, and Gramma was a head nurse during the war. They were a safe space for my siblings and me. Near the end of Grampa's life, he went deaf, but would still play the piano.

Kaia and I visited a year before he passed, and he played a small concert. At first his notes were off. We could see confusion in his 96-year-old eyes. Then his wrinkled fingers began playing on their own. Slow at first, and then like dancers. I have never cried tears like that—joy, sadness, and wonder. Imagine not being able to hear your own final symphony.

## MOM AND DAD

My mom is incredibly brave, direct, and clever. She left a tricky home at seventeen and hitched west to live on the islands. She became a forester because she loved trees, and met my dad down Kimbasket Lake doing timber layout. *They fell in love,* which I now see as a mysterious domino, tipping a beautiful sequence of events. My mom is my best friend.

Dad grew up in Vancouver but peeled 'er to the Rockies after university. He's also a forester, and together my parents started their own consulting company. They wanted to change the clear-cut mentality, but mostly they just loved being in the woods. All us kids were taken out regularly, and one of my first jobs was planting seedlings (25 cents a plug). We had cook-outs on slash-piles, drove quads and ski-doos, and would ride in the back of the truck. It was awesome. *Thank you.*

## ALEXIS NORWELL

Lexi and I were close growing up. I looked like her, and we were often mistaken as sisters. She has travelled countless countries and sailed across the Atlantic Ocean! What an inspiration. She now has a baby named Wrenly, *who is beautiful.* She lives on Vancouver Island with her infinitely kind partner, Gavin Millar. To both, a bear hug and *thank you,* for keeping it real and living so courageously.

## ARRON NORWELL

I grew up watching my brother play Magic cards and computer games. These are my safest, happiest childhood memories. At 17, he wrote his own science fiction novel! It made me believe I could write a book too. His wife, Sanaz Arabzadeh, is wonderful and has a huge honest smile—the kind that changes your whole day. A mega thank you for all the support and love.

## JEN NORWELL

You might have heard my sister on the radio. She works for CBC and has been an asset to my writing and creative process. She is multi-talented, warm-hearted, and mind-bendingly artistic. She also stands up for what is right, no matter what. This has affected me deeply. She lives in Kamloops with her fantastic husband, Ian Reedman (who is unbelievably good at listening and including people), and their Lego-king-son, Paul. *Thank you.*

## MY MOUNTAIN FAMILY

To Liz, Brian, Karen, Reiner, Hannah, Matthias, Sepp, Will, the baby still to come, and all the McKirdys, thanks for being stewards of the mountains, and showing me how to load trailers and pick blueberries. My love to Janey, Bob, Vern, and Shelby for everything, and for taking me to the ocean when I was a kid. To Ross, *thank you* for rescuing me, and showing me there is so much more.

## ELEMENTARY SCHOOL

I grew up in Kamloops till age 13. My gratitude to the teachers at Beattie Elementary and Sahali Secondary. And tons of love to the Setkas, Thomsons, Thompson Tigers, and Gagnier-Ruckerts for being second families, especially, Joel, Jer, Stefan, Andreas, Rylan, Lief Amundson, Aaron Shippit, Adrienne Rempel, Steven Loynachan and Greg Wagner, and Spencer T.

## HIGH SCHOOL

PG is a rough timber town. The reason I survived is the wonderful people at Lakewood middle school, PGSS, the PG Mafia skate-crew, The Boys, and everyone else who molded me in those early years. Special thanks to Rick and Penny Fahlman, Jess Higgs, Spendo Girard, and Brad Pichler.

## VICTORIA

In Vic I lived in a communal house with fifty different roomates over four years. Big Love to all. Especially: Matt Mo, Julie Wolf, Fin Bones, Audrey Lane, Alyssa Lefort, Erika Hiroko, Moss Types, Henri and Josie Simpson and family, Justin Ming, Nash Laj, Sophie Noel, Paige Kato, Michelle Ania, Wylie Fuller, Blake Malo, Jackson Franchetto, and The Ouldalis: Jaqui, Ben, Soleia, Mo. And everyone at the Kings and Fairburn Houses. Special thanks to Denise McGowan, Andrew Ellis, Lochlan Ellis, and Harrison Ellis.

## UNIVERSITY

Deep thanks to Brian Starzomski, James Rowe, David Duffus, Eric & Logan Higgs, Phil Dearden, Trisalyn Nelson, Kara Shaw, Chris Darimont, my profs in the Geography and ES departments, the *Martlet*, ESSA, ESSENCE, The Community Cabbage, The UVic rowing team, Georgia Klap and the Klap family, Aviva Lessard, Mike Graeme, Inanna So, Alex Browne, John Brans, Emma Louise Bles, Josie Simpson, Adrian Esau, Bridget Woods, Simon Wilson, Luke Robertson, Kelly Toots, Thom Hoff, Michael Nyquist, Ian Cruickshank, Navi Smith, Kate Williams, Ryder Bergerud, Kalina Hunter, Andrew Sheriff, and everyone else.

## SUMMERS

Warm regards to Ted Hunter and Ryan Dragoman and their wonderful families. Thanks to Issac Fage, Shawn Ryan, Cathy Wood, all the GroundTruthers, Hannah Findlay-Brook, and the lovely people who make Dawson City anything but a city.

A big consensual hug to Peter Carson, Luke Ferris, Peter Gibbs, Alyx MacAdams, Tracey Proverbs, all LD1s and 2s and every kid, counselor, and human living and learning nature-values.

## PIERS

Dear Kaia, my deepest gratitude and respect for your precious company, clever edits, gracious encouragement, and endless kindness. This book would not have been possible without you. Thank you for teaching me to sail. To Taise, Alan, Uta, Keito, and everyone on Piers, thank you for being such a warm, open-minded, musical community—a template for humanity.

## HAKAI

Dear Eric, Christina, Erin Foster, Maartje Korver, Ben Millard-Martin, Julia Fisher, Sara Wickham, Bill Floyd, and all the Hakaites: *Thank you dearly.*

## INDIA

Lots of love to Buddha Kyab, Manjushri Educational Services, the entire Tibetan community, HHDL, Ringo, Miranda, the BBC team, Neha, and the infinitely sweet Srinidhi Iyer. Special thanks to Deborah Smith, Bella Lindsey, Baptiste Gueguen, Anouchka, Alex, and baby Jonakin.

## PADDLERS / SEA SALTS

Big ups to Kate Hives and all guides and oceanists making sure people are safe on the water. Special thanks to Catherine and Ted in Ketchikan. Devon, Paul, Henri, and James from Sitka. Sue White in Washington, Manu and Florian from France. Simon Behman, Kayak Kelly, Just Jen, and Dave on the *Albee Rose!*

## HERITAGE HOUSE

A warm thank you to Lara, Nandini, Setareh, Monica, Renée, Rodger, Kimiko, Marial, and all the Heritage authors. *Thank you.* Many hands make amazing work.

## OTHERS

My respect to Alan and Peter Thomas, Sarah Daamgard, Hans Henrik, Sidsel, Anna Viale, Bobby Lee Daniels, Bob McDonald, David Attenborough, the Haywoods, Suvitcha, Wayo, and Waree Pakkrasa, Maturot Intarabutra, Jen Liao, Harmony Hub (Pai) S.N. Goenka, the Vipassana meditation community, and everyone helping us learn the laws of nature. To anyone I have missed, and everyone who has picked me up, housed, and/or fed me, I love you too! My brain is just too full and uncoordinated, please forgive me.

## THE FIRST AND LAST THANK YOU

I could not have done this trip without the stewardship and support of coastal Indigenous Peoples. On my journey, I was fed and housed, and if I ever needed rescue, the first responders would have been the local Indigenous people. The writing of this book and each leg of the journey took place on the traditional and, in almost all cases, unceded territory of Indigenous Peoples. Thank you to the current, past, and future generations who care, protect, and live for the land. A special debt of gratitude to HIRMD, the Guardian Watchmen, the entire Heiltsuk Nation, Denise and Chester Starr, the Brown and Housty families, *Qatuwas* Jess Brown, Larry Jorgenson, Rick Wilson, the Qqs Projects Society, and everyone at Koeye.

### STEWARDSHIP (NOUN)

1. the careful and responsible management of something entrusted to one's care.

Stewardship requires us to first know and love something; only then can we care properly. Science and politics often fail because they know but do not love. Environmentalism and activism can falter in reverse. The Indigenous Peoples I met loved and knew the land deeply, in a way I don't think I'm capable of yet.

Even though I was living in my tent and mostly alone, I was a guest. It's hard for me to understand this whole coast and country is the living-home of people who have cultivated and cared for ecosystems since time immemorial—a time beyond remembering.

### RECONCILIATION (NOUN)

1. the act of reconciling or the state of being reconciled.

2. the process of making consistent or compatible.

3. A reestablishment of friendship, harmony, or cordial relations.

I'm not sure if this is the right word for a country to lean on. It implies previous "cordial relations." Settlers came to exploit, colonize, and capitalize. Reconciliation requires both Indigenous and non-Indigenous people to work, and much of the heavy reflection, work, and compromises need to be done by those with the most (current) power. For this, a process is necessary, so let's get going—earnestly and openly. I'm overwhelmed by this; it's natural to want to ignore the societally sanctioned geno-cide. No one likes looking in the ugly-mirror (past and present).

But we have to. The unmarked graves, lost languages, sexual abuse, murders, old-growth clear cuts, and the historical policies that allowed for these actions won't disappear. The people who went through all this, and the settlers who continue this cycle, won't disappear. We are in this together now. The important thing: *the process must be on Indigenous terms*. We cannot fix this with the same machine that created it. Again, I point to the Heiltsuk who have their own reconciliation agenda and word: Háɫcístut. There are many communities outlining their own process and how best settlers can engage.

I hope this helps. Please forgive me if the above is triggering or not-done-perfect. I'm learning here, and don't feel comfortable writing this at all, but messy honesty is often better than nothing.

CEDAR

# RESOURCES

If you are inspired to do your own journey—of whatever kind—these resources may help. I highly recommend some training if you are paddling alone.

## KAYAKING AND SALTY ADVENTURES

1. Sea Kayak Guides Alliance of BC (SKGABC): guide certification courses.
2. Paddle Canada: skill and instructor courses.
3. SKILS: BC kayak-hive offering skill courses, expeditions, and more.
4. *Navigation, Sea State and Weather: A Paddler's Manual. Freedom of the Seas Volume 1,* second edition, by Michael Pardy, J.F. Marleau, Andrew Woodford, and Piper Harris (Ucluelet, BC: SKILS, 2020). Don't leave home without this paddler's bible. As a solo paddler it saved my life, and was my constant reference.
5. Sea Kayak Canada Facebook group for paddling tips, tricks, and community.
6. *The Curve of Time* by M. Wylie Blanchet (Sidney, BC: Gray's Pub., 1968). This book should be taken on every coastal adventure. A profound reflection from a single mama, adventuring with her cubs.

## SCIENCE

1. Raincoast Conservation Foundation: they do fantastic work and offer a free online "wolf-school."
2. Quirks and Quarks: CBC Radio's longest running science podcast with legend Bob McDonald!
3. *Hakai Magazine:* Compelling marine stories from all over the world. They have in-depth articles on marine mammal intelligence.

## SPECIES GUIDES

1. *Plants of the Pacific Northwest Coast,* third edition, by Jim Pojar and Andy MacKinnon (Tukwila, WA: Lone Pine International, 2016).
2. *Whelks to Whales: Coastal Marine Life of the Pacific Northwest,* revised third edition, by Rick M. Harbo (Madeira Park, BC: Harbour Publishing: 2022).
3. *Mushrooms of the Pacific Northwest* by Steve Trudell and Joe Ammirati (Portland, OR: Timber Press, 2009).
4. Central Coast biodiversity species app and website: centralcoastbiodiversity.org.

## TRADITIONAL ECOLOGICAL KNOWLEDGE (TEK)

1. Nativelands (native-land.ca): an amazing global mapping project.
2. Coastal First Nations (coastalfirstnations.ca): a union of Nations working in the Great Bear Rainforest. Lots of inspiring videos and links to TEK and science in the Great Bear Rainforest.

## RECONCILIATION

1. Beyond 94: a cool CBC initiative holding the Canadian government accountable.
2. The Canadian Encyclopedia (thecanadianencyclopedia.ca). Search for the collection by Indigenous peoples.
3. National Centre for Truth and Reconciliation memorial register (nctr.ca/memorial/): a list of the names of children who never returned home from residential school, and their stories.
4. Haíɫcístut (heiltsuknation.ca/departments/reconciliation): Heiltsuk reconciliation.

## PHILOSOPHY AND MENTAL HEALTH

1. Vipassana meditation (dhamma.org): they offer 10-day silent retreats to stabilize, understand, and purify the mind.
2. Birken Forest Monastery (birken.ca): Ajahn Sona is a Canadian monk with a monastery close to Kamloops, BC. He has many videos/discourses reflecting on western society from a Buddhist perspective.

## PORN ADDICTION

1. Sexual sanity (sexualsanity.com): a neat site looking at the issue from many angles.

*Rest easy, Catly-Do. We will always love you.*

# ENDNOTES

Countless hours have been spent down these black-rabbit-holes. *Beware.*

## INTRODUCTION: LIFE IN THE BACK EDDY

1 *Modern samsara.* In the *Lokavipatti Sutta*, Buddha explains: "Monks, these eight worldly conditions spin after the world, and the world spins after these eight worldly conditions. Which eight? Gain, loss, status, disgrace, censure, praise, pleasure, and pain."

2 *Privilege.* "Unpacking the Invisible Knapsack" by Peggy McIntosh first appeared in *Peace and Freedom Magazine* (July/August, 1989, pp. 10-12); it is available online. This essay was one of the first good discussions on privilege, which McIntosh defines as "an invisible package of unearned assets that [a person] can count on cashing in each day." In the essay she lists twenty six conditions for us to consider where we are on the privilege ladder.

3 *Kayak packing.* For a thorough kayak packing list see *www.kayakguidance.com/kayak-camping-list*

## CHAPTER 1: WOLVES OF THE DEEP

1 *Dumpster Diving.* In 2015, Kaia, John Bransfield, Sophie Noel, Matt Morrison, myself, and a handful of other UVic friends started the *UVic Community Cabbage*. Each week, we reclaimed dumpster goodies, cooked them up at the local church kitchen, and then served them for free on campus. We would engage with people about food, where it comes from, and the industrial food-rammer we so happily accept today.

2 *Lord of the Rings.* My sister Lex and I were obsessed with the film trilogy, and would rewatch parts every day after school, memorizing lines and acting out the scenes. The classic journey-in-to-the-darkness narrative deeply influenced me and was part of my motivation for this trip. I wanted to know what was beyond the Shire.

3 *Piers Island.* In the 1930s Piers was a penal colony for the Sons of Freedom (a group of Christian Doukhobor extremists.) These Russian *Freedomites* were self-proclaimed as *God's People*, opposing land ownership, public education, and using animals for work. They are best known for protesting nude. Many BC and Alaska islands have strange, slightly disturbing tales. For a culty adventure, look up the history of DeCourcy Island with Madame Z and Brother XII; there's a good article online at *Atlas Obscura*, and an episode on CBC's podcast, *Ideas*.

4 *Whales!* For more details about the whale-human relationship and the aquarium culture/history of Victoria and other cities, see the documentary *Black Fish*. It stars UVic geography professor Dr. David Duffus.

5 *Chester "Lone Wolf" Starr.* You can look up a charming biography on the Raincoast Conservation Foundation website. Search "Chester Starr." He grew up in Bella Bella immersed in nature—fishing, hunting, clam digging, and spending hours navigating the Heiltsuk Territory island-maze. In 2000 he began helping and guiding Raincoast's wolf research, and in 2004 Lone Wolf and Chris Darimont were given the Compassion in Science Award from the International Fund for Animal Welfare. At the event in Ottawa (Chester's first time out of BC), Chris relates: "Jane Goodall was... there for a Lifetime Achievement Award. *They were drawn to one another.* They hung out all throughout the mingler before the event. And they sat beside one another as we took our seats. At one point, as Chester's achievements were being read aloud, she reached over to hold his hand. It was very, very sweet."

6 *Mammalian intelligence.* The cerebral cortex is held as the best measure for intelligence and emotional complexity, giving rise to the expression *don't be so cerebral.* In total neurons, the African elephant leads the charge. To measure brains and neural connectivity, scientists turn the brain into soup, then count neurons! They also use MRIs, which show that marine mammals have extra *folds* that humans don't. For a whale-human head-to-head, go to YouTube and watch *Orca Brains and Intelligence: The Evolutionary Story,* by Dr. Lori Marino.

7 *Humpback and wolf cortex information.* Neural data for humpbacks is from their closest cousin, the fin whale. Wolf brain data is from dogs. Wolves must have more neurons, but science is fresh in this field, and data is lacking for many species. Also, it's hard to get intact brains.

8 *GPS.* Backcountry trekkers and coastal mariners can now use their phones with accurate GPS results. I use MAPS.ME and OsmAnd (phone apps) for mapping. However, don't get dependent! You need paper charts. My dad downloaded all the charts on his phone as a reference, and dropped it in the water on the second day. At least a chart atlas you can dry out.

9 *Oysters.* Shucking requires an intuitive hand, a strong blade, and perseverance. It is the coconut of the PNW.

10  *Careful of red tide.* Once upon a time, a harvester raw-popped an oysie on low tide, then became paralyzed. Slowly the water came up and began to cover his body, so he could feel everything but couldn't move. Luckily, a friend found him right before the water came over his nose! So the legend goes.

## CHAPTER 2: CAPE CAUTION

1  *Berries.* While working on the Central Coast with the Heiltsuk First Nation, I learned that *tarp picking* berries has been tried and trusted for thousands of years. Wild berries are full of vitamins, minerals, and antioxidants, and complement a protein-rich diet of fish and deer.

2  *Currents and tidal surges.* Tidal currents are different from *ocean* currents, which are the global-mama-flows circulating the entire earth. Ocean currents are created by gravity, the Coriolis effect, and temperature differences between the poles and equator.

3  *When math stops making sense.* These are my dad's thoughts: "The introduction of mechanical calculators (1700s), then computers (1900s) has changed the way we perceive the world. Circa 1850 we thought the world was entirely predictable but now we have discovered fractal and chaotic mathematics, and multi-dimensional topology. Also, the social world view has gradually changed to try and keep up with these new understandings. Today we have an interconnected social network that has unforeseen implications for the development of individuals, societies, and nations. Additionally the naive, western mechanical worldview is giving way to an appreciation of the energetic arts like acupuncture and healing touch that at one time were beyond scientific enquiry. This appreciation has come about through a renaissance of research in recent decades in brain research and psychology enabled by new measuring technology (we are more like flocks of birds and schools of fish than we realize)." In short: science is evolving and although limited currently by its own methodology/perspective, it doesn't have to remain that way.

4  *Kaia's journey.* To solo a 25-foot sailboat down this coast with a kitten is an unbelievable feat. She wrote an article about her experience in the magazine *48 North* (April 2016 edition, pages 38-42). This article has incredibly cute kitten-sailing pictures. It also details the sailing trip we did together that summer, giving the other important perspective on our shared story. You can access it at *issuu: www.issuu.com/48north/docs/48-north-april-2016.*

6  *Love vs science.* For a more in-depth look, please see: *Aroused: The History of Hormones and How They Control Just About Everything* by Randi Hutter Epstein (New York: W.W. Norton, 2018).

## CHAPTER 3: LET GO OF EVERYTHING

1  *Meditative dissolution.* A state called *bhanga-nana* in the Pali language. In this stage of vipassana, a meditator experiences *nama* (mind) and *rupa* (matter) continually arising and passing in great rapidity in the framework of the body. From this experience, a meditator begins to see all phenomena as (1) impermanent, (2) without a self, and (3) unsatisfactory.

2  *Kayak sails.* Since writing this, awesome sailing setups have been innovated and are gaining acceptance (though some people are strict *paddlers*). Look up "Best Kayak Sail" on kayakhelp.com for the definitive guide (accessed at www.kayakhelp.com/best-kayak-sail on September 30, 2022).

3  *Spirit Bear.* The white fur is the result of a double recessive gene (unique to the subspecies), which causes the bear to create adenine rather than guanine.

4  *Salmon osmoregulation.* Basically, they drink loads of water and shut down their kidneys' urine production until Na and other electrolyte levels balance.

## CHAPTER 4: MY DAD

1  *Dad's knitting.* When entering our house, there is a dedicated knitting corner for my dad, where you will see knitting pattern graph paper with my dad's own mathematical designs, custom needles, and a spinning machine. He has made sweaters, baby blankets, and everything else warm.

2  *Lighthouses.* Some lighthouses are now fully automated, but many still have *keepers*. You can see what a day in the life is like by looking on the famous YouTube channel: *BC Lighthouse Keeper.*

3  *Haíɫcístut.* There is information on Heiltsuk Nation website mentioned in the resource section. This other link is from the federal government: *https://www.canada.ca/en/crown-in-digenous-relations-northern-affairs/news/2019/07/canada-and-heiltsuk-sign-the-haicistut-incremental-house-post-agreement.html.*

4  *Solar-powered nudies.* The Blue Dragon NB (*Pteraeolidia semperi*) eats algae-rich coral and absorbs the algae's chloroplasts (zooxanthellae) into its cerata, which photosynthesizes, creating nutrients that can

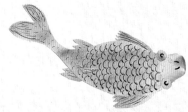

sustain the nudibranch for months. Other nude-units have evolved other ways of farming zooxanthellae, storing them in their digestive glands.

5 *Race to Alaska.* This is an annual (usually June) no-engines-allowed human-and-wind-powered race from Port Townsend, WA, to Ketchikan, AK (750 nautical miles). The only check points are Victoria and Bella Bella, leaving it up to each boat on how to thread the islands (or to take the outside route). The winner gets USD$10 000 and second place gets a set of steak knives. No other official prizes are given, although many side-bets are made.

6 *Ketchikan.* The creek flowing through the town was a fish camp for the Tlingit called "kitschk-hin," translating to the creek of "thundering wings of an eagle."

## CHAPTER 5: JUST DON'T DIE OUT THERE, OK?

1 *Sea kayaking deaths.* There was one accident that changed the fate of sea kayaking on the BC coast. In July 1993, "Nine sea-kayakers led by two guides, were on passage to Vertical Point, Louise Island, [Haida Gwaii], BC. On encountering adverse weather conditions near Heming Head, four kayaks were overwhelmed and capsized. Two members of the group were rescued immediately and two others were swept away by the waves. They were discovered in the water three hours later during a Search and Rescue mission. One was suffering from acute hypothermia. The other was later determined to have died from hypothermia and drowning." This is from the marine investigation report by the Transportation Safety Board of Canada (TSB). After this accident the government asked the kayak community to come up with a plan, and SKGABC formed in 1994 to train and certify guides in what was before an unregulated tourism industry. This trip report is quite revealing and can be found at: *www.bst-tsb. gc.ca/eng/rapports-reports/marine/1993/m93w0008/ m93w0008.html* on the TSB website.

2 *Cetacean sleep.* Studies show marine mammals have what's called unihemispheric slow-wave sleep, where half the brain remains awake while the other hemisphere sleeps, then the brain switches sides! This allows the creature to breathe, consolidate memories, and do bodily repair while staying with members of its group and being aware of danger.

3 *Sea otter recovery.* From 1969 to 1972, eighty-nine otters were reintroduced to Checleset Bay (west coast of Vancouver Island). As of 2017 that population has grown to over 8,000. They eat 20 percent of their body weight a day and are taking over the urchin barrens by storm. There is a hilariously narrated old documentary documenting the reintroduction efforts in Alaska that took place at the same time, on YouTube: *The Warm Coat (1969) Sea Otter Transplant Documentary.*

## CHAPTER 6: A CAMPFIRE STORY

1 *Campfire characters.* My nephew is named Paul. My niece is Wrenly. My sister is Lexi. Ottaline is a character from Rupert Bear (an illustrated children's comic book), who I used to have a crush on when I was a little boy, if that is even possible (Ottaline was an anthropomorphized river otter character).

## CHAPTER 7: SPAWNING SALMON

1 *Alaskan fishing fatalities.* In the 1970s, in Alaskan waters, an average of 34 fishing vessels and 24 lives were lost each year in the commercial fishing industry, an occupational fatality rate 20 times the national average. As of 2018, it's leveled out at around 3.5 deaths per year.

## CHAPTER 8: SEPTEMBER STORMS

1 *Profound nature moments.* "A walk in nature, walks the soul back home." –Mary Davis. "And into the forest I go, to lose my mind and find my soul." –John Muir.

2 *Porn addiction.* I first wrote on Medium about my experience with porn and sexual abuse in an article titled: Raised by Porn.

3 *Sunflower star.* Beginning in 2013, the population of sunflower stars began to crash due to the mysterious sea star wasting syndrome. Since then, 5.75 billion individuals died (90 percent of the population). Scientists still don't know why this crash happened and *what* the syndrome is; some hypothesize warmer oceans and a pathogen/parasite.

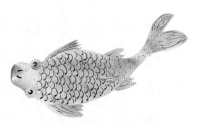

# ABOUT
# THE AUTHOR

**DAVID NORWELL** is an author, illustrator, and world traveller. He holds a BSc in Geography from the University of Victoria, and has worked for eight seasons conducting biological and geological surveys in BC, Alberta, and the Yukon. His passion is communicating science in a way that accesses the human heart. David has visited thirty-three countries, sailed across the Atlantic and Indian oceans, trekked over the Himalayas with a kitten, and hitchhiked over two hundred rides. He is dedicated to understanding the human experience and sharing his findings. When not working on books, he is volunteering at schools, studying the Buddha's teachings, and practising meditation.